The

Texas Homestead Hoax

Harvella Jones

Order this book online at www.trafford.com
or email orders@trafford.com

Most Trafford titles are also available at major online book retailers.

Print information available on the last page.

ISBN: 978-1-4120-4458-5 (sc)
ISBN: 978-1-6987-1698-5 (e)

Trafford rev. 05/20/2024

 www.trafford.com

North America & international
toll-free: 844-688-6899 (USA & Canada)
fax: 812 355 4082

Each year, thousands of homeowners in the State of Texas unknowingly sign away their homestead rights at the closing table. My family and I were part of that figure in 1988. Each year, many homeowners across this state receive foreclosure-threatening letters. My family and I were part of that figure in 1991. However, very few actually are foreclosed strictly for maintenance fee non-payments, even when they are up-to-date on their mortgage payment. My family and I were among that small figure in 1995.

This book is dedicated to my beloved husband Johnnie Jones, my two daughters Paula and Karen, the dedicated advocate members of The Texas Homeowner's Advocate Group (T.H.A.G.) and to all homeowners everywhere.

"Trust no future, suffer no disappointments."

---- Lois Gray

CONTENTS

CONTENTS

CONTENTS

The

Texas Homestead Hoax

When the call came in I had been waiting to get for several years, I remember what I was doing on that day in 1996. It was a day full of sunshine. It was a good day and I had just gone upstairs when the call came in. The phone had a special ring to it, when I picked it up, and heard the voice on the other end say, "Mrs. Jones, what can we do to get you out of our hair?"

So began a closing of one chapter and the opening of another. Little did we know that it was only the lull before yet another storm and another foreclosure.

Let me start from the beginning.

Our arrival in Houston, Texas, was uneventful. Our drive down was peaceful and except for our German Shepard named Sebastian peeing on Karen, our youngest daughter, it was a pleasant drive. We came directly from Bedford Heights, Ohio, with a brief stay on the West side of Houston and finally settled in at 2026 Oak Shores Drive, Kingwood, Texas, August, 1988, approximately one year after the little known case Inwood vs. Harris had been affirmed by the Texas Supreme Court. We quietly moved into a planned community thinking we had homestead protection on our retirement home.

Prior to that case law, homesteads were protected by Article XVI, Section 50 of the Texas Constitution from forced sale by a homeowner's association for nonpayment of maintenance fees.

I will never forget how it felt to own a home with a swimming pool. It was such a beautiful house. It reminded us of the one we had left behind in Ohio, we thought!

The first year and a half were great. We were all so very happy. Our girls had adjusted very well. Paula was eleven (11) and Karen was nine (9). We were all overjoyed our loyal Sebastian had tolerated the long trip down and was with us and he loved his new home too. I remember looking up one day from the pool and noticed our next door neighbor was looking down at us with great interest. We were having such a great time. Well, needless to say, it did not last long. In retrospect, it is a scene that, I am sure, has played over and over again across this state after 1987, in many, many homes.

Things began to change in 1990, when we first learned there was a homeowner association in our neighborhood that collected annual maintenance fees. We had never heard of homeowner associations. What was an association that expected money every year from us? Back in Ohio, at the time we left in '88, a neighborhood group was one that gave block parties and you had lots of fun. We thought the fee we paid at closing was a one-time fee for some kind of service organization, like the one you pay for pest control. I guess in retrospect, we turned out to be the pest they were trying to control. Somebody sure dropped the ball on that one.

To make a long story longer, I mean, shorter, we eventually found out and then discovered the association was assessing fees incorrectly. We challenged that, thinking they would correct it, we would pay it, and that would be the end of that. Unfortunately, it did not work out that way and that was when the gates of hell opened up and enveloped us for many years. We could not get any attorney to take our case and believe me we tried. We called the ACLU and they turned us down. We contacted the NAACP and they turned us down. We tried everybody and were turned down by everyone. No one wanted to tackle Goliath, so we did. After all, we had cut our eyetooth on a case without representation in 1990, so we did not think it would be a big deal to represent ourselves, after all, we had beaten Royce Homes, Inc.

Therefore, we took on the awesome and dubious task of defending ourselves once again. Johnnie is retired from the Government and I am trained as a Certified Professional Secretary (CPS). Most of my work assignments were titled an administrative assistant. We still make the coffee though. My familiarity with the keyboard and such, won me the honors of doing all the research, typing the motions and making the argument in court. I came cheap. All I asked for was at least two good meals a day, company when I went to the law library to do research, peace and quiet while I was trying to type and a roof over my head. Well, maybe that was not so cheap. So Johnnie cooked (even though at first, my appetite was gone), rode with me to the law library, kept the kids away from me while I typed way into the night and day and he paid the bills so I could continue to have that roof over my head. It was quite a learning and eye-opening experience.

Our lives, once peaceful, joyful and full of tranquility, quickly became dark, depressing and filled with evil thoughts about evil people. It was a time when Office Depot, Kinko's and the Law Library downtown Houston became our second, third and fourth home. Johnnie, as the "banker"; and me, as the "lead attorney", for this "do-it-yourself" legal team. I recall writing and typing for several hours' straight, releasing my anger first on paper and then on the computer. Most of what I first wrote did not make sense and if filed with the Court, would have caused us to be sanctioned and possibly some jail time.

The anger and the hate started then and did not begin to subside until December 5, 1995, but more on that day later. We began to dream of ways to retaliate violently and were frequently on our knees praying and asking God to help us, and to forgive us for our evil thoughts and to guide us. He did. He transformed us from trusting ourselves and the system to trusting Him totally. You know as Christians, sometimes we have the tendency to pray but then try to fix things ourselves. Well, this was an educational experience. We learned to "let go and let God."

The Trails Association claimed they had served us regarding their lawsuit; but we never got the notice. We successfully turned this first homeowner association lawsuit around and on April 1, 1993, the First District Court of Appeals reversed the judgment against us and remanded the cause back to the 270th District Court of Harris County, Texas.

The Woodland Hills Trail Association had sued us on September 17, 1991, for unpaid annual maintenance assessments and for foreclosure of its lien securing payment of the assessments. A default judgment was entered May 27, 1992.

Our pro se writ of error contained 15 points of error. It was our tenth point of error, contending we were not served that won the reversal. Woodland Hills Trail Association was ordered to pay all costs incurred because of this appeal. Nice job for a couple of pro se litigants. It was going to be smooth sailing from now on. Poor us, we have a lot to learn.

Judges do not like to be wrong and a reversal is embarrassing to them; so Judge Ann Cochran recused herself and a new judge by the name of Harriet O'Neill was assigned to the case and we got a chance to defend our homestead. Attorney Michael Treece, with Laviage & Steinmann, had given up or been fired. We are not sure what happened to him but he had called us after the case was reversed and remanded and wanted to cut a deal as in "pay the bill and we will forget about the lawsuit."

We turned him down because first of all The Woodland Hills Trails Association was not a "real" homeowner association that could foreclose, right? Secondly, we knew if we accepted that deal, they would be back again the following year with a lawsuit unless we got the maintenance fees corrected finally.

Attorney Michael Treece left and that was when the Trails Association brought in Attorney Jeffrey Ewalt.

All that talk from the trails association about foreclosure was nerve-racking. What are they talking about? They cannot take our home. We protected it at closing when we signed the document stating we would be using it as our main domicile and it was our homestead property, we thought. How could a trails association foreclose on your homestead? Not only were we confused about how they could foreclose but also the fact it was a trails association was even more puzzling to us.

After the case had been remanded back to the Court, we were able to prepare an answer and a defense. We found out our maintenance fees included an amount that had not been voted on by the homeowners. We told them take that out and we will pay it. They would not. Therefore, we had no choice but to counter sue. We brought in witnesses from the association. We took very good depositions. We were able to subpoena the former

9

President at the "association" and former officers who were involved with the unauthorized assessment hike, along with homeowners willing to help us win our case. We were able to do excellent discovery on this case.

On my way back to the courtroom from the restroom, Travis McCormick, the Accountant for the associations in Kingwood, Texas, insulted me. I immediately told Johnnie. He found Travis still in the hallway and Johnnie asked him not to confront me like that again. Travis left after that. I wondered what Johnnie said to him. I never had that problem with Travis again.

Overall the trial went well and the judge agreed with our position that the association had breached the covenants when they decided to have a third illegal meeting to raise the fees and accumulate their proxies, even counting them at home outside the meeting.

One of the pieces of evidence uncovered was a proxy sheet with Jeff Ewalt's name on it. How did that happen when he was not at the homeowner's meeting held in the 80's? Why is he now handling and counting proxies? Our witnesses cleared that up for us with some of the best testimony I have heard to date. In fact, one participant in the actual counting of the proxies admitted they were counted outside the meeting and at their homes and that is why there were blanks on the minutes' page for the Special Meeting held October 1, 1985. The blanks were never filled in.

We hired an excellent court reporting firm. They came to the house and did the depositions. The only downside regarding it was the fact Attorney Jeff Ewalt had to enter our homestead to witness the proceedings for his client, the Woodland Hills Trails Association. I never felt the same living there after he contaminated the CO_2 in the family room. I also noticed him surveying the family room and the rest of the lower level of the house as though he were taking a mental inventory of his future real estate and he wanted to remember the way everything looked in the event there was exit damage.

The day the board member was being deposed who admitted counting the proxies at home after the third unauthorized meeting and accumulating them, Ewalt was not there. He sent his partner David Dickinson. It is always interesting to watch the face of an attorney when his client makes a confession. They try so hard to look like nothing important has been said to not alert you to the goodie you just got.

There were about eleven (11) depositions to take. Among the worst ones was the former board member who had an amnesia problem. She could not remember anything. Most everything was "I don't remember", or a variation of it. I had to ask her did she have some kind of memory problem. The answer was, of course, "no". The next worst one was the accounting firm. We wondered how the books could have been correctly audited during the year the illegal increase was made without the auditors knowing. They

11

thought we were a joke or I should say they thought I was a joke since I was asking the questions. They gave clever little answers to all my questions but when I left, I knew they had put together a false audit because they tried too hard to dodge all my questions. If you have nothing to hide, you do not need to dodge. Johnnie and I both maintained our cool. In all the years we litigated, we never went "postal".

Being a neophyte was costly. We won some things and lost some things. We paid dearly and lost a lot of damages because I did not calculate my damages correctly in this particular case. I did not realize until later just how much my ignorance of the law cost me at this juncture. I would say thousands and thousands of dollars. It was like winning the battle but losing the war.

For me the testimony was extremely tough as not only did I have the burden of presenting our case but also during the trial, my beloved mother died and I had the additional burden of mourning her death while trying to testify and enter our damages. The trial had to be recessed momentarily as I broke down and cried.

At the end of the day, the association won attorney fees and we won attorney fees. They won more attorney fees than we did because they pled more. While the Findings of Facts and Conclusion of Law reflected the breach and more detail of the trial, the Final Judgment did not as Ewalt drafted it and Judge Harvey Brown signed it on August 25, 1995 after we had appealed Judge O'Neill's decision to grant attorney fees to the association and lost. We were surprised the original judge still said the Trails was entitled to foreclose and that was why they were awarded attorney fees as well. Guess she did not notice we challenged the Trails having the ability to foreclose, it was not a "real" association and they had unclean hands because of the breach.

Up to this point, no one seemed to know how we could lose our homestead over maintenance fees when we had Homestead Protection. Finally, we found one who knew, Senator Jack Fields. He has since left politics. When we called Sen. Fields' office for help, we received no help. In fact, they supported foreclosures and directed us to this Inwood vs. Harris case law. So back in those days, the only people who seemed to know about Inwood vs. Harris was Sen. Jack Fields, Inwood's attorney Lou Burton and other Community Associations Institute attorneys and special interest groups and it was quite clear we were not going to get any help from any of them to stop our foreclosure proceedings.

We had two associations in our village, the wannabe community association, The Woodland Hills Trails Association; and the real association, North Woodland Hills Village Community Association, Kingwood, Texas.

Their lawsuit progressed through the system as we continued to learn about Inwood vs. Harris. We finally wrote the Attorney General's office at the time, who was Dan Morales. I think he is in jail now. We thought maybe we could get some help from his office. Well we did not get any help from his office directly but we did get an interesting letter from both associations' attorneys, Roy D. Hailey for the Woodland Hills Trails Association and Jeffrey H. Ewalt for the North Woodland Hills Village Community Association in response to our Attorney General complaints filed January 31, 1992. We were billed $650.00 for each letter (their response to our complaint to the Attorney General), but it was educational. We finally learned what Inwood vs. Harris was all about and was able to use that information in our counter suits and other lawsuits.

Somehow, Inwood vs. Harris had given homeowner associations across the State of Texas the right to foreclose on one's homestead in spite of the fact we were suppose to have Homestead Protection. CAI Attorney Roy D. Hailey in his Attorney General response said, "The association is a legal entity whose lien rights arise by contract." Back then in 1992, a CAI attorney, Roy D. Hailey, agreed homeowners are entitled to review "the financials". CAI attorney, Jeff Ewalt, agreed, the same year of 1992, that homeowners are entitled to inspect "the books and records of the Association". What happened to those beliefs?

So did the Inwood case take away our rights? How did it get around the Texas Constitution? Is not the Constitution more powerful than a case law? Why do not more people know about this? I could not find much on the case law at the law library other than the Shepard's copy of it. I needed to know more about the law that had taken away our homestead rights. What place could I go that would tell me more? Austin, of course. My valedictorian skills had not failed me. I could still think.

Johnnie and I drove to Austin and asked for the Inwood file. For hours, we studied it. So, there were also other respondents, one by the name of Roland M. Pamilar as well as Charlie Harris. There were a Jorge Custodio, John A. Cruz and his wife Christina; Victor L. Cardenas and his wife Concepcion and Joseph A. Villarreal. None of them ever showed up to defend themselves. It was a default judgment. How tragic.

There were quite a few Amicus Curiae (friend of the court) briefs. There was one prepared by the Legal Committee of the Greater Houston Chapter of The Community Associations Institute. At the time of the brief on February 16, 1987, it appeared they did not have any homeowners as members. The brief stated, "the Community Associations Institute is a national organization comprised of eight thousand (8,000) members in forty-five (45) City Chapters, including chapters in Dallas, San Antonio, Austin and Houston. The Greater Houston chapter is comprised of 394 members who are developers, condominium, townhouse or subdivision community associations, management companies, attorneys, accountants, city and state officials and other persons who service community associations. The attorneys who prepared this brief represent, collectively, some six hundred seventy-three (673) community associations in the city of Houston and have knowledge of the existence of 2,200 community associations in Harris County."

What I found interesting about this brief were the signatures on it. There was Bruce Ian Schimmel with Schimmel & Associates; Jeffrey H. Ewalt with Butler, Langford & Ewalt; Roy Hailey; Charles S. Parrish with Eikenburg & Stiles; Marc D. Markel with Roberts, Markel & Folger; Howard M. Bookstaff with Hoover, Cox & Shearer; David L. Cook, Jr. with Polland & Cook; Christina Stone with Stone & Stone; Joel W. Mohrman with Tudzin & Tobor; Robin A. Hartman; Richard C. Waites with Richard C. Waites & Associates; Harvey A. Ford with Harpold, McDonald, Fitzgerald & Hall; Marilyn Mieszkuc with Gregg, Jones & Mieszkuc; Mitchell Katine with Jack C. Ogg & Associates; Richard Lievens with Frank, Elmore & Lievens and Austin Barsalou with Barsalou & Associates.

Two names jumped out at me—*Jeffrey H. Ewalt* with Butler, Langford & Ewalt and *Roy Hailey*. Marc D. Markel with Roberts, Markel & Folger meant nothing to me until later. At the time of studying the file, only Ewalt and Hailey

16

were familiar to me. Were not they the ones involved in the association's lawsuit against us? Were not they the ones who wrote those expensive replies to the Attorney General?

All the way up to the first hearing, it looked like the Texas Supreme Court denied Inwood North Homeowners' Association the right to foreclose on their contractual lien. It was not until the motion for rehearing that three Supreme Court judges including Justice Ted Robertson decided December 17, 1986, to grant a "consolidated motion for rehearing and withdrew its order of September 10, 1986 refusing the application, no reversible error." It was granted on Point of Error No. 3. The cause was "set for submission and oral argument for Wednesday, February 18, 1987 at 9:00 a.m." Regrettably, it was my daughter Paula's birthday. Had I known ten (10) years earlier that ten (10) years later, she would be sharing her birthday with an egregious law such as Inwood that would eventually rob us of our homestead, I would have done a better job planning my pregnancy.

I was truly amazed at the begging on the part of the various special interest groups, particularly one by the name of Marshall T. Gaspard, who stated in his October 10, 1986, letter to the Court "the granting of a writ of error is critical. It is not just a function of judicial review, but a necessity that the people of this State be granted (through Inwood North Homeowner's Association) an opportunity to argue their case." What people of this State? My goodness, the people of this state never spoke in Inwood. Then Mr.

Gaspard further states, "The consequences of this Court's decision may not have been fully appreciated by the Justices. There are thousands of homeowner associations in this State, effectively maintaining billions of dollars worth of real property. We must have the right to have our Supreme Court Justices hear this case." Well, one thing for sure, it certainly appeared as though it was their Supreme Court Justices in the end and not the people of Texas Supreme Court Justices.

Looking at the file made me angrier than before. It appeared the homeowners had been ganged up on by every CAI attorney, developer, homeowner association and special interest group in the State of Texas.

Why did only two dissenting Justices--Mauzy and Gonzales—have the real spirit of the law in their medulla oblongata? I felt like shouting at the copy machine as I copied the file (in case it disappears), it is a homestead issue, stupid! In fact, Justice Ted Robertson in his July 15, 1987, opinion stated in the first paragraph *the issue before this court is whether the homestead laws of Texas protect the homeowners against foreclosure for their failure to pay the assessments."*

As I read more of Justice Robertson's opinion, I disagreed more and more with what it said. It just did not make sense to me. It spoke of "deeds given to the various homeowners contained specific references to the maintenance charges, or in some cases to the property records where the declaration was filed." I thought, so what? Then in his opinion, he mentioned the words "'vendor's lien'" was "contained in the declaration". I have seen vendor's liens and this is no vendor's lien. Then at the end of the opinion, the words "contractual lien" appeared. He stated, "We recognize the harshness of the remedy of foreclosure, particularly when such a small sum is compared with the immeasurable value of a homestead. Under the laws of this state, however, we are bound to enforce the agreements into which the homeowners entered concerning the payment of assessments." I left the table in the room where I was reading this more confused than when I sat down because I was wondering when did the homeowners involved in this case enter an "agreement".

Then Justice Robertson said earlier, "in conclusion, we hold that under the facts in the present case, the Homeowners' Association is entitled to the foreclosure of the contractual lien it has on the houses of delinquent owners."

The sad part about cases like this is an error was made and now this "*present case*" is affecting every homeowner in the state and we have not had a chance to speak to straighten this mess out. The seeds of the group my husband Johnnie and I formed, The Texas Homeowner's Advocate Group, were being planted.

Armed with more knowledge than when we arrived, we made more copies and left Austin with thoughts of our next field trip, this time to a Public Library to study the Texas Constitution.

Once we got back home, we were exhausted. It was a long trip and hard on the eyes. There was a lot to read. The Point that Inwood won on was the evidence we were looking for. Point of Error Three read "the court erred in not granting the applications for writ of error upon Point of Error Three which reads: The Court of Appeals erred in affirming the judgment of the trial court which judgment denied foreclosure of the lien retained in the Declaration of Covenants and Restrictions – Inwood North, Sections Five and Six and order for sale pursuant to Article XVI, Section 50 of the Texas Constitution because petitioner held a valid and subsisting lien to secure payment of assessments which attached to and encumbered the respective lots of each respondent prior to such lots becoming homestead."

I looked at the copy of the Declaration of Covenants and Restrictions I had for Inwood North, Section 6, and I read Section 8, the effect of nonpayment of assessments and remedies of the association and it said, "Any assessments or charges which are not paid when due shall be delinquent. If an assessment or charge is not paid within thirty (30) days after the due date, the Association may bring an action at law against the Owner personally obligated to pay the same, or to foreclose the Vendor's Lien herein retained against the lot. Interest accruing on past due assessments at the maximum rate permitted by law, costs and reasonable attorney's fees incurred in any such action shall be added to the amount of such assessment or charge."

The section troubled me. Why was it referring to a "Vendor's Lien"? In the case law, they also mentioned a "contractual lien" and admitted this was no "Vendor's Lien". Also, the section of the covenants that stated "each such Owner, by his acceptance of a Deed to a Lot, hereby expressly vests in the Association or its agents, the right and power to bring all actions against such Owner personally for the collection of such assessments and charges as a debt and to enforce the Vendor's Lien by all methods available for the enforcement of such liens, including foreclosure by an action brought in the name of the Association either judicially or non-judicially by power of sale, and such Owner expressly grants to the Association a power of sale in connection with the nonjudicial foreclosure of the Vendor's Lien. Non-judicial foreclosure shall be conducted by notice and posting of sale in accordance with the then applicable laws of the State of Texas. No Owner may waive or otherwise escape liability for the assessments provided for herein by non-use of the Community Properties or abandonment of his Lot."

I looked at my Shepard's copy of Inwood and saw where the court acknowledged this was no "Vendor's lien". I was eager to see what the Texas Constitution would reveal about "contractual liens" and "Vendor Liens".

Johnnie had just given me my cup of water in the Law Library and I could barely keep my excitement level down. What I had just read blew me away. I immediately got up, paid for a copy card, and went into the copy room to preserve this exciting moment.

I have in my hand The Texas Constitution, Homestead Law, Article XVI, Section 50; and I could not find any reference to "contractual liens" nor any reference to developers having a higher lien right than a homeowner; and the description for a Vendor's Lien did not fit what I found in the *Inwood* case law.

Earlier that day, God sent an angel to the library by way of a black attorney whom Johnnie approached to help me out. I did not have a clue as to what section of the library to be in to do research, let alone what to do with the book once I found it. Wherever that angel is today, may God bless him and his family always.

Once I got that excellent start, I was like a toddler learning to walk; once they get up to walk, they do not look back. Once I learned how to research in a law library, I never looked back. I had my special table where we would mostly sit. The library even had rooms to make phone calls and had rooms to type in. It really helped to have this at our disposal because sometimes it was necessary to type a quick motion.

Over the years, I was surprised to see how many attorneys came to the law library to do research. I thought they all had those big offices with reference libraries in them. They certainly collected enough attorney fees from homeowners to build a library in their office.

Once we got back home with the Homestead Act clutched in my hands, I immediately went to my office that was in Karen's bedroom. I often felt so guilty typing way into the night so often and probably disturbing her precious sleep. This was not a good time for any of us.

I carefully read the Homestead Act in its entirety as I have many times since then, and there was definitely no exception for "contractual liens" as referenced in the case law Inwood and there were no reference to developers being able to place one-party contracts on land prior to our homestead designation at closing.

I went on-line to try to find other homeowners I could discuss this with and found no Texas groups on-line at the time. Most of the groups I joined in those days, the early nineties, were in other states and mostly engaged in their own problems in their own states. Once or twice, I sent out an email asking if anyone from Texas was on-line but did not get back any responses, so I assumed I was the only Texan having difficulty.

I began to realize that I was sitting on top of a minefield. How many legislators really knew about this and were not addressing it because they were benefiting either financially from it or politically from it? How could something so clear in the Homestead Act be abused like this? Then I thought about where I was—in Texas. The state where President John F. Kennedy had been assassinated. The state where the slaves had been emancipated three years before they knew about it. The state where some of the biggest violators of the S & L scandal came from.

Each time we had to go to court, we dug deeper into the Texas Constitution to find or confirm information. In those days, I made a complete circle. What I innocently saw as a virgin litigate, I saw later as a seasoned litigate. In the beginning, the homeowner associations' attorneys tried to convince the court I was wrong in my legal position but I kept on stating them because I knew I was right. I learned early on that not only was I right but they knew I was right and tried to discredit me in court with their favorite alert statement to their judges—she is "pro se, your honor".

By saying I was "pro se" was to alert the Court that it is okay to grant the attorney's motion even though they were wrong. It is okay to take away the Joneses' rights because they are ignorant of the law. However, I was thinking, wait a minute, Mr. Attorney, was that not you I saw fleeing the library when you saw me there? I know where the books are now too thanks to my angel.

The more we began to spread the word about Texas's dirty little secret, the more assertive the lawyers became and the association became. One night we were "visited" by three men. Two appeared at the door and one hid in the shadows. Johnnie opened the door with his one hand behind his back as in "I have a weapon in my hand". The two men at the door and the one in the shadows noted all of that and I guess they said, there would be no crime tonight. They said they were looking for a family down the street and wondered if we knew them. After hearing the name, we did not. Of course, no such person lived on that street.

This visit came after the association's attorney Jeffrey Ewalt had to pay us sanctions for not complying with discovery. We were now engaged in a lawsuit with the real association, North Woodland Hills Village Community Association, and their attorney was Jeffrey Ewalt. They decided to proceed with their lawsuit after the Trails lawsuit had been remanded back from the Court of Appeals. It is called, "let's rush the pro se all at once and confuse them."

We had counter sued and were putting up a good fight. The judge on this case was Eugene Chambers, who was a former librarian. Once he resigned from the bench, we use to see him at the law library. He was known as the "sleeping judge" because he would sometimes fall asleep in the middle of a case and is now deceased.

On February 9, 1994, we received a letter from Rep. Craig Washington stating, "Your understanding of the Homestead Act is correct in that a foreclosure can only be affected due to failure to make payments of mortgage, home repair loans, or taxes. There are no exceptions. You should rest assured that nonpayment of assessment fees does not constitute grounds for foreclosure. Enclosed you will find additional information regarding the Homestead Act. I hope you find it helpful."

Why would a member of the Congress of the United States say that about his home state constitution unless it was true?

Jeffrey H. Ewalt, formerly with Butler, Ewalt & Hailey, owed us sanction money so we arranged to go to his office and collect our sanction Judge Eugene Chambers had awarded us. We were early into our counter suit against The Woodland Hills Village Community Association and had won our right not only to get the information we were seeking but also to get the sanction we had sought as well.

We had counter sued our association. This association had filed their lawsuit against us when the Trails Association lawsuit had been reversed and remanded. It was called a two-prong attack led by Jeff Ewalt. Therefore, we were fighting both associations at the same time.

When we walked into Ewalt's office, we were taken aback. Oh, my Lord, what an office. I have never been in one before or since like it. Beautiful dark wood (believe it was mahogany) furniture and high-end wall paneling. It was breathtaking. Then I stopped and thought. Wait a minute. There are tons of attorneys in Houston, how can you make this kind of money for this kind of office when there is so much competition?

I then began to notice that the receptionist was taking calls from homeowners regarding paying debts. She asked each caller what homeowner association they lived in. Not one call received while we were in his office involved a non-HOA matter. It was a collection agency. I thought about the names I had seen on the Amicus Curiae for the Inwood case and I began to derive a conclusion. This is really nothing but a collection agency.

Roy Hailey and Jeffrey Ewalt were two of the names I recognized on one of those Inwood Amicus Curiae briefs and now I was in their office. I recall thinking, this is a racket. Instead of chasing the ambulance in the traditional way of an attorney, these attorneys here in Harris County, have created, supported and benefited from stealing homeowners' homestead protection and making it look legal. Oh my God!

I left rather hurriedly because I was beginning to get physically ill and that night I took an extremely long bath. I felt like I had been raped!

I awakened the next day more determined than ever to stop this electronic fornication of homeowners. Johnnie and I decided to go to the Harris County Courthouse downtown Houston and research the records to find out how many lawsuits the attorneys we had met thus far had filed. We found Jeff Ewalt, Roy Hailey, Michael J. Treece, and Rick S. Butler had filed quite a few foreclosure filings. The king of the foreclosure filings, though, was Jeff Ewalt. This man loved to file foreclosures and most of them seemed to be in areas where the price of the home was under $100,000. We noticed that some of them were filed under their firm's name, Butler, Ewalt and Hailey, so we could not get an accurate total. We had copies made of what we found showing the pattern of increased foreclosures from 1987 to the current

28

time—1993 and decided to start notifying the State Bar, District Attorney, any agency or entity that we could interest in this obvious abuse.

We began to bring it to our legislators' attention as well as other homeowner advocates. We never got a satisfying result from this research. We are not certain what was done with our research. It appeared any progress made forward was lost at the State Bar. We filed complaints with the State Bar over the years but nothing happened there either. It was a total waste of our time to file the complaints. The Houston State Bar appears to be an alert system for the offending attorney to let him or her know what complaint has been lodged and then nothing happens. One time, we and other advocates picketed the State Bar and while nothing may have been accomplished from it, we had a surge of accomplishment from letting others know how ineffective the organization is.

I suppose you can liken it to going to a turkey and reporting the wrong activity of another turkey. We did notice, though, once we started investigating into the activity of this particular attorney, Jeff Ewalt, his foreclosure filings subsided somewhat. Of course, once all the lawsuits were over, he resumed his activity. Later, down the line, when I learned he had left Butler, Ewalt and Hailey, and formed his own firm with another attorney by the name of David B. Dickinson, I thought, good. I bet they kicked him out because he was lower than a snake and worse than the Devil in hell. He is an antichrist and I am not sure how he sleeps at night.

I have personally witnessed the pain and suffering, besides ours, that he has caused other homeowners. He is a hated man. He has taken homes from cancer patients, single women trying to raise their families by themselves. He has no mercy for anyone, there is nothing that he will not do to win, and there is no rock low enough that he will not crawl under. He is the poster boy for the Devil. He is not fit to be an attorney and should be disbarred. I encourage anyone that see his name anywhere running for any public office, do your self a favor, and do not vote for him.

I knew I was under a lot of stress but I was too busy to notice the small round bright red spot on the top left side of my head. My daughter Karen was the first to discover it. She was combing my hair one day while we were looking at television and exclaimed when she saw it. I checked it out with a mirror but was not too concerned and attributed it to my poor diet (even though Johnnie was trying to feed me, I was not that hungry most of the time), lack of sleep and increased stress.

It spread fast because the next time she worked on my hair, she screamed. I ran to the bathroom, grabbed a mirror, and screamed myself. The small, insignificant spot had turned into a bigger red circular spot on the left side of my head. What in the world was it?

I started calling doctors and asking around and finally, I got a name for the Mars' like circles that kept appearing on my head, Alopecia Areata, baldness. Oh Great! Now I am going to be bald on top of everything else I am going through right now.

I, of course, went out and invested a small fortune on wigs. Although at some point, there was so much hair loss at one time, there was not enough hair to pin the wig to.

Every time I had a stressful day at court, by the time I went to bed that night, I would have a new circle. They began to occur near the medulla oblongata area of my head. The spots were no longer red, just big and slick to the feel. When I stressed, it began to feel like something inside my head was eating my hair follicles and once I felt that pressure inside my hair, a new spot would be there.

I began to look at Johnnie's thick head of hair with envy. Why was this not happening to his hair? Is this not a male baldness thing? Then I recalled, oh yeah, I am the lead attorney. Remember? The one with all the pressure, all the research, and doing all the arguing in Court.

Being the type of person I am, though, I decided to fight this male baldness called Alopecia Areata, so I began calling doctors again as well as hair clinics and everyone else I could think of who would know what to do. No one knew what to do in my particular case. "There is no cure for it," they said. "We don't know what could have caused it." "There is nothing you can do." I do not think so! The defeatist attitude does not work well for me so I started going to health food stores again, buying herbs and vitamins. I tried ointments on my spots. Prayed fervent prayers. Improved my eating habits with less chocolate candy in my diet. Tried to decrease my stress level and not think about my head circles so much. Tried head massages—the whole nine yards.

Then miraculously (and I do believe in miracles), the original spot began to sprout new hair growth. During a routine check by Karen, she became very excited when she noticed fuzz on the original spot. Of course,

I had to check it out immediately and became excited with her. We were all pleased with that discovery. So, your hair can grow back, I thought. Thank you, God, for answering my prayers.

Over the next couple of years, I lost all of my hair except the hair close to my face in the front and on the sides. As soon as hair would grow back in one spot, it would come out in another spot. Sometimes hair would come out again in spots that had just grown back in. It depended upon whether or not I had a good day in Court. There were not many good days in Court. Stress had attacked my immune system and caused my hair loss at least that was my self-diagnosis.

Eventually, I learned to control my stress levels and to eat the meals Johnnie was preparing for me. My weight gain was tremendous due to all the sitting at the computer.

The day we met Roberta Jones Hanna, C.D.E. (Certified Document Examiner), was one of the worst days of my life. God must have been working on someone else's problems when she entered our lives. She apparently sensed we had a few extra dollars in our possession that she was determined to make sure when she left, the money would go with her. In the words of my deceased mother, she must have thought we had "money stacked up to the ceiling".

Next to homeowner association attorneys that foreclose on homeowners are greedy certified document examiners that feed on scared, vulnerable homeowners trying to save their homes from foreclosure.

Roberta came across as a nice, caring senior citizen. However, when challenged, her true nature emerged, which was a "pit bull on steroids".

I clearly remember the day she came into our lives. We had just learned during our discovery process in the North Woodland Hills Community Association lawsuit we had filed that some of the association documents had been altered.

We had two law firms on the ropes, including the one that handled the foreclosure on our homestead. We had 316 documents copied in Travis McCormick's office. If you recall, he was the accountant for the associations in Kingwood, Texas, that insulted me in Court during the Woodland Hills Trails Association trial.

The cost for the documents was 25 cents per page for a total of $79.00. It was well worth it. We had them! Or so we thought, until we brought in our forensic expert, our handwriting expert Hannah Jones. She is no relation to us.

This was dynamite information regarding the altered documents and we did not want to blow this opportunity to bring down the law firm of Roberts, Markel & Folger, L.L.P. and the association, so we looked in the yellow pages for a document examiner.

We had used one a couple of years' ago and wanted to use the same one, Lillian I. Hutchison & Associates. She had done such a wonderful job for us last time and only cost us $300.00. She understood my budget and complied. She did a good job and we wanted to use her again. She only took 2.4 hours at $125.00 per hour and brought in good results.

Oh, No! She is not available this time. It seemed she was on her way out of town and I need someone quick. I called down the list and everyone was either out of business or not available forcing me to leave a message. I had left my name and number at a couple of places and was hoping one would call back.

As the phone rang, I leaped to pick it up before it stopped. It was someone that shared part of our name—Jones. I explained to her my terms.

The job should not exceed $300.00, I had a couple of documents I had found during discovery that appeared to have been altered, and I needed confirmation. She said she could do it for $350.00. I thought that was not bad because, after all, it had been about two (2) years since I had gone to a document examiner so prices would have gone up a little bit. I have gone over that conversation many, many times because I wanted to make sure in my own mind that I had not misrepresented myself to Roberta. I never start projects without knowing what they will cost in the beginning so if it is too much, I get someone else. I do not believe in open-ended deals. My checkbook has a bottom to it. My mind was totally focused on what she was saying, as I did not want to misunderstand anything and even wrote down $350.00 the amount we had agreed upon.

When we got there, I paid her but I did not get a receipt. I did not think about a receipt until I left. I thought my canceled check would suffice. Johnnie and I were caught up in the excitement of our find. We told her we would need her report by August 28. We were in the year of our Lord 1995. She said she could meet the deadline.

There was no mention of additional money or any mention of it being a Phase 1 and 2 to the examination of the documents. We left and began to get calls from Roberta regarding this, that and the other. She said she needed an original. We went to the attorney's office but they did not produce the original, so she agreed to examine the copy.

We filed our motion to report violation of Penal Code 37.09 and needed her report for the August 28 hearing. Our biggest mistake aside from hiring her was failing to take the report and presenting it ourselves. Instead she insisted she needed to present the report and we agreed thinking it would help our motion. We did not find out until it was too late that she had been in contact with the association's attorney behind our backs.

Every time we would go to her home office, there was more money she needed. She kept saying, "This was more complicated than she originally thought." She realized through me how important her report was as we had received a Court order with contempt of order sanctions in the amount of $350.00 for the association failing to respond to our request for certain documents which included the original of the document she had examined. The altered documents were an attempt on the part of the association to influence the outcome of the lawsuit during the discovery process so that we would ultimately lose our homestead.

My mistake was I did not listen to Johnnie and that is why we got "sucker punched". He tried to tell me to drop her when she wanted money above the $350.00 I had agreed to but I was so desperate to get the information I thought we needed so badly to win the Motion.

Johnnie has a "crook-detector" Geiger counter attached to his brain. He is excellent at reading good or bad character and whenever I do not listen to him, history will record, I always pay a high price. So, since I did not listen, a $350.00 total fee turned into a $350.00 down payment and the entire job ended up costing us $2,628.75, which I was never able to recover.

As though that was not enough, at the trial, she wanted more money. As always, I did not know until the day she arrived in Court with her report to testify. She whispered to me as she sat next to be on the bench, "it is going to cost $600.00 for me to testify". I was forced to write a check, which she accused me of stopping payment on later.

What a greedy woman. Did she not have enough of my money already? At any rate, she whispered again, when I was showing hesitation about writing the check, "if you don't pay me $600.00, I will not testify." This was the Dr. Hyde side of her personality. Who would have believed this was a handicap woman suffering from Lupus acting like this. I should have held her to her verbal threat. It would have been the best move of the day. Her testimony is what killed our motion. However, as they say, "hind sight is twenty twenty".

God was trying to help us out but I was not listening. I missed his first and second warning, and paid the price for not listening. She destroyed our motion. She confused Judge Dwight Jefferson so badly; he appeared to have become a bit impatient with it all. He started being very respectful and eager to learn of this Penal Code Violation. It soon became clear that our document expert Roberta Jones Hanna did not have a clue as to what she was doing. She made a simple alteration of documents look like the most complicated operation in the word. We have all heard of cut and paste. Simply stated, someone cut out information pertaining to a material fact in our case and pasted the irrelevant material in its place. There was a line in the document, which I noticed during discovery, and the other document had weird changes in it as well.

This was such an important motion, so much so, that they had brought in a team against us. Three members from the Roberts, Markel & Folger firm were there—Patricia A. Quinn (brought in by the firm to work on some cases; ours was one of them she worked on), Marc D. Markel and Jeffrey D. Roberts. Also in attendance was Jeffrey H. Ewalt now with his own new firm--Ewalt & Dickinson. On my way to the restroom, I had seen them all huddled in a football circle discussing their strategy. They had pulled Marc Markel out as the lead man and substituted him with Patricia A. Quinn to counter me—woman against woman. Patricia had made sure she came into the courtroom pulling behind her this big box of documents. I requested she open the box and produce the documents we were still missing but by then the Judge was still recovering from Roberta's antics with her pointer and lack of knowledge so he ultimately denied our motion.

We processed Roberta through the complaint system. We certainly had plenty of experience in doing that by now. We filed an Attorney General complaint on September 5, 1995. We reported her to the Better Business Bureau and we filed a small claims lawsuit against her for her Deceptive

Trade Practices. One of the things she did was she "failed to disclose fee of service with intent to induce us to transaction and continued to work and accrue fees even after being told several, several times not to." The woman was crazed with the smell of someone else's money.

When she was served with our Notice of Contempt of Court and Sanctions Hearing several years' later with an order compelling her to respond to our First Set of Interrogatories and Production, she finally took our lawsuit seriously and hired an attorney. She won. We filed an appeal and it went to the County Court level, where Judge Cynthia Crowe, Court at Law Number 4, voluntarily recused herself. Roberta won there too. Although we lost in the Small Claims Court and County Court, we chose not to appeal higher after our previous experience with appellate courts.

We never recovered our money; but we would like to think it taught her a lesson of respect for other people's money. She was a cocky woman but we know we taught her fear and respect. Perhaps she treated her next clients better and did not try to suck every penny from them.

Driving to Kinko's on Westheimer in Houston from Kingwood, Texas, after midnight was quite a drive. Nevertheless, we had to meet the United States Supreme Court deadline in a couple of days and needed to make the appropriate copies.

We were on the last leg of our journey to save our homestead from foreclosure. While we now totally understood how it had happened, we wondered why it had happened. Why would the State of Texas allow such egregious behavior when we had a Homestead Law that protected our homes or I should say was supposed to protect our homes?

We had fought the same battle with the Woodland Hills Village Community Association as we did with the Woodland Hills Trails Association regarding illegally raising the maintenance fees and in the Community Association lawsuit, we also challenged the ability to pay monthly, especially when we discovered during discovery that many other families had been allowed to do so.

While this was not racial discrimination, it was a privileged-membergroup discriminatory matter. Everyone must be treated the same in the association. You cannot give one family their request to pay monthly and then deny another family their request to make payments monthly. If you do, you are discriminating.

We had the option on the last leg of this lawsuit to either allow the Texas Supreme Court or the United States Supreme Court to hear our foreclosure issue. Taking into account, The Texas Supreme Court was the Court who had erred in their foreclosure decision in 1987 with Inwood, we decided it would be easier to walk on water than to get them to agree with our legal position on that issue. After our loss in the Court of Appeals, I began to understand better what happens in Texas, stays in Texas.

On June 28, 1995, we lost our case in the Fourteenth Court of Appeals, which had to be one of our more disappointing losses. We had hoped to be heard but once again, it was reinforced at our hearing that coming to Court, especially as a black female pro se litigant, was not always successful. While these words were not said, you felt the aura. However, let it be said that it really does not matter what sex, what age, what color you are or how much you paid for your house in Texas. When they come after you, it could be any profile.

Never in any of our lawsuits, did we use the race card, although our white friends have told us that is why we were foreclosed because we are black. In our opinion, it is about the "Benjamin's," "greenbacks," money. It does not matter what color, sex or age you are.

The Justices started out by clearing the Court and believe me when you see that happening, it is a clear sign that something unethical is about to take place. We were not surprised when it did, just extremely disappointed. We are citizens of these United States and we believe that you have the right, no matter who you are, to go to Court for justice. The Court system tells you as a pro se litigant you have the right to represent yourself but you must prepare yourself as though you are an attorney and do not expect special treatment.

We did not expect special treatment but we certainly did not expect the oppression we received 99% of the time while trying to save our homestead and while trying to get retribution against the perpetrators who had indulged in taking away our Constitutional right to jury trials and due process.

At the outset, we thought if we came to Court with the truth, we would emerge with a victory. If we prepared ourselves like an attorney, we would be respected and heard, and leave with the win we deserved. Instead, we emerged having sustained an injury we could not be treated for. How do you treat a bruised spirit? Or a broken heart? Or a dead soul? Where do you go for treatment when you have been raped by the system setup to help you get justice?

On June 7, 1994, at 1:30 p.m. on the ninth floor in the Fourteenth Court of Appeals courtroom, Justices Ross A. Sears, Norman R. Lee and William E. Junell permitted oral argument. I probably should correct that and say they permitted Attorney Jeffrey Ewalt to orally complain about how we had caused him so much pain and suffering and how we were not entitled to

43

win because it is an established right that the HOA's have here in Texas to foreclose and we were not going to win anyway. In other words, he told the Court what a pain in the buttocks we were to him, slackers; and we did not have a right to be there and were not going to win anyway. We were virtually wasting the Court's time and money.

I can certainly see why the Courts have fought cameras in the Courtroom and metal detectors. The Courtroom is a nasty place to be with many nasty, arrogant judges dressed in the legal version of the Ku Klux Klan with black robes instead of white robes.

They vigorously and humbly seek your votes or appointments and as soon as they enter the Courtroom, they transform into a god.

Whenever I tried to speak, I was told I would not win. At all costs, this Court was not going to make an exception when it came to the homeowner association's ability to foreclose.

Back in those days, when it came to homeowner association foreclosure disputes; and I believe our public dispute was among the first, it was extremely difficult to get past the tunnel vision of the judicial system. From the District Court to the Texas Supreme Court, every court was on the same page as far as protecting the rights of the homeowner associations to foreclose on our homesteads.

Therefore, we sat in the Fourteenth Court of Appeals that day June 7, three days from our wedding anniversary and sat through yet another deprivation of our right to be heard. We could not yell, scream or shout as we sat through Ewalt sucking up our time with lies, deceit and pity party testimony. All the time we had waited for this moment and it was lost in a few moments of Ewalt's testimony. How could this poor excuse for an attorney and a man, a man that should be disbarred, be respected in this high Court?

This time when I looked across the room, I did not panic. I was beginning to have another "white out". A white out for me was when I temporarily went blind. When it first happened, I thought smoke was slowly coming from somewhere in the Courtroom as I began to lose sight of the occupants in the room. I am sure all the pressure I was under caused it. All that stress. The first time it happened was during the Woodland Hills Trails Association trial but it came and went quickly. This time it lingered a bit longer. I only have them in Courtrooms under circumstances such as the one we were going through at that moment. I thought, I am sure it will clear up in a moment. I will just give it some time. I hope that by the time this farce is over, I will be able to see how to get out of here without Johnnie's assistance.

While I was giving it some time, I was half listening to the cunning Mr. Ewalt and at the same time thinking about the day I could have saved our house.

Ewalt had filed a summary judgment for his client, The North Woodland Hills Village Community Association, and had attached the wrong exhibit to it. According to my research, the paperwork on a summary judgment has to be perfect. I filed a response to the summary judgment highlighting this error with the hopes the Court would reverse their decision for the association.

Johnnie and I went to the records room at the Harris County Courthouse to get a copy of the incorrect document that was filed. Normally, I would have immediately had a copy made; but as fate would have it, that day I had a migraine headache (something I had inherited since all the litigation) and did not feel well enough to wait to get copies made of the page, so we decided to return Tuesday after the holiday.

We returned after the holiday and that was when we got the shock of our lives—the page had been replaced with the correct one and I had not made a copy of the old page in the file so I could not prove the switch.

We lost a little bit of our spirit that day. It was a hard lesson and another hard day at the Courthouse. We wondered who could have made the switch for Ewalt. We narrowed it down to Court 215's female court clerk, who was still there when Judge Dwight Jefferson arrived. God forbid she tried anything else. She worked for Judge Eugene Chambers and his replacement Judge Dwight Jefferson. She had a long tenure. We were appalled that anyone would do such a thing. We prayed for her. We really did. It was not a vengeful prayer.

We filed our lawsuit, not our counter lawsuit (it had been already filed); but, this time, it was our lawsuit filed. We found it rather odd that we got the same Court as the association's lawsuit against us—Court 215. Were these not supposed to be random balls picked? We thought we might as well give this up but God knew what He was doing when He allowed it to be put back in Court 215; as unknown to us, Judge Chambers had retired and returned to the library for good and had been replaced by one of the fairest judges we have ever been before--Judge Dwight Jefferson.

Well it looks like Ewalt has finished his argument. Time to go home and await the results of this shameful hearing.

The denials came back in rapid succession. The Supreme Court of the United States denied our petition for a writ of certiorari on June 12, 1995. A quick decision given the fact it had only been docketed on April 11, 1995. On June 28, 1995, the Fourteenth Court of Appeals issued the Mandate.

"Keep it simple." Funny, I would remember those words. It came from the mouth of one of Houston's most interesting judges. Colorful, loud, charismatic, scary, insulting, rude, wannabe comedian, and unfair are just a few words to describe Judge David West.

He would look me in the eye with a look of steel and say, "don't think I am going to help a pro se". The word "pro se" would roll off his lips like a bad piece of steak had just been ejected from his teeth.

Some of the early advocates would come as Court watchers to give us support. One in particular was killed due to being roughed up one day in Court, causing hospitalization and his subsequent death.

The snakes protect each other but who protects the homeowners? Who will step up to the plate?

The lawsuit before Judge West was filed against Jeffrey H. Ewalt and his new law firm Ewalt & Dickinson. His partner David B. Dickinson was the attorney for both of them. Is it amazing when an unethical attorney is caught, how they never have the guts to defend themselves? They are only strong when someone else's house is in jeopardy.

The first thing we did when this lawsuit was returned to the docket after abatement was to file a Demand for Jury Trial. A Demand for Jury Trial is another waste of energy and money. The money must go to each Court's coffee and doughnut fund, because most of the time, you sure do not get that Constitutional jury trial you are entitled to.

This lawsuit against the association's attorney had been abated on April 17, 1995, until the two associations' lawsuits became final.

When the case had been abated, we tried to recuse the judge but he refused to recuse himself.

On May 6, 1996, we all agreed, Johnnie, Attorney Dickinson and I agreed to reinstate the lawsuit.

Discovery started and we looked forward to finally getting some answers to so much deceit. Not surprisingly, we ran into opposition and found it necessary to file a Motion to Compel Production. Surprisingly Judge West signed an order to produce but not surprising Judge West refused to sanction him. He said, "We will just let it accumulate. That's the way I like to do it." It did not seem like he was just letting "it accumulate" for other litigates.

When the attorneys approached the bench, there was gaiety, laughter, and a joke from the bench. When we approached, the demeanor changed. The gaiety ended the laughter, and the jokes. It was distracting and disturbing. In addition, a pro se litigant's argument time is cut down; and sometimes even if it is your motion, you do not get to speak first. Sometimes the Judge will even look at the opposing attorney while talking to you about your motion, waiting for the opposing attorney to answer the question put to you.

Since none of the associations' attorneys was fair, it was constantly a battle of wits and good timing to jump in when you could so that you could explain your case and win your motion.

On the day of the Motion to Compel Production Hearing, Ewalt made an anonymous call to the Court pretending to be someone else and stating Dickinson would not be there. Did Ewalt not think I could identify his voice over the phone? Even with that testimony, Judge West did not see fit to sanction Ewalt.

We never really got much information during discovery. Several months' later, Dickinson filed their Summary Judgment and set it two days before our trial. However, we were scheduled in another court and filed a Motion for Continuance. Judge West denied our motion, assured us it was "not required", and actually wrote the words on our June 3, 1996 cover letter to the Court, which you may inspect in the back of this book in the "Documents" section marked "Chapter 11".

The Summary Judgment filed is one of the Community Association Institute's (CAI) favorite trial killing devices. Claiming there are "no disputed issues of material fact in the case and therefore—as a matter of law-- they were entitled to a summary judgment as to all matters." The other device they use to abuse level is dismissals. The court system takes you through mock preparation then allows the attorneys to snatch it away from you at the last minute with the dismissals and summary judgment motions. The jury trial or trial before a judge is only going to work if the judge is fair and how do you really know the judge is fair? Or will be fair to you even if he or she is fair to someone else? Answer: You do not.

At any rate, we filed fraud charges against Ewalt for his misrepresentation while handling the two homeowner association cases. The saying "if you are not part of the solution, you are part of the problem" fits this scenario. Ewalt was always overseeing all the cases, putting his special touch on everything flowing in and out of the two Kingwood Homeowner association cases until we sued him and then he went into hibernation where he needed to be represented by his partner in crime, Atty. David Dickinson. It is so stressful, when circumstances are reversed.

Judge West was timid about disciplining Ewalt but swift in his punishment for us. He was not the first judge to act as co-counsel for the defendant and unfortunately, for us, he was not the last. Little did we know the granddaddy of jury trial violation was about to take place.

Remember that coffee and doughnut fund donation I talked about earlier? Here is why I said it. The jury trial was set. We were placed on the docket and even though, Ewalt had filed a summary judgment, the hearing had taken place in our absence, not continued, when the Judge knew and approved our absence, so we were not concerned about the summary judgment because we had the judge's "word" that a Motion for Continuance was "not required".

Approximately one to two days before the trial was to begin, we inadvertently learned a summary judgment had been granted to Ewalt. I called just to see where we were on the docket so I could get an idea what time to be at the Court for the trial and what time to tell the witnesses to be there. We had thirteen (13) witnesses on hold. They were Attorney Roy D. Hailey (Testimony as a fact and expert witness), Ms. Barbara Adams (Proxy Count and Deposition Testimony), Robert O. Little, Jr. (Proxy Count and Deposition Testimony), Joseph J. Fareed (Attorney Fees), Lynn Travis McCormick (Attorney Fees), Marc D. Markel (Attorney Fees), Jeffrey D. Roberts (Subject to the first lien testimony), John C. Clifton (Foreclosure purchase Testimony), Ms. Carole Cossey (Purchase of former house testimony), Ralph Murdock (Sale Procedures), Constable Wayne E. Eason (Sale Procedures), Deputy Wayne Chumley (Sale Procedures) and Captain Cecil D. Lacey (Sale Procedures).

The clerk said she would call me back. When she called me back and told me Ewalt had received a summary judgment and there would be no jury trial, we came as close to losing our minds as we have ever come since becoming advocates trying to protect our homestead. I cannot speak for Johnnie's mind. I know he was extremely mad.

However, here is what was going on inside my mind. It was in a surreal state. I had shifted into autopilot and entered a new dimension of reality. I was moving about physically but mentally I was trying to hold onto my sanity, hoping that I would not stay in this mental state because I would be rendered insane for the first time in my life. I remember thinking how could this have happened? The judge had given us permission to not be there because he understood you could not be in two places at the same time. We trusted him. We relied on his representation. We recalled how during the Motion to Produce, the Judge had failed to sanction Ewalt for not being there even though Ewalt had not produced a good reason for not being there.

You could say our litigation life ran before us. Then we wondered why he would rule a death penalty decision on Ewalt's Summary Judgment in our absence when he had authorized the absence? We recalled him referring to accumulating sanctions and then understood he was obviously accumulating them against us.

While I was operating on my third field of mental juices, I remembered to call a member of the advocate Court watchers to meet us in the Courtroom. We literally flew down there, only we used our car. We were suspended in some three-dimensional time warp.

I remembered quickly dressing in jeans and a blouse that were not Court attire but sufficient for the moment. We thought if we got down there fast enough and protested to the Judge, we could stop this latest violation of our due process rights.

I kept saying, "I don't believe this," "I don't believe this," "I don't believe this." I was shouting it, as I got ready to go. I truly felt as close to being crazy or we both were momentarily as crazy as we will ever get. We thank God for snatching us back from the final snap.

Once we got to Court, we entered Court 269 and spoke with his Clerk. Court was not in session so we set a date for a Motion for Rehearing. I remember going to the law library to use their typewriter and hurriedly put together a motion, thanking God along the way for making me aware earlier there was a room with a typewriter in it. In fact, I believe that was the day I actually saw Ewalt's partner Dickinson in the library and I informed him they could expect the motion. I did a certificate of conference right there in the library.

We rushed back during our lucid interval to the 269th Court and set the hearing, which I inserted into the motion and filed it.

When we returned for the hearing, we refreshed the Court's memory we had authorized absence from the Summary Judgment hearing. In addition, Ewalt had indicated in his Order, which the judge had signed, "The parties appeared before the court for the hearing on the motion." We questioned "what parties?"

Our Court watchers were there and we were unable to turn the situation around. We filed another Motion to Recuse the Judge. Guess what? This time he recused himself voluntarily on October 3, 1996. I suppose his thought was mission accomplished; now I can be excused. He had successfully protected Ewalt's right to continue to file egregious motions against third-party litigants for his HOA clients.

Judge West, with a stroke of his pen, had successfully set the stage for more homeowners to be extorted out of their money through boilerplate default or summary judgment filings by the clever Mr. Ewalt. Judge West, with a stroke of his pen, had tossed out $689.00 in subpoena fees and may have permanently blocked one of the biggest exposures of homeowner association foreclosure scam and extortion in the history of Harris County because we had subpoenaed all the players in the foreclosure, auction and "chill sale" of our former homestead.

The problem with all of this is there must be a law in each state to end third-party damage by attorneys that litigate for homeowner associations. Not only is it important to be able to sue your lawyer one-onone, you should also be able to sue your association's attorney when they step over the line as Attorney Jeffrey Ewalt did. Oh, my gosh! Even as I say his name Jeffrey, Jeffrey. Jeffrey is a name assigned to little boys with small toys. A cute, innocent little boy that would do no harm to anyone. I recommend a name change for Jeffrey Ewalt from Jeffrey to Lucifer.

As we looked around the room, we spotted the faces of some of the Court watchers who had supported us throughout many of our hearings. The room was full—"standing room only". More than 125 homeowners had gathered to vote for changes in our deed restrictions for the North Woodland Hills Village Community Association and the Woodland Hills Trail Association.

One of the mistakes we had made while living in Kingwood, Texas, was we never attended a board meeting. In fact, we did not know anything about them and by the time we did, we were in arrears with the associations because of our maintenance fee dispute over the unauthorized increases. Many people at the meeting had never been to a board meeting either because of the hostile climate between the association and its members— the homeowners.

There were only two anti-homeowner watchers in the group so that was not a bad average. The President of the North Woodland Hills Village Community Association was one and an unknown shouter of the message, "why don't you just move out of the community?" As she ran out the door. We got one call like that too; may have been the same woman. Not a bad average. We did not have ID caller then. It appeared most residents were on our side, because when you thought about it, what sane homeowner would want the type of oppression in their neighborhood an HOA delivers.

Johnnie, Paula, Karen and I had walked the entire North and South Woodland Hills Village area and collected signatures on form letters supporting us in our Texas Supreme Court appeal case earlier in the year and many of them were now in the audience supporting my efforts to amend the deed restrictions of both associations.

The meeting was successful and I received enough votes to make the amendments. "No opposing votes were cast in any of the actions," was reported in the Kingwood Sun, Wednesday, January 3, 1996, on the front page.

By the time the article hit the paper, we had moved out. When I called the meeting, we had started to box up our items and were preparing to move.

When the President of the Association, John Clifton, was later asked why he foreclosed on us, he stated, "If we had not foreclosed, they would have never moved."

The Request for Writ of Execution was filed once the association found out about our meeting to amend the declarations. They had sat on the foreclosure action until our final Court action in this matter had been denied. Ewalt executed the Request for Writ of Execution on October 18, 1995. The amount of the judgment was "$11,023.89 plus court cost and interest at 10% per annum."

We were the first homeowner-getting-kicked-out-of-home Texas realty show, years before Winona Blevins. A reporter from Channel 11, Michael Barnes, covered us for three (3) days and accompanied us to the Family Law Center that final reality day, December 5, 1995. The first Tuesday of each month, the homestead auctions are held at the Family Law Center in Harris County, downtown Houston.

The sun was out and it was weather wise not a bad day. While people who had seen us on television said Johnnie looked a bit strained, this day we both looked and felt resigned to our fate.

We had fought a good fight and were now accepting our doom. We wanted the event forever in the archives and appreciated Michael being there for us. Had it not been for Channel 11's Michael Barnes, I am not sure what would have happened to us, as we were extremely depressed during those last few days.

I recalled when I realized Johnnie had given up all hope of saving the homestead when he stopped planting and stopped talking about the fence replacement he was going to do before the foreclosure.

I wish I had not replaced the carpet, repainted rooms and installed wallpaper. I did those upgrades for us not for a new family.

When Michael entered the Harris County Family Law Center with his camera mounted firmly on his shoulder, he aroused great interest. Many there had already heard about us, the "slackers" as we were called in the spin-doctor circles. "Why didn't you just pay your fees?" (Ever heard of ratification?) "Why don't you just move?" (Why should we?) "I don't want to get involved." (Why not?) "I just want to be left alone." (Being left alone is not going to save you from a homestead loss.)

When others do not step up to the plate, someone else has to. On December 5, 1995, we stepped up to the plate because no one else had. Except for us, other violated homeowners had not come out of the closet yet.

Michael had found his target, Jeff Ewalt, who was now camera shy and began to ask him why he was foreclosing. I believe the answer was because we had not paid his client their authorized maintenance fees. It is amazing to me now, how a professionally trained certified liar can sum up all his malicious actions into one complete rational statement for all to hear and judge.

While it was interesting watching Ewalt being interviewed, rather uncomfortably at that, I caught someone else moving rather quickly across the room that looked like part of the Ewalt team. It was. It was Patricia Quinn, with a hugh smile on her face. If I had not known better, I would have thought I was attending a party. Maybe I was except there was no dancing or food. The two met in the middle of the room and began to talk.

By now, our attention was on the man who calls out the bidding. I immediately noticed something strange in this bidding process and fortunately, Michael's camera caught it for the archives.

What was strange was the way Captain Cecil D. Lacey looked right at the President of the Association, John C. Clifton, and then practically whispered the bid of $448.00. The house had a market value of $75,000. Lacey waited a few seconds and then affirmed the bid, while never breaking his eye contact with Clifton. There were no other bids as none were being solicited. The lien holder Union Planters Mortgage Company was not there although we tried to get them involved; and even though they were well aware of the auction, they chose not to participate or to pay the maintenance fees for us or to do anything to save the house. The bid was very low and did not cover anything. Why was the bid so low? Why was the bid accepted? How can you buy a $75,000 house for $448.00? It is almost a free house. I hope Ewalt told his client they are going to have to pay the mortgage.

The sale was recorded and we all walked away with a permanent realty film on record with Channel 11 for anyone's future review. We had just witnessed a "chill sale", where the bid is controlled and the buyer is already known. Everything pertaining to that sale was orchestrated whereby the house ended up in the possession of the President of the Association that had foreclosed on our homestead.

The outward happiness that had been expressed by Patricia Quinn and Jeffrey Ewalt was now subdued and it made me wonder, should they not be happier? Is this not what they wanted? Our house. I saw Clifton hand something to Ewalt with some kind of comment. A lip reader told me that the words from Ewalt were, "No, No". Wonder why he said that? The association now had our house. Now all they have to do is assume the monthly payments. Guess they forgot about that. We learned then, it is not the foreclosure they pursue, where they actually have your house in their possession. It is the threat of the foreclosure that nets proceeds for them. The "threat" of being foreclosed is the real weapon, the real hammer for the HOA. The "threat" is accomplished through the "filing" of the foreclosure. They do not have a clue as to what to do with the homes they actually foreclose and have in their possession, especially if there is a mortgage still on the property. If the victim does not make a loud noise to alert everyone, the foreclosed home is usually sold to investors for very little and resold to make a profit and the victim is stuck with the mortgage payment. If the home is paid for or has a large equity in it, and these are the homes the industry prey on, any amount they sell it for is a profit to the homeowner association and their lawyers. Non-profit corporations buying our auctioned homesteads and financially benefiting from the sale, how can this be?

When Johnnie and I stepped back and let our home go for auction, we had alerted everyone; and the homeowner association and their attorneys really did not know what to do with our mortgaged house since all eyes were upon the disposing of it.

This "cottage industry" is indeed an extortion racket where the threat of foreclosure brings in the money for the CAI attorneys and not the actual foreclosures.

Hence, we left the Family Law Center and as it say in Luke 9:5, "shake off the very dust from your feet."

As we walked away from the Family Law Center, we knew we had left one zone of our life and entered another. We found out later through discovery in our lawsuit against the North Woodland Hills Village Community Association they had actually paid only $184.92, for the $75,000 house. We saw the canceled check and so can you by checking the document section at the back of this book. How can you buy a $75,000 house at auction with a $184.92 check that you bidded $448.00 on?

We felt unusually free. It was as though 20 extra pounds of pressure and stress were suddenly lifted from each of our shoulders, although outwardly we looked the same, inwardly we were calm.

The day we had been avoiding for the past five (5) years had finally arrived. We had made one last attempt to save our homestead by filing an injunction to stop the foreclosure. The judge really left it in the hands of Atty. Jeffrey Ewalt as to whether or not we would be foreclosed. Ewalt held our whole world in his hands. He chose to take our homestead because he wanted the attorney fees the association he represented had not expended.

The judge then asked after we returned from our brief meeting with Ewalt during the injunction hearing if we had $13,000. The answer to that, of course, was "no". She then said, "I cannot stop the foreclosure." She continued to speak and said, "If you want to change the law, go to your legislators for change."

So our move-out day had arrived and it was once again a realty day. It was a cloudy day mixed with heavy then light sporadic rain. It was Wednesday, December 27, 1995; and Reporter Michael Barnes from Channel 11, who had been covering us, was there once again with cameras rolling to get the last shot of us moving out. We had not put up our Christmas tree that year and everything pertaining to Christmas had been boxed up early.

We felt very alone. There was no support. Our neighbor across the street, who had asked not to be involved when we had gone to him to sign our petition, was looking out a window at us, and probably thinking he knew he was right when he did not get involved. When you do not become involved, you are not right; you just delay your time at the turnstile.

Michael asked if there was someone he could call to be a part of the filming. The person we recommended we had helped, even while in the midst of our predicament, by taking time out from our dilemma to accompany her to Kingwood High School to meet with the Principal regarding her son. Her son had an attention deficit disorder and the teacher had tied him to the desk.

I even managed to send a fax as a character witness for her in the middle of my personal crisis. There were approximately 50 black families that lived in Kingwood, Texas, at the time we were there, collectively in all the villages that comprised Kingwood. George Forman was a resident of Kingwood also. He lived in one of the more expensive homes of Kingwood. The lady we were trying to reach knew him or rather her son knew his daughter.

When Forman won his fight, there was a sign announcing his win and his residency in the community posted at the entranceway. The sign stayed a short time and was ordered removed by one of the associations.

I complained and they returned it. George Forman is not aware of that little bit of advocacy work I did on his behalf. One last thought before I left my home.

Michael was unable to get our "friend" on the phone. Another lady showed up who I had just met at the meeting we had to amend the deed restrictions. She handed me one of my lamps, Channel 11 took that picture, and she gave us all hugs. We really appreciated that visit. One of our neighbors brought us home-baked cookies the night before. They were delicious. We maintain friendship with many still in that community. We gave Michael and his cameraman a hug and a sincere thank you for without his presence at one of the most vulnerable times in our lives, it would have been extremely difficult to get through it all. God surely sent him to us.

We gave away our dog Sebastian—our beloved Sebastian. He was too big to keep in the small apartment we were going to. The girls went back to college. Fortunately, for us, they are intelligent young women; Montessori trained and started college early. Paula started at 16; Karen started at 15. We ended up selling quite a bit of furniture and gave away many things too. We got storage for the items we could not fit into our apartment and which we were too sentimentally attached to sell or give away. When you live somewhere for seven (7) years, you accumulate a lot of stuff.

We moved into an apartment not too far from the Galleria on Briar Forest in what we later called "roaches run" (it had four types of roaches in it) and within a month moved again into a four-bedroom townhouse not too far from the Galleria. The townhouse was larger than the house we had just lost but it was not the same as our homestead.

With the loss of our homestead, the "hostage" had been killed. We still had a live lawsuit against the North Woodland Hills Village Community Association and they had "killed the hostage", or foreclosed on our homestead and taken it away from us. They expected us to go away, to drop our lawsuit or to commit suicide. We are not sure what they expected us to do. Something snapped. The boomerang effect had begun. What do you do when you have nothing to lose? You keep on fighting for your rights, only harder.

Ewalt had slipped through our hands in his lawsuit. Our lawsuit against him and his law firm were finished. Our discovery of two separate sets of attorney fees during our association discovery uncovered one set of attorney fees the North Woodland Hills Village Community Association had actually expended in the amount of $2,597.02. We also found another set of attorney fees he had put together while at Butler, Ewalt & Hailey that totaled $26,033.16. Thirty-seven pages, sequentially numbered by stamp, were submitted to Johnnie and me during our discovery. The figure included The North Woodland Hills Trails Association lawsuit and $18,004.17 was applied against the North Woodland Hills Village Community Association as debt owing for attorney fees that were actually not expended.

We learned through our lawsuit that Ewalt had made an agreement with the association that would allow him to collect what he could from us and it would not cost the association anything. In other words, the association turned their association loose on us. The $2,597.02 was what the association's expenditure was and Ewalt and his law firm fabricated the $18,004.17 figure at the time. The words found on the top sheet of page 1 of the fabricated fees speak for themselves, "Jeff, I also found this." It appears the feeding frenzy had begun.

Legislators must introduce legislation to capture this type of extortion on third-party litigants in homeowner association actions. Attorneys that do this type of extortion must be held accountable beyond their State Bars. Homeowner Associations must become regulated entities to ensure that there is oversight for malicious releasing of their Community Associations Institute (CAI) Attorneys on homeowners.

Before we left our homestead, one of the association's attorneys, Patricia Quinn, scheduled oral and video depositions duces tecum for September 27 and 28 after the court had indicated it was attempting to mediate in our lawsuit against The North Woodland Hills Village Community Association.

We decided once we had lost our homestead to go ahead with our lawsuit and to go ahead with the depositions. We had stepped up our attack and had filed a report with the Federal Bureau of Investigation (FBI), Internal Revenue Service (IRS), Post Office and The U.S. Dept. of Housing & Urban Development (HUD).

The District Attorney's office, John B. Holmes, Jr., surprised us by writing a letter to Mark Markel and Patricia Quinn on October 26, 1995, regarding the altered documents, which came on the heels of the Forgery Complaint we filed with the Houston Police Department September 7, 1995, Incident No. 103021195-E. We also talked extensively with Karen A. Barney, Assistant District Attorney, regarding the matter. Sometimes if you cannot get through the front door (Court), you have to go through the back door (agencies). If it sounds like we lined all our ducks in a row, we did.

When we reported our homestead loss to HUD, the Clinton Administration began to investigate the matter. It dragged on for years and once Bush got in office, the investigation stopped cold and so far, we have been unable to revive it. We have written letters to Senator Kay Bailey Hutchison to look into the foreclosure. We are requesting damages in the minimum amount of "$150,000, plus interest of $2,554.59 for a total of $152,554.59" which was "in the registry" at the time of our Federal complaint; and for some reason, while it should have been offered to us, was not. Kathleen Riska with Finance said, "We cannot make a payment of $201,304.68; therefore, I ask again, why wasn't the $152,554.59 presented?

Senator Hutchison received a response December 1999, from Hal C. DeCell III, Assistant Secretary with HUD, in which he dodged the bullet. Of course, we will continue to pursue this matter until it is resolved to our satisfaction. Our former homestead will never be able to be sold with a clear title until HUD resolves the matter with Johnnie and me.

When we entered the Court room for the Motion to Determine Market Value March 5, 1996, we were not surprised to see the association's entire legal team again, which included Jeff Ewalt, Marc Markel, Patricia Quinn and Jeffrey D. Roberts.

I had fought long and hard to get this hearing because, frankly, Judge Jefferson had become weary of this case since we had failed to have a successful mediation. He was trying to stop the foreclosure action and have us agree on attorney fees and such but Ewalt arrived at the Court with an affidavit that showed he wanted over $20,000 in attorney fees for the combined two lawsuits for his two clients—The Woodland Hills Trails Association and The North Woodland Hills Village Community Association, so Ewalt's request killed the mediation.

It is hard to mediate a lawsuit when attorneys are involved. They are a bit distracting because of the attorney fees; but it was imperative for us to determine the market value at the time of the foreclosure and to establish who created the deficiency (the association). It was not Johnnie and I who created the deficiency.

Getting past his Court Clerk was important though because she was the one we suspected replaced the incorrect summary judgment document with the correct one for Ewalt in the association's lawsuit, which led to the final demise of our homestead. Once we told her we really needed to set this hearing up to determine the market value of the homestead property at the time of the foreclosure sale, she relayed that message to Judge Jefferson and he agreed to the hearing. This was his first knowledge the homestead had been auctioned.

Once the attorneys learned we had attained the hearing, they decided to file a Second Summary Judgment Motion, which weighed almost five (5) pounds. Boy that thing was heavy. To this day, I am amazed they were able to staple it. They must have had to special order the staples and used a sledgehammer to staple it.

I thought, Oh, Great! Now Judge Jefferson is really going to be upset with this if they come in with the "baby whale" Summary Judgment.

It was one of my best hearings. It showed what I could do when the Judge is not bias, when the Judge is willing to listen to both sides, when the Judge does not interrupt either party, and when the Judge respects everyone in the Courtroom. It was an atmosphere to die for. My ability to express my opinion had finally found a Courtroom willing to hear it.

When I first saw the colored pictures, I knew something was wrong. Ewalt handed them to me. Yes, the man, I had learned to hate but who I had asked God to help me overcome my hate so that I can go to Heaven when I die. I looked at them very carefully and my suspicion meter went off. I was on the witness stand and Ewalt wanted me to help him destroy our Motion to Determine the Market Value of our former house at the time it was foreclosed. After looking at all the pictures of the house inside and outside, the swimming pool peaked my interest.

I know when we left the house everything was in top shape and we mailed the keys via certified mail to John Clifton immediately. Anything that happened to the house after we left was not our fault. However, here was Ewalt trying to get me to accept the pictures. The Market Value was important because that was part of the damages we were asking in our lawsuit and Ewalt was trying to reduce it or eliminate it all together.

When Judge Jefferson asked me if the pictures were a true copy of the house at the time of the foreclosure December 5, 1995, so that Ewalt could enter them into evidence, I said no. Fortunately, for me I was the one who cleaned the pool. I knew how long it took the pool to get a certain color. What I was looking at was a dark green color the pool had acquired, which meant the pictures had just been taken and reflected what the pool looked like closer to the hearing as opposed to when we left the house. When we left, the pool was a light blue because I cleaned it before we left.

Another suspicious point was the pictures were not dated. To me that is evidence 101. If these were legitimate pictures, they would have been dated. The fact they were not said it all. I told the Judge the pictures were not representative of the way everything looked when we left, especially the pool. The Judge granted our motion and determined the house was valued at $75,000 on the day of the foreclosure, December 5, 1995. The Judge took no action on their "baby whale" summary judgment. They were unable to use any of the depositions they took from us due to the fact we mentioned throughout the documents that their client had altered the documents we received during discovery.

In fact, I was bored listening to the questions presented to Johnnie during the taking of the depositions. They questioned him first. He hardly ever speaks in Court and they probably thought he would tell them something interesting. He actually told us all something interesting because they were trying to get him to agree to an old document to confirm a new one. A bait-and-switch type question. I remember Johnnie saying, "Wait a minute. What document are you reading from?" I was suddenly more alert.

Back in the Motion to Determine the Fair Market Value Courtroom, I thanked God. At last, I have beaten Ewalt. Maybe not in the way I expected but in a way I could appreciate and enjoy. One on one, without his co-counsel Judges, he was no match for me. I knew the law in this regard as well as he and he knew that and that is why it was so important to him to do all the underhanded techniques he had committed against my family and me.

In his tireless pursuit to destroy our homestead rights and to perpetuate the cottage industry he had helped create, he inadvertently stripped away his dignity, honor and bared his soul for all to see. When he left the Court, he was a short, old, cheap, embarrassed and defeated man because this pro se litigant with her fair Judge had finally exposed him to lady Justice. I do not mind losing anything; I just do not want to be cheated out of it. If you beat me fairly at something, then that is the way it is. If I beat you honestly, I expect my reward. Before we left that day, God motivated Ewalt's fellow cohort, Jeffrey D. Roberts, to say, "You know you are supposed to pay for that house." He said it in front of the Judge and everyone.

Right about early 1996, Johnnie and I decided to form an advocate support group for other homeowners to have someone to talk to about their problems with their HOA. We wanted to permanently stop homeowner association foreclosures and were greatly motivated by what had happened to us in Kingwood, Texas, and wanted to make sure that what happened to our family never, ever, ever happen to another family again.

The Texas Homeowner's Advocate Group was officially registered with the State of Texas and we opened our mailbox at P. O. Box 420925, Houston, Texas 77242. We opened a telephone line at 713-639-4991 and we were ready to help. One of our members gave us the nickname T.H.A.G. We liked it and decided to call ourselves that for short.

All the advocates, we had encountered so far, we networked with. This was the first time Texas had an official homeowner advocate group registered with the State of Texas in which actual homeowners could join and be helped with their various homeowner association problems. They can also help bring about a change.

Being pro se litigants, we cannot litigate for anyone else, but we can share our personal experiences with others and inform people how we would take on a particular situation. We eventually added an inhouse attorney to our group, who was ready to work with troubled homeowners on their legal issues. T.H.A.G. was always updating its work to help homeowners and we are flexible in what we are trying to do for the homeowners. We are your support group. (As an update, on April 5, 2006, The National Homeowners Advocate Group, LLC was created and oh my, what an organization. www.thenationalhomeownersadvocategroup.com, harvellajones1234@gmail.com) The Texas group (THAG) is now a 501(c)(3) group, depending on donations to help homeowners in various ways.

After years of litigating as a pro se, I realized how difficult it is for the average person due to time constraints, among other things, to protect their rights. We need reliable legal help to survive the attack of a homeowner association's Community Associations Institute trained attorney who is experienced in filing foreclosure pleadings against our property.

One day while speaking at a property rights meeting, a contact person for Prepaid Legal approached me and I was extremely excited about this idea of offering this wonderful plan to other homeowners who need legal help. I certainly wish I could have had it when I was learning to protect my rights. However, I subsequently discontinued being a part of Pre-paid legal because the organization began to fail in its help to the homeowners referred to them from my organizations.

There are very few homeowner friendly attorneys in this State who are willing to help the homeowner with their fight against a homeowner association and I want our group to be able to assist homeowners in all ways possible. While we do not go into the neighborhoods any longer, we are working on developing safer ways to communicate via our website www.thenationalhomeownersadvocategroup.com and give homeowners the latest information on bills that are before the legislators, if we are in session. We are not attorneys and cannot litigate for you; but we can share our experiences with you as there are many ways to communicate on-line these days with you and point you to your Constitutional rights, statutes, books, and other information that will help you save your homestead and document the activity of the perpetrator(s)

We encourage all homeowners everywhere to contact your legislators with all problems you are incurring with your homeowner association via your board and the association's attorney. If legislators do not hear from you, they think everything is okay.

Attend your board meetings because if you are out of the loop, you do not know what three, five, or more board members are doing to make your life miserable. If you attend the meetings, you are in a better position to know what is going on and can fix it before it gets out of hand.

Together we can accomplish something. It is extremely difficult to do something by yourself. When our associations and their attorneys were violating us, there was no one around to direct us to the correct source for help. One of T.H.A.G.'s task was to direct you to the correct source and (now the baton has been passed to the National Homeowners Advocate Group to do so.)

Our group gets emails from all over the country from people having HOA problems of some sort. We see emails from homeowners in cities in Texas I have never heard of. Places where CAI attorneys have gone into the community and encouraged homeowner association formation where none was before. On the other hand, places where there were dead homeowner associations but CAI attorneys have gone in and reactivated them; other homeowners who have formed homeowner associations without the approval of the entire neighborhood; homeowners collecting money from other homeowners and not authorized to do so. People are becoming ill over homeowner association issues. I personally hear from homeowners regarding all types of situations from "attorney fee" problems to being hit in the mouth by their board member.

CAI moles are constantly infiltrating advocate groups across the country. They want to get into the groups and break them up with disruptive statements so that the advocates can become disorganized. They usually start this around legislative session time. Most of the groups, including T.H.A.G. (and now TNHAG) have instituted a system to weed out moles before they get into the groups. If a mole happens to slip by, my group is smart. They can tell a mole a mile away and as soon as the mole is found, he or she is removed from the group. We need homeowners. We do not need CAI moles.

The description on our THAG website stated: "The Texas Homeowner's Advocate Group is a nonprofit group dedicated to protect the homestead rights of Texans; to support, monitor and help write laws pertaining to Texas homesteads; to permanently stop homeowner association homestead foreclosures and to support the removal of all HOA Homestead foreclosure language from the Texas Property Codes. " (The National group did and continues to do just that.) We encourage voters and homeowners to protect their property rights by attending their neighborhood HOA meetings and closely monitoring everything that takes place and by writing their legislators to encourage them to support any anti foreclosure pro homeowner bills." On March 19, 2000, the group went on-line and later became a 501(c)(3) organization. (Now we are operating under The National Homeowners Advocate Group, LLC) To join our group, simply send an email to harvellajones1234@gmail.com There is a small fee-based membership that helps pay our website hosting cost and other operating costs. Information is on our website for membership at http://www.thenationalhomeownersadvocategroup.com.

We had a National on-line petition asking homeowners across the nation to sign. The website was http://www.petitiononline.com/homeback/petition.html. We work hard as a group and we have made a difference in our state. Many of us go to hearings in Austin to support various homeowner friendly bills and we tried to get support for a proposed bill I wrote called Revised Jones Bill No. 1. This is the second bill I have written. I wrote one in the last session. This session's bill (2005) is shorter and more to the point (in other words, short and sweet) and is as follows:

By: _____ A BILL TO BE ENTITLED   **Revised**
Jones Bill No. 1
AN ACT

relating to homeowner associations' practice of foreclosing on homestead property through the use of "contractual liens" that run with the land and that are created by developers. These "contractual liens" are not on the "exception to foreclosure" list of the Texas Constitution Homestead Law, Article 16, Section 50. Therefore, homeowner associations, property owner associations, any neighborhood association in the State of Texas, no matter what the association is called, that foreclose "contractual liens" on homestead property, either judicially or non-judicially, are violating the Texas Constitution Homestead Law, Article 16, Section 50, and the practice of foreclosing on these "contractual liens" is hereby prohibited.

Effective: January 1, 2005, or sooner.

Also, we asked the Attorney General, through Rep. Fred Hill, to give his opinion on a question we asked: "Whether the placement of one-party foreclosable contractual liens on the land by the developer that supersede the homestead rights created in Article XVI, Section 50 of the Texas Constitution violate the Texas Homestead Act?"

Unfortunately, for advocates, our message does not get out often in the manner we want because we have limited access to the media.

When we were foreclosed, there was one television station that consistently followed our story, Channel 11. The reporter was Michael Barnes. I am not sure he is still with Channel 11; but wherever he is, I am confident he is doing the same fine, thorough job he did with us. He was our family when we needed one. Just his presence was comforting.

The only newspaper that was consistent in covering our story was the Kingwood Sun, Kingwood, Texas. The Reporter was Walker C. Wooding, Jr. He also was a fine reporter and would report our stories accurately.

Perhaps if the North Woodland Hills Village Community Association's attorney Jeffrey Ewalt had not shut down our other potential stories, we would have been able to stop any future foreclosures due to the publicity about us. The Houston Chronicle, our major paper in Houston, took an extensive interview in their office and took our picture for the front page but never printed the story. We learned later Ewalt had destroyed the story. Back in those days, being the first homeowners to come out of the closet about their homestead loss, easily gave us the titles of "slackers", "deadbeats", "troublemakers" and such. So all he had to do was say something to the tune of "it was a legitimate debt". "We are entitled to collect maintenance fees and to foreclose if we don't get the money." "They could have paid to save their house." They are just "slackers".

This was enough for the balance of the newspapers and television stations to back off for fear of being sued. It would not surprise me if they were threatened in that manner as well, such as you print it, we sue. If our story had been more widely spread, we are certain subsequent foreclosures would not have occurred. However, enough print did manage to seep through to get the attention of several legislators, such as Sen. Jerry Patterson and Sen. Rodney Ellis, who were concerned about notice requirements and homeowner association foreclosure power respectively.

As far as we know, back then on December 5, 1995, and probably not too many since then, we were the only family who actually lost our homestead because of non-payment of maintenance fees, in spite of the fact we were up to date with our mortgage payments. As no one else had revealed a homestead loss due to maintenance fees only prior to ours, one must only assume there were no such losses prior to December 5, 1995.

We were asked, "Why don't you file bankruptcy so you can save your house?" We had never filed bankruptcy and we did not want to have that mark on our record as well.

The day I met Geneva Kirk Brooks, sometime in 1997, I immediately liked her. We met through a mutual friend who was also an advocate who had contacted me after seeing Johnnie and me on television. Geneva showed me a letter that she had written to the then Governor Bush to complain about an attempt to foreclose on one of her properties because of a tree stump. Governor Bush did not do anything about the complaint or any other HOA property complaint that crossed his desk.

Geneva was best known for her advocacy work against pornography in Houston. I remembered her telling me one day she was traveling down one of our highways and she suddenly looked up at a hugh billboard that, I believe, had breasts on it or something like that. Whatever it was, it was naked, lewd, big and offensive. She became an activist against pornography then.

When I met her, she was putting together a group of people she knew that were advocates in a variety of other areas and who were beginning to have problems with their homeowner associations. We would meet in various places and she was able to get a room at a facility in one of the parks off Richmond Road in Houston.

I remember at the beginning of her lawsuit that was to become a class-action lawsuit, she was looking for other homeowners to join her. She successfully put together a group of Plaintiffs and secured the services of a capable ACLU attorney by the name of David Kahne.

Geneva would call me to accompany her at various speaking opportunities and I would speak, if I could, during my lunch hour. Everyone that knew Geneva knew if you were on the same program as she, you may or may not get a chance to speak. She was a feisty, colorful speaker, who would have you rolling in the aisles with laughter. She was an entertainer but determined to get results.

I remember one time she called me to put some signs together and join her downtown to march in front of the Harris County Courthouse. I called the few advocates I knew at the time to see who was available and my daughter Karen and I went downtown with the signs we had made and marched in front of the Harris County Courthouse.

Geneva passed away at the age of 79 in 2002. The lawsuit she started survived and the issue of no foreclosure on fines only, no raising of maintenance fees over $60.00, and no accumulation of fees were won for the Plaintiffs in her homeowner association. It confirmed the premise that if your deed restriction did not allow an increase over a certain amount or a maintenance fee accumulation from year to year, then you could not do it. It also confirms that the case law that allowed HOA/POA foreclosures did not allow foreclosures on fines only. The association's Motion for Rehearing was denied.

Unfortunately, though, I was unable to relay to Geneva how the Inwood case law had taken our homestead rights from us and caused the foreclosures for non-payment of maintenance fees, which is unconstitutional also. If I had been able to relay that message to her, it would not have been necessary for me or others to continue to fight this issue. However, we are forever grateful for all of her efforts to attain justice for the homeowners and to expose the wrongdoing of the homeowner associations and what she was able to accomplish through her lawsuit. She was the publisher for the Metro Media News and she did an excellent job of getting her message out.

Suddenly in March of 1996, we received a call from the North Woodland Hills Village Community Association's attorney Patricia Quinn and it was over. We settled out of Court and were placed under a gag order for that particular situation.

On or about March of 1996, we began to get letters from a debt collection agency in Dallas, Texas, called Barrett, Burke, Wilson, Castle, Daffin & Frappier, L.L.P., representing our former lien holder Union Planters Mortgage Corporation formerly known as Leader Federal Bank for Savings.

One Wednesday we called an attorney hotline and were given the advice that all we had to do was send the deed with the association's name on it (the Deed Under Order of Sale) and we would be able to correct the misunderstanding regarding the lien holder's attempt to foreclose on us. This Deed Under Order of Sale would show the transfer of title. It sounds easy enough.

If anyone had told us then that our attempts to stop a second foreclosure would be futile, we would have recommended they commit themselves to a mental institution.

We are still looking for the real answer to our question, "How can you get foreclosed again when you do not own the house?" Another question: "Should you not foreclose on the real owners of the house?"

One of the most interesting aspects of law is called the legal version of "ring around the Rosie, a pocket full of posies." To Johnnie and I, that is when the attorneys would pull a lie out of their pockets and run behind us trying to make us believe they were right. The sentence that was the kicker for the second foreclosure was "the title obtained by the Association by virtue of the constable's deed was acquired subject to the first lien held by Leader and that acquisition of title by the Association did not release you from liability on the above-referenced loan." Wow, talking about justification. Of course, it is all a bunch of hogwash.

The fifth paragraph of the letter was interesting too. It stated, "Pursuant to the Federal Fair Debt Collection Practices Act, we advise you that this firm is a debt collector attempting to collect the indebtedness referred to in the above paragraphs and any information we obtain from you will be used for that purpose." This is a Federal law and it would seem more practical that the debtor you are pursuing actually owed the debt. During this incredible second foreclosure, we felt as though we had eaten the original cow that caused the "mad cow" disease. My God, when was this going to end? How much more of this persecution were we going to have to endure before this nightmare was over?

We kept our former lien holder in the loop, giving them the opportunity to save us if they complied with the Deed of Trust. They chose to watch us hang. They did not show up at the first foreclosure December 5, 1995 auction.

For the second time in less than a year, we found ourselves standing and watching our (former) property being foreclosed and auctioned on the first Tuesday of May, 1996. Only this time, we did not own the house.

The association that purchased the house they foreclosed on December 5, 1995, for $184.92, decided they were not going to take over the mortgage payments and Ewalt also made the decision he was not going to cooperate with the lien holder in sending them the filed copy of the Deed Under Order of Sale conveying title to the homeowner association.

When contacted by Union Planters, they recorded in their foreclosure process notes on January 3, 1996, Ewalt "was smart and said just what can you do but foreclose on property again." Ewalt "wanted the name of someone rather than just a collector to call back." He was given a name and extension and our "phone number" was taken "off the system". The Lien holder indicated in their notes not to call us but to call Jeff Ewalt, Attorney. "Ewalt was to call the association to see what they wanted to do." It was quite apparent everyone that should have known who to foreclose on at Union Planters, actually did know.

The simple fact is Union Planters could not get the association to file the transfer deed or assume the loan, which would have put the paperwork in the association's name, so they came after us since the "Mortgage Insurance Certificate", was in our name from the initial purchase with them.

Union Planters ran over us with a lawn mower and got HUD's help to make it look legitimate.

So, once again here we were the first Tuesday of May, 1996, hearing our property we no longer lived in, no longer had a deed in our name, and no longer obligated to pay, being foreclosed the second time. The lien holder's attorney Mitchell's words were ringing in our ears, "what does it matter, your credit is already messed up from the other (homeowner association) foreclosure." He assured us though, "a deficiency judgment would not be pursued." Oh goody, I thought. Since we did not cause a deficiency, how nice of him not to file a deficiency judgment against us; proof positive that we did not default. If we had, no such generosity would have occurred.

We were here because our name was on the Insurance Certificate for this property and our former lien holder could get their money back by foreclosing in our name. To them, it was quicker, easier, and much more efficient. Why bother spending money chasing the lien holder when you had a captivated audience already in us? In their notes, Union Planters reported, "I went to the Sheriff's office and he said that he was ordered not to give me the deed." In addition, reported, I "said I spoke with an attorney with FHA and said that we can do something other than get deed from them to get this put in the homeowner association's name."

Angela Richardson in a February 12, 1996 memo to Diane Floyd, both with Union Planters, admitted, "We can do nothing else, at this time until we receive a transfer deed." I thought it also interesting in the memo that the president of the North Woodland Hills Village Community Association, John C. Clifton, was indicating, "The Association was awarded the property in a sale." I guess if you only paid $184.92 for it, it was awarded to you. I also found it interesting that he was admitting that "the back door was left wide open" after a lock change and this after trying to pass off pictures with damage on them to us during the Motion to Determine Market Value hearing I spoke about earlier.

Wait a minute! This auction sounds different! The person calling out the bid started at a higher price, he was louder and there was more participation. HUD ended up with the house but the auction was conducted differently than the auction in which the association purchased the house.

Now that we had not only lost our house twice, our credit history now in total ruin, evidenced by receipt of bankruptcy letters which we did not get during our first foreclosure, encouraging us to file bankruptcy even though we no longer owned the homestead; it was time to fight back once again.

We filed a lawsuit against our lien holder for wrongful foreclosure. It was an interesting odyssey. During our discovery, we uncovered documents that verified our legal position of a wrongful foreclosure. Among them was an interesting Foreclosure Process Note posted June 4, 1996, that acknowledged "Association foreclosed 12-1-95 (they got the date wrong though, it was foreclosed 12-5-95) but LFB (Leader Federal Bank) lien superior—their foreclosure sale was for $12,000. This may create a problem when it comes time to get title policy issued. If BBW (Barrett Burke Wilson Castle Daffin & Frappier, L.L.P.) did this foreclosure and not make sure

LFB was clean on this foreclosure, LFB should pass any losses on to BBW/ discussed with SL."

The HUD package was sent to Washington on June 4, 1996. Washington knows what is going on in Texas with these bogus foreclosures.

We had a tape recording of a conversation between our former lien holder and ourselves in which they admitted they were waiting to take action against the association if they did not pay but needed the transfer title.

Union Planters falsely accused Johnnie and I of defaulting when we in fact, no longer owned the property. They illegally received money from a Federal agency using our name when they knew we no longer own the property, in other words a fraudulent transaction was conducted using our name to pull it off. The documents can be viewed in the back of this book under Chapter 16 documents, pages marked 000089 and 000090.

What should have been an easy transfer turned into a witch's hunt and subsequently nothing we produced, by way of subsequent depositions with explicit admissions or documentation verifying our legal position, deterred Union Planters from pursuing us for the insurance money.

The title to the house at 2026 Oak Shores Drive, Kingwood, Texas 77339, is tainted and clouded and causing the house not to be sold. It is currently being held under the name of a trustee by the name of Carol Nagel.

We got one lucky break in this matter when Leslie Bromer from HUD actually sent us an email May 6, 1997, at 3:20 p.m. in which she attempted to suppress the Credit Alert pertaining to this second foreclosure and indicated the default was the homeowners association and not ours.

Once this fax hit the fan, so to speak, Leslie tried to back off from it and so did her co-workers. We persisted and were able to get an investigation started under the Clinton administration; however, when Bush came into office, the investigation died. We are still working on it through a legislative resolution and we discussed it more detail in Chapter 14.

Our lawsuit failed because of Judge Tracy Christopher, more on her later. We initially went to Federal Court seeking an injunction but the action was dismissed without prejudice and Judge Vanessa Gilmore told us, to return once we resolved the State lawsuit. Had we not filed a lawsuit, filing a complaint with the Comptroller of the Currency Administrator of National Banks may have been a better path to take.

We started out with a lot of hope. We had filed our lawsuit and requested a jury trial, still believing in the Constitutional right to have a jury trial. This time we actually had the jury trial but with a new twist, we had not anticipated.

In the beginning, we were getting fair treatment from the Court. Initially, Union Planters Mortgage Corporation formerly Leader Federal Bank for Savings' Attorney Ronald Mitchell, was not taking our ability to litigate seriously and kept paraphrasing his statement, "what does it matter, your credit is already messed up from the other (homeowner association) foreclosure." Of course, when we told the judge what he said, he denied it.

We always did well in each of our lawsuits with discovery and this was no exception. On July 29, 1996, Judge Tracy Christopher signed our Order compelling Leader Federal Bank for Savings to respond to our discovery "requests on or before August 19, 1996," and ordered them to pay us "$50.00 for expenses incurred in preparing the motion and attending the hearing."

As we followed Mitchell to his office to collect the money, we knew it was all he could do to control himself. He was the maddest we had ever seen him. He was actually outraged, seething like a pit bull. He was going to make us pay big for this humiliating experience.

We were in Court after that to file some paperwork and spotted Mitchell in the Court reporter's office. We thought it interesting but not unusual. Since that day we believe he may have had ex parte communication with the judge as so many of the attorneys have done to win their cases. After that Mitchell sighting, the judge's demeanor changed. She became bias in her rulings, bitter and rude toward us in Court.

I put the finishing touches on the material for the trial. All my ducks were lined up and we were ready to go. Witnesses had been subpoenaed and were ready to testify.

During the trial, I knew we were in trouble when Judge Christopher would not allow me to enter impeachment evidence in the form of a taped recording I was trying to introduce, even though it was on the evidence list. This was the one I told you about earlier in Chapter 16 in which there was a "tape recording of a conversation between our former lien holder and ourselves in which they admitted they were waiting to take action against the association if they did not pay but needed the transfer title."

The recording would have proven without any doubt that Union Planters maliciously executed a wrongful foreclosure against us but as the Judge glared at me, she denied my entering it into the record stating I could not surprise him.

I found that extremely disturbing as I was "surprised" once in a lawsuit I was involved in that did not pertain to HOA's; however, it was an automobile accident in which I had been hit from the rear and had filed a lawsuit against the driver of the car. However, his attorney turned the entire situation around by introducing a tape showing me bending over in my yard and the tape was a surprise. It was to impeach my testimony that I had a back injury; however, on the day they taped, I had gone to the doctor and was rendered fine so I was doing some yard work. It was not a day that I had claimed damages for.

Impeachment material is mainly for theatrical purposes as far as I am concerned but every now and then, they really do show good stuff. The tape I wanted to enter in the Union Planters' case was good stuff. The judge in my accident case was Judge Crowe, County Court 4. She later recused herself on the Expert Witness Case involving Roberta Jones Hanna that was before her because of the accident case.

The light from the projector slides I was showing disturbed the court reporter, the same reporter Atty. Mitchell was visiting the day we were filing documents. I knew I was in trouble with the Court; however, we had lucked out on the jury. Voir Dire went well for both sides and we had a wonderful group of Jurors. One of them was actually taking notes with a sympathetic look every time I spoke. One was leaning forward so as not to miss anything and they all appeared attentive and respectful.

The jury was sent out to deliberate and then it got sci-fi. I knew something weird was about to occur when the Judge sent the court reporter out of the room so as not to have any written evidence of what was about to occur. She then engaged in a conversation with Atty. Mitchell as she was getting the jury instructions together that included her saying, "if the jury returns with a favorable verdict," she would "JNOV it." Then she stated while preparing the questions, "I happened to think you (Atty. Mitchell) are right." It is a good thing Lady Justice was blind that day; Judge Christopher would have embarrassed her.

Judge Christopher then became the co-counsel for Union Planters and submitted the following question even though Johnnie and I objected; but, of course, remember, the court reporter had been sent out the room so there was no record of the objection for the appeal:

Question No. 1

Did Leader Federal Bank wrongfully foreclose on the Deed of Trust on the property in the name of Johnnie and Harvella Jones?

This is where the question should have stopped; but the Judge went further and added the following *facts and legal commentary.*

"The Joneses are the original note holders.

The homeowner's association held a junior lien position on the property in question, and is a junior lien holder.

Leader Federal Bank held the senior lien, and is a senior lien holder.

If a junior lien holder purchases the property, it must service the senior lien in order for the junior lien holder to retain possession of the property without foreclosure on the senior lien.

If the junior lien holder refuses to service the senior lien, and does not assume the debt, the senior lien holder can foreclose on the original note holder under the Deed of Trust.

A lien holder does not have to pay cash at a foreclosure sale."

Answer "Yes" or "No"

The jury came back with this statement: "Is the statement below question a statement of law."?

Judge Christopher's response was: "yes, it's a statement of law and fact."

Shortly after that unethical opinion from the Judge, the foreman sent the following note out: "We have enough votes to support a verdict. Do we need all 12 votes? One person needs more time before voting." She responded with, "Please follow paragraph 6 on page 2 of the charge."

I had another white out when I lost this case. While sitting there in the courtroom trying to see again, I thought about how hard I had worked in preparing this airtight case. In accordance with the law, I prepared my case my self like any "attorney" would have, and yet, we were robbed of our justice, once again, by, this time, Judge Tracy Christopher. I am always amazed at no matter what you do or how well you prepare; you still lose in the courtroom if the Judge wants it that way.

I kept thinking how could the judge decide the facts for the jury? Wasn't that the job of the jury? How could she make legal conclusions that overrode what Texas auction law prescribes and neither Mitchell nor I presented that to the jury? How could she have made such a fast turnaround since we first stepped into her Courtroom?

I use to think it was the attorneys who messed you up but Johnnie said no, it is the judges. He was right once again.

At the elevator, one of the jurors was waiting. I believe he was the one who needed more time to vote. He told us they stopped looking at the evidence when they read the Judge's statement of law and fact and she verified that was what it was.

My faith keeps me from verbalizing the description I would like to bestow on the Judge. What a pitiful day it was for lady justice on February 25, 1998; but I believe in justice. While I did not get justice that day, justice is not dead. Eventually the voters will weed out the trash and Judge Tracy Christopher will be collected and discarded back into the sewer from where she came, for Justice is not yours to abuse and misuse in your black robe, it is for the benefit of the people. Judges are not to mete out justice as though they own it but to protect what is already ours and issue it to the ones who have proven through their legal and factual presentation that it belongs to them.

It is harder to get reconsideration when you have a jury trial but because of the misuse of power conducted by Judge Christopher, I asked for it anyway. The juror that had inside information about what had occurred in the jury room and who we had talked to after the trial was over, was successfully subpoenaed and ready to testify at our Motion for New Trial.

In the final judgment, she misrepresented the jury's deliberation efforts by stating, "The jury made findings that the court received...." Since we knew the jury had not deliberated thanks to her "opinion" on the question, we felt compelled to right this wrong.

Now that the tide had turned and we were on Judge Christopher's "bad people" list, it was extremely difficult to get court business accomplished in a civil manner. We tried recusal. No success. It was necessary to file a motion for sanctions against her staff and that was when Christopher almost forgot she was a judge. Her look of venom, that made me feel as though I had been bitten by 100 rattlesnakes, put concern about my safety in the courtroom into my mind. It made me wonder what exactly she had under that black robe. Perhaps a gun? If looks could kill, I would be dead.

She proceeded to express her outrage at my nerve for challenging her sacred staff by blocking our motion for a new trial by refusing to let subpoenaed witnesses testify. She continued to block every attempt we had launched to get justice against our lien holder for their wrongful foreclosure.

We revisited our previous thought, shared with you in Chapter 10, regarding why Texas Judges, for the most part, do not want cameras in their courtrooms and why they fought so hard against them. If cameras were in their courtrooms, they probably would have to act like Judges.

The judges and their courts want to be treated like God or royalty, when in fact most of them conduct themselves in a manner that encourages disrespect from pro se litigates. They want to be omnipotent. Why can they just do their job and be fair to both parties? Why can they just respect all litigants no matter who they are? Why can they just stop blocking justice? Why do they have to use the courtroom as a political arena laced in bias juice?

After such dismal failures at State level, we bought into the idea of attaining justice at the Federal level. We began to file the balance of our lawsuits in the Federal court thinking that the judges there were from out of-state and we would get a non-bias judge, not from Texas, who would listen to what we were saying.

We had enough of the State courts with their bias judges and unfair jaundice rulings. Oh my goodness, were we in for a rude awakening. On the other hand, a better description would be "out of the frying pan into the fire". Not only were the judges we faced in Federal court homegrown Texans but they were four times as lethal as the State Judges. Let us just say it was an eye-opening experience.

Our first encounter with a Federal judge was when we filed the Federal injunction to stop the second foreclosure. I recall Judge Vanessa D. Gilmore, medium height, average size black woman, coming out with an air of self-importance, as though someone else had already ruined her day. She snapped at Union Planters' attorney Ronald Glen Mitchell and there was real fear in the Courtroom. She obviously had been disrespected in her previous life and was going to make sure it did not happen again.

Atty. Mitchell feared her and rightfully so. She spoke in sharp, loud insulting tones. She was one of those no nonsense kind of judges. At the time, she appeared fair to us and dismissed our injunction without prejudice so we could come back when we had completed our process in State Court.

We returned almost two years later, on March 20, 1998; but this time we had Judge Lynn N. Hughes for the Union Planters Mortgage Company issue. We did not know then, but we had just been assigned to a judge known to blacks to be one of the most racist judges in the Federal Court and we do not think being assigned to him was an accident. He has an extremely poor reputation among blacks in the city of Houston and has a reputation of manipulating the cases of black litigants. Of course, I am sure there are white litigants that could testify to bias decisions from him as well. He certainly lived up to his reputation and then some.

Just eight (8) days after the second foreclosure by Union Planters Mortgage Company, we filed a $50,225,000 compensatory and punitive damages lawsuit against the State of Texas for making and enforcing case law that is in violation of the fourteenth amendment's prohibition against depriving citizens of property without due process or equal protection of the laws. Judge Vanessa Gilmore was the judge on this case.

The foreclosure (first foreclosure) proceedings were unconstitutional. I had fine-tuned my skills as a pro se litigant. I had a certain amount of years to file lawsuits for the wrong that had occurred in our lives and sometimes I would be juggling three cases at once.

One clever technique attorneys do when litigating, especially against pro se litigants, is to confuse the Court as much as possible. If you present a clear case, they will confuse it as best they can. While the Court system allows you to defend yourself, most judges are not happy to see you in their Courtroom as a pro se litigant and will believe whatever the other side is stating in their pleadings and during their argument. Remember I told you about our experience in Judge David West's court in Chapter 11. If you are in the Courtroom with a rattlesnake attorney for the other side, you are at the mercy of what that attorney will portray to the Judge.

Therefore, we found out the hard way that Federal Court was not better than State Court for justice. I would say it was worse.

This lawsuit against the State of Texas was a direct assault to their unconstitutional case law Inwood vs. Harris, the source of our homeowner association foreclosure problems here in Texas. The case was dismissed by the Court as Magistrate Mary Milloy was able to convince Judge Vanessa Gilmore that the issues were "'inextricably intertwined'" "with a state judgment". Or I should say the attorneys for the state were able to convince Judge Vanessa Gilmore, They were a team of attorneys including The State of Texas Attorney General Dan Morales (who I believe is now in jail as mentioned in Chapter 3), Attorney Jorge Vega, Attorney Laquita A. Hamilton, Attorney Toni Hunter and Attorney G. Stewart Whitehead.

I found it particularly interesting that Attorney General Dan Morales could not help us in our original complaint to him in 1992 but now he was part of the defense team for the state. What kind of protection do we have from the Attorney General for this egregious law the state support called Inwood vs. Harris? What kind of protection do we have from the state for misconduct on the part of the homeowner associations in this state? Is justice only set up to protect the strong and hurt the weak? Who do we have to protect our rights in this state?

One rainy day on our way to Federal Court for our former lien holder's lawsuit (Union Planters Mortgage Corporation formerly Leader Federal Bank for Savings) we witnessed an automobile accident in which a pedestrian was walking across the street and was hit dead center, thrown into the air, bounced off the car onto the street and then momentarily left to crawl to the curb where he sat in a daze.

We were stunned but manage to get the license number; and the driver must have seen me write the number down because he slowed down, pulled over to the curb, got out of his car and walked back. We called the police, waited, gave them our name, phone number and then proceeded to continue our journey to the Judge's chamber where we were to get the decision on our Default Judgment against our lien holder.

For whatever unknown reason, Union Planters' attorney David Kirkendall had failed to respond to the lawsuit notice and now was faced with a default judgment. We had successfully served it. It was 23 days past the answer time and it was in default. We had requested entry of default judgment.

Now we had been called to Judge Lynn Hughes' office for the pretrial conference. We knew when we entered the chambers; there was a "dead cat on the line". The Judge knew way too much about the state case outside of the Motion as he began to lay the case out for us; and we knew, yet again, ex parte communication had taken place; this time between he and the lien holder's attorney David Kirkendall and the attorney from the state case Ronald Mitchell, who were also in the judge's chambers when we got there.

Once again, a judge in a case we were trying had become the cocounsel for the other side and we felt like the pedestrian who had been knocked into the air on our way to court. His accident had set the tone for our day. It was not going to be a good day for any of us.

I just hate it when you are being raped by a judge, they hold you down with their condescending voice and their cold, uncaring stare while they are stripping you of all your rights and then when it is over, they talk to you in a conciliatory manner as though you are some idiot and dare you to fight back or you will be sanctioned.

Johnnie finally exploded that day. I think he felt like he had been raped as well and used the "N" word. No one objected to its use as the deposition will show but the appeal court used it to "try" to sanction us, but I am getting ahead of myself.

Our rights were roasted that day. It was a good thing Lady Justice is blind, as I have said before. We would not have wanted her to see what happened that day. Federal Court was certainly worse than State Court. There is much more abuse of the rules and disrespect for the rules are on a larger scale.

Judge Lynn Hughes definitely proved why he should be retired and in a senior citizen facility getting lessons on how to become a human being. He not only became a co-counsel for the lien holder, he tried to prevent us from speaking on our own behalf. His behavior would have been an embarrassment to a prostitute. He snatched away our rights and gave them to his two "adopted sons"—Kirkendall and Mitchell.

Hughes was more concerned about ruining the careers of his two "adopted sons" than he was about following the law. Our rights did not matter.

Why was there not this kind of concern when Inwood won its default judgment, which affected every homeowner in the State of Texas? Now, here we were before a racist Judge and he was concerned about ruining the career of two inept white attorneys by the name of David Kirkendall and Ronald Mitchell, who had underestimated our ability in Federal Court; and what does an attorney do when he cannot beat you fair and square?

He does ex parte communication with the Judge and impresses upon the Judge how right he is and how wrong you are? It works if you are pro se, a woman and black. Going through the Texas judicial system with those three marks against you is worse than any roller coaster ride you could take.

I am not saying it is not rough going through the system as a white, male or female, pro se litigate. In this business, it is probably just as bad; but like anything else, I can only speak about what I know. Justice is the little green spot on the other side of the fence when you are pro se, a woman and black.

The only defense Kirkendall had for his default judgment was "your honor, you wouldn't do that to us would you because you wouldn't do it to them?"

At 2:30 p.m., on June 22, 1998, the final nail was driven into our casket containing all of our civil rights. After the burial, our $5,000,000 default judgment had been denied and the case was dismissed. The Judge tried to stop me from speaking short of sanctioning me.

I did not care what the Judge thought about me at that point. My rights had been violated and I was going to speak and spoke I did. I had to speak to preserve our objections or they would be lost forever. The two "adopted" boys had been well trained by their co-counsel Judge Hughes. The only words they said in their defense were "yes" and "no". They did not have to open their mouths. They sat there and let the Judge litigate for them.

By then, I had made full circle. There were no tears, no white outs, no hope, no nothing. I no longer respected the men or women in the black robe. They had lost my respect. They were the underground KKK (Ku Klux Klan for those who have been living on Mars). I had the right to speak and defend myself and that is what I was going to do.

I looked at Kirkendall and Mitchell sitting across from me and wondered what it felt like to be a white male attorney in a Federal Courtroom where you did not even have to open your mouth to defend yourself because you were so privileged and so protected that a Federal judge litigate for you and tell a couple of black pro se litigants "….you'd be a lot smarter if you'd listen occasionally and not just talk." The purpose being to stop us from preserving our objections for the obvious appeal.

I wondered how I could have ever thought that we were going to get justice in a Federal Court, especially a Federal Court in Texas. What does it take to get justice in this State? Where is Lady Justice hiding in this State? How many times are we going to be punished for buying a house in Kingwood, Texas? How many times will we be foreclosed before it is considered enough? When is someone going to think that what we went through is enough, enough, enough? I cried out to God, is there any justice anywhere? What do I have to do to get this evasive, rare thing called justice?

We filed a Notice of Appeal on June 24, 1998. On July 2, 1998, Hughes took it upon himself, even though he had no jurisdiction now, to file an order

107

stating, "It has become apparent that they have abused the system with their multiple filings for the same complaints." He listed six cases we were supposed to have filed in the last two years. Of course, his list was wrong. He also included in the order, we "may not file another suit in this district without permission of this judge." Where did this man get his training?

As the last bit of dirt from Hughes' shovel hit our casket, we tried to recuse the bias, senile, incompetent Judge Hughes. He signed an order denying the recusal on November 9, 1998. Surprise! Surprise!

His order set the stage for our Appeal in Louisiana. While we may have been able to turn the $5,000,000 default judgment around, we were unable to because of Hughes' tainted and bias order that he filed when he had no jurisdiction to do so. He filed the order after we had filed our Notice of Appeal, which successfully removed our case from his jurisdiction.

So powerful was his order, done to ensure we would not be successful, the Court of Appeals, issued sanctions against us for language in our Application, when the wording was merely verbatim what had occurred in Hughes' chambers that day of the automobile accident. Remember when I told you Johnnie used the "N" word and no one objected; now they wanted to assess sanctions on undisputed testimony.

We, of course, filed an objection to the sanctions and the Court of Appeals never contested our refusal to pay but we were denied our appeal in retaliation in record time.

In 1996, we filed a flurry of Federal Cases. We took our Jeffrey Ewalt case to the Federal Court along with his Judge, David West, his partner David Dickinson and the Judge that got the case when West recused himself, Shearn Smith.

What is the sense of recusing yourself if you are going to train the next Judge? West finally recused himself after giving Ewalt a summary judgment but he trained the next judge, Shearn Smith to block our attempts to get a new trial or correction to get a trial. It seemed like West was still in the courtroom, only an older version.

I have only looked into the eyes of one other person, a Judge of course in another case, and saw what the occupants of hell must look like. For one split second, I felt like I was before a Court in the early 1920's, when my ancestor's were being accused of a crime and were before the justice of the peace at that time. Such hate in those eyes! Such evil in those eyes! Such bias in those eyes! I wondered as with Tracy Christopher was he packing a gun under that black robe; and if he shot me, would I be considered wrong? I truly felt threatened.

The smile on my face froze when I looked into those eyes of hate. I thought Judges are protected from our vengeance when we go through a metal detector. Who protects the litigant when they stand before a hateful judge filled with his or her own loathing for anyone who dare speak up and out for their rights, their justice, their bottom line?

My smile was gone now and a deep anger was swelling in my gut and for the first time I was coming very close to being sanctioned for an actual offense. However, I rethought my position. No, why should I break my record and say or do something sanction able in the Courtroom. So instead of crossing over the line, I decided to come as close to it as I could get without crossing it.

I looked Judge Shearn Smith, the second evilest Judge I had ever been before, straight in the eye and fought for my rights. I did not let his evil stare distract me. I remained focus on my argument. It began to dawn on me that Judge Smith already had made his decision on this matter and that he really was not paying much attention to what I was saying. He just wanted to make sure I could not accuse him of a due process violation. For the record, I kept speaking and making my argument. Upon completion, he denied our Motion for Rehearing.

On December 10, 1996, we went a few blocks over to the Federal Court and filed our Federal case for violation of our civil rights. It ended like all the others filed in the Federal Court, dismissed.

The one difference in Federal Court is you get the impression you are going to get justice because you do the Case Management Plan and joint discovery. In fact, in the Union Planters Federal Case, we had permission to do discovery. Of course, when we sent our first set of interrogatories to the

Defendant and they saw the questions, a Motion to Dismiss was quickly filed and they won.

Johnnie picked up a middle name "Mae" through the filing process that we tried the duration of the lawsuit to have removed with no success. Apparently, the efficiency level was not very high in the Federal Court. We left the system with a different perspective. We strongly recommend voters take a closer look at the judges they vote for because one day you may be looking him or her in the eye and pleading for justice.

The Community Associations Institute, aka the CAI and not to be confused with the CIA, the Central Intelligence Agency, which "provides the President and his senior advisors with accurate, comprehensive, and timely foreign intelligence relating to national security. Conducts counterintelligence activities and other operations relating to foreign intelligence."

The Community Associations Institute (CAI) is a national group whose members are the architect for the homeowner association foreclosures we suffer from today.

If every state dug deep into their Covenants, conditions and restrictions (CC&R) documents, they would find a CAI foreclosure blueprint. In fact, CAI should stand for Control and Intimidate.

Somewhere in the 80's, members of the CAI across the country formed legal committees and drafted boiler-plate documents that took away our property rights as we know it and created bulletproof terminology that makes it almost impossible to defend oneself in court.

In Texas, it started with the filing of an Amicus Curiae brief filed February 18, 1987, with the Texas Supreme Court, supporting a little known case law (at the time) called *Inwood vs. Harris*.

The Legal Committee of the Greater Houston Chapter of The Community Associations Institute described themselves in 1987 as "a national organization comprised of eight thousand (8,000) members in forty-five (45) City Chapters, including chapters in Dallas, San Antonio, Austin and Houston. The Greater Houston chapter is comprised of 394 members who are developers, condominium, townhouse or subdivision community associations, management companies, attorneys, accountants, city and state officials and other persons who service community associations."

The Legal Committee spoke of their "retailed liens against the property of homeowners, whether the property is in the form of individual lots, townhouses, or condominium units. The collection of these fees is absolutely essential for the existence of these quasi-governmental authorities. These quasi-governmental authorities provide the same services to their residences, as do many governments, even though these authorities may be within incorporated city limits. Some of the services provided included private or constable provided security services, recreational facilities, meeting houses, trash pickup, street light electricity, maintenance of esplanades in public areas and, most importantly, policing of the neighborhood and litigation in support of the enforcement of deed restrictions. The budgets of these associations range from several thousand dollars per year to several hundreds of thousands of dollars per year. In the state of Texas, there may be as many as 20,000 such organizations.

It is vitally important, therefore, that this Court resolve the question of the validity of their liens for the collection of their maintenance fees as many billions of dollars of public services that would otherwise have to be raised by cities or the state would not be collected by community associations who provide these services. Many of these quasi-governmental authorities have thousands of residential citizens and absentee landowners subject to their jurisdiction. In contrast, with only 600 residents, a city can be formed in Texas under Article 961 et seq. which can take land on a tax lien or arrest and imprison for violations of city ordinances."

While I did not see any homeowner inclusion on the membership roll of the CAI list, Attorney Richard C. Lievens with Frank, Elmore & Lievens, on October 20, 1986, stated, "I am also the President-elect of the Greater Houston Chapter of CAI, which is a nationwide non-profit organization which promotes education and interaction among community associations, builder-developers, homeowners, public officials, and managers relative to issues involving community associations, including the rights and remedies available to homeowners and/or associations in the collection of maintenance assessments."

What a bunch of garbage. We must as homeowners exorcise ourselves from these demons—CAI attorneys. They have created a "cottage industry". They created a foreclosure cancer. This cancer feeds on the fear people have of losing the roof over their heads. A cancerous cell planted in each state's homeowner associations by CAI attorneys and protected by legislators, judges, constables, HUD, real estate companies and mortgage companies.

It is a cancerous system, fed by the lies of CAI attorneys to keep it alive and well so they will benefit from it on a financial level. Think about it. What is greater than the actual maintenance fees they foreclose on? The attorney fees, of course. In my particular case, $13,000 attorney fees were added to $842.00 in maintenance fees.

A funding system has been setup across the country by CAI attorneys. Once a CAI attorney has his foot in your homeowner association's door, he has a fee attached to everything he or she does. Often there is no contract between the association and the attorney and the sky is the limit as to what you will be charged. The association, in essence, sets the attorney loose on you, such as what happened to my family and me in Kingwood, Texas. We were fortunate enough to find a January 26, 1993, letter during discovery from one of the foreclosing kingpins, Roy D. Hailey, that was sent to Chuck Venezia with Houston Management Service Company, regarding Woodland Hills Trail Association, Kingwood, Texas.

In the letter, Hailey is trying to sell the "collection work on a contingency basis", which is not only unethical and a violation of the Barratry Law; but it explains why the rat activity increased in many of our associations. Enjoy it. It is at the back of this book in the document section in the Chapter 19 section.

Getting back to CAI control--the foreclosure system is then good to go with the loss of property rights secured either through legislation or case law that guarantees judicial support for the association when you arrive at Court for justice.

The next task for the CAI attorney is to visit each homeowner association they want to pollute. CAI attorneys look mainly for homeowner associations that have an abundance of minorities, whether they are blacks, Hispanics or Vietnamese homeowners. Another vulnerable group of people they choose is senior citizens. It is extremely important to these CAI attorneys that they pick areas where there is vulnerability.

Earlier I shared information pertaining to the type of soliciting CAI attorneys do with the management company. Sometimes they bypass the management company and go directly to the board of directors to solicit. Once the board is convinced they do not have to do any work, the attorney is in because after all the boards are all volunteers that are usually too busy or too old to actually run the community without help from the CAI attorneys. They just want to make sure "property values" don't drop and the neighbor from hell does not continue to live next door to them with all the cars and the oil spots and weeds between the expansion joints of *their* driveway,

The Management Companies are usually already chosen before the CAI attorneys arrive with their boilerplate forms and sales talk. Sometimes the Management Company is created or selected by the developer to ensure that the running of the community stays on-line with what the developer had intended.

To keep everything up and running and keep the "troublemakers" from trying to take over the community, it is important to "train" the board members and to keep the training flowing to any and all new board members "fortunate" enough to be on the board. This usually involves a friendly visit from the friendly and caring CAI attorney. who will talk to the newly appointed, selected or elected board members at no charge, after all this will ensure the attorney gets to stay and help watch the "kitty".

Since the homeowner association is really an extortion ring under cover, it is important to have a course in place to make sure all homeowner association training is on the same page no matter where it may take place. The homeowners themselves, as maintenance fees are used to pay for each board member's training, foot the cost of the course. Katharine Rosenberry wrote the "ABCs a Basic Course for Community Associations" and the CAI in 2002 and one of the CAI attorneys that reviewed it was Marc D. Markel, one of the members of the Legal Committee who participated in the amicus curiae brief support for Texas's *Inwood vs. Harris* foreclosure lawsuit.

My question is why does one have to take a CAI course to keep homeowners in line? Why can't homeowners who want to do something different than what the CAI attorneys suggest run these homeowner associations? It is about control. If you show up at your homeowner association meeting, you might find out what is really going on in your neighborhood.

When you do not show up at your meetings, the board can do whatever they want behind your back and before you know it, you are in a property rights' warp.

Now that everything is in place, let's see; your rights are gone, your association has brought in a management company with a CAI attorney, the judicial system is ready to deny you any and all rights (even if you know what you are doing) and the fear of losing your home is always near and dear. Now that the money machine is set up and ready to go for years and years, welcome to a planned development community and the real world. You cannot run to a place where there are no HOA's because they will come and they will find you and attach CC&R's to your property illegally or legally. They will go into old neighborhoods and create new CC&R's with foreclosure ability attached to them.

If you discover the scam and want to fight, your neighbors usually have not discovered the scam and you find yourself fighting the battle alone. If you happen to be successfully elected to the board, once they find out, they cannot control you; they find a way to remove you.

If there is a dispute about maintenance fees, they win unless it is so outrageous and hit the newspaper and then they may withdraw out of fear of arousing a legislator who just might take action to stop permanently the offense.

Once you step into the developer's dream world, you find that you have entered into one of the worse living arrangements on the face of the earth. You realize you have signed up for thirty (30) years of torture. Most of the time you have received no notice of what has happened to your rights or the association you supposedly freely joined.

Instead of being a new, happy, free property owner who has the full ability to make decisions about their own property, you have unknowingly transcended into the world of the slackers, the deadbeats, the troublemakers.

The attorneys who are members of the Community Associations Institute must ensure that their "cottage industry" never goes away, so with the financial power and manpower they enjoy, they outgun you at the legislative hearings held throughout the country held every year or every other year, depending upon where you live.

They even help write and create "band-aid" laws that are self-serving and guaranteed to block, stop and lock up any chances you have of getting relief from the oppression you live under every day. They also want to ensure that nothing worthwhile ever pass for the homeowners--that would hurt their industry.

They are always thinking of ways to guarantee their hands stay in your money pockets so that they can afford their lifestyle. After all, with all these attorneys around, how can they live unless they feed off homeowners? How many ambulances can you chase? In addition, tort reform would cut down on excessive attorney fees. Therefore, a scheme had to be conceived that would benefit attorneys. Attorneys are legislators. Attorneys are judges. Attorneys are inextricably intertwined in every facet of our lives. CAI attorneys are always looking for greener pastures, new places to feed; new ways to collect HOA/POA fees to make sure their "cottage industry" continues to thrive.

Every time homeowners and advocate homeowners testify at a legislative hearing, CAI attorneys, homeowner associations and other special interest groups counter with such testimony as lower "property values", living next to "purple houses", or "slackers", "deadbeats", etc., etc. They paint a dismal, unsubstantiated picture of total community chaos if they do not have the power to foreclose, their hammer, because they need to have a way to collect their fees so the neighborhood will not fall apart because if some people do not pay, then others will have to hold up their end.

One of the worst things a CAI attorney could see is an informed homeowner. It is always on their agenda to keep information from the homeowner regarding the association's financial records, what is going on in the board meetings, what is going on behind closed doors with homeowner legislation, and anything else that is relevant to the homeowner and important. CAI attorneys are always scurrying around during session looking for ways to legalize their foreclosure honey pot because they know sooner or later it will come to a resounding end and not a day too soon for homeowners.

Everything is based on fear, fear, fear and more fear. Architectural Review Boards, deed restriction enforcement and payment of maintenance fees have all been merged to confuse the homeowner, the legislators and the court system. It is a lot easier to complicate when everything is presented as one theory.

In Texas, legislators are not paid much and they meet every other year. Many of the legislators are developers or involved in some kind of way with this "cottage industry" created by CAI attorneys. One Senator in particular stands out because of his self-serving, conflicting association with being a legislator and involved in the bill making process as are many of the CAI attorneys who created the industry. Senator John J. Corona, District 16, comes to mind. Whenever important bills are created by brave legislators such as Senator Jon Lindsay, District 7, Senator Carona is there to make sure the bills are watered down if not destroyed all together.

Senator John J. Carona is President of the Principal Management Group, which is one of the largest Management Companies in Texas. If that is not a conflict of interest, I do not know what is. His ability to sit in on important legislative bill creation to ensure the bills go nowhere is troubling to me and many other advocates. A couple of us have even filed complaints against him with no success. I wonder why we were not successful. He is the fox watching the hen house to make certain that no hens escape intact.

Whenever a good pro homeowner bill is made known, CAI attorneys and other special interest groups converge upon Austin to shoot it down with fabrications and misrepresentations, as well as tearing up fax machines to submit their lies and keep the fax line busy so pro-homeowner material cannot get through.

When Johnnie and I first started going to the Austin hearings to testify for various homeowner friendly bills, we were alone. We started testifying right after our first foreclosure as Sen. Rodney Ellis wrote a "no foreclosure" bill right after we were foreclosed and everyone on the industry side knew who we were when we arrived to testify. They were waiting for us, well prepared to shoot down everything we said. We did not know them but they knew us.

Sen. Ellis realized then what a powerful bill he had written and how much it was hated by the industry.

It is always a revelation to the legislators when they write homeowner friendly bills, set up hearings, and get overrun by special interest groups who invariably destroy their good bills.

After testifying before these legislators several times, it dawned on me that the legislators were no longer innocent of what was happening to homeowners in the State of Texas, most of them just did not care enough to correct, change, or create better law.

The legislators that had tried to make a difference were becoming rapidly discouraged by the lopsided support they were receiving. Very little homeowner support was filtering through and a hugh amount of industry advocacy was present, which oftentimes gave the impression the bill was not worthy of passing.

Now, the bottom line is after being extruded through a well-oiled system, Johnnie and I know what will work and what will not.

Filing one-party lawsuits do not work. Class-action lawsuits work better. Plain and simple. One-party lawsuits do not work because the law, until we change it, is mainly on the side of the homeowner association and their attorneys. When homeowners and voters were looking in another direction quietly moving into their new homes, tiny, CAI attorneys were putting chameleon maneuvers in place.

The CAI attorneys put the laws in place and they are going to make sure they stay in place, so going before committees for various homeowner friendly bills may or may not be productive. It depends upon the writer of the bill and his or her determination to support it all the way through the system, making sure they get the amount of support they need to pass the bill and get it signed. The bill should not be amended much once it has been originally drafted because it weakens the bill too much. Once it has been weakened, advocates or homeowners should not support it. It should not be a long bill because long bills are more vulnerable to change. Short bills are better to digest and easier to pass.

Unless something positive happens at the hearings for homeowners, it is my growing belief that they are nothing more than a way to find out what our strategy is, how we think and how fervent we are about it. Are we mad enough to start a revolution? Are we mad enough to get violent? How much further can we be pushed before we explode into violence? I believe these hearings are conducted more to show the world how sincerely legislators are relating to their constituents when in fact we are just pawns. It reminds me when we use to picket the State Bar and file complaints against CAI attorneys, when all that was happening was to wire up the offender and let them know what we had on him or her.

In August, 1997, then Lieutenant Governor Bob Bullock "charged the Senate Interim Committee on State Affairs to study the legal powers, duties, and structure of homeowners associations in Texas, including lien and foreclosure abilities, Senator Kenneth Armbrister, D-Victoria, as the Chair of this Committee." Nothing significant came of the study. Several years later, Sen. Jon Lindsay, R-District 7, became the Chair of this Committee to do the same kind of study. Everyone had input, some more than others. The result was his bill SB949, which did not get out of committee. It was so badly bruised; it would have harmed homeowners in its altered condition. CAI attorneys ravaged it.

Legislators must create a homeowner-advocate committee, which would allow us to give input to the legislators as to what we want since it is our money supporting the cottage industry. This committee should not contain any attorneys—pro homeowners or anti homeowners. Attorneys have a different outlook than homeowners and advocate homeowners. Moreover, you never really know the true agenda of an attorney. No one can speak for a homeowner better than a homeowner. Legislators must stop treating us like we are mentally challenged.

The legislators should also set up a panel of legislators that ask homeowners and advocates questions about any proposed homeowner bill and questions about problems in the community to make sure the proposed bill will fix the problems. The legislators during hearings should not filibuster during the hearings to eat up homeowner and advocate witness time as we are aware of this procedure and it affects our opinion about the legislator and will affect our voting incentive for him or her.

Now, I said earlier "the law, until we change it, is mainly on the side of the homeowner association and their attorneys;" but we have a small window in which we can get justice. It is important when we use the system that we go to Court with a cause of action recognized by that state, such as Breach of Contract, Discrimination, something like that. When we appear in Court with "gray" ambiguous cause of actions that we have created, we are not going to win. We are going to spend a bunch of money for nothing.

As long as we have homeowner associations, we will have to try first to resolve the matter with our HOA. When that fails, we are going to have to get legal representation or represent ourselves. We are going to have to be ready to fight for at least four (4) years minimum. We are going to have to be willing to go through the back door and by that I mean reporting the egregious behavior to everyone—Attorney General, District Attorney, Banking, the Post Office (I learned that if you unknowingly pay an unauthorized maintenance fee because you got your maintenance fee in the mail, you can file a complaint with the Post Office), Internal Revenue Service (I learned that some homeowner associations may not have reported income because they are masquerading as non-profit organizations and should not have income but the IRS should know this), since these are debt collecting agencies aka CAI attorneys file a complaint under the Consumer Credit Protection Act (amended by The Fair Debt Collection Practices Act on September 30, 1996), and write the President of the United States (make sure it is when a Democratic President is in because you won't get a response from a Republican President, no offense intended to Republicans). Please send me a letter or an email when something works to relieve your pain and suffering and it is not a court action.

Doing all of the above at the same time works well. In addition, it does not hurt to picket, notify the news media, and post on your website (if you do not have one, I think it is smart to create one). Additionally, always contact your legislators and all the other legislators to let them know you are having a problem so they can monitor the type of problem you are having and will know there are problems in our HOA's. During our testifying at hearings, some legislators have stated they have not heard from their constituents regarding HOA problems. Some legislators like Sen. Juan "Chuy" Hinojosa, District 20, will aggressively act on their constituents' complaints and really want to help you resolve your issue. This Senator will even send a team of representatives to your home to talk about and resolve the problem you are having.

There are many Senators and Representatives who have tried to present good bills for homeowners such as SB949 that Sen. Jon Lindsay introduced last session 2003, but his bill as mentioned earlier was ravaged by CAI attorneys, developers, homeowner associations, board members, and the list goes on. Of course, T.H.A.G. members were there to deflect the lies told by the anti homeowner bill speakers.

Every session it is always the same old rhetoric from the anti homeowner bill speakers. They never have any proof of what they support but they are part of the CAI food chain. The homeowner never gets the proper amount of time to speak and has to grab the few minutes allowed to speak. Thank God, I talk fast and minutes are given to me by Johnnie and sometimes other T.H.A.G. members so I can present our case with time to spare; but the time I get does not match the time the opponents get and the opportunity to answer questions they get. We call it stalling or filibustering. Many of us must stay way into the night to be heard. Nevertheless, most of us stay to support the ones who speak later.

The CAI attorneys who foreclose the most are flamboyant, touchy, sensitive and defensive in their message. They are offended that we, the homeowners, have the nerve to show up and try to stop malicious foreclosure filings against our property, or to stop unreasonable, arrogant board member behavior. We are truly sick and tired of the crumbs being thrown from the association we live in, especially when we are footing the bill.

Homeowners are being permanently forced out of their homes because their board members have initiated "drive by's" to see if the weeds have been removed, the mat removed from the driveway, the grass cut, the mailbox fixed, house painted, and other busy-body fund raising deed restriction complaints. If you have followed your deed restriction regarding your architectural improvements and added your fence, painted your house, put your new roof on, and a new board comes in and tells you to take it out, if you do not take it out or replace the "violation", you will be involved in a foreclosure filing. They know the average person is not going to lose their house over a failure to cut their grass, or painting their house the wrong color or whatever; just like they know you will pay your maintenance fees whether you belong to a homeowner association or not.

CAI attorneys have key hauled board members into thinking pursuing homeowners with lawsuits is advantageous to the property values in their community, when in fact it is moving against gravity. I will let you do the math. Take the association's lawsuit against us for instance, approximately $2,998.20 actually expended by the association as opposed to collecting $842.00. How is this better for the neighborhood? Would it not be better to allow a family like this to pay monthly until collected? Is it not clear to everyone involved, that this is not a productive way to run associations in any state? Is it not clear that this is just an open-check book for special interest groups?

Homeowners do not want to be treated as if they are mentally challenged. They must like good things or they would not be in a nice community. Is it fair that developers have bought up all the land and placed restrictions on it and now board members want us to move out and find the few acres left that do not have an association on it?

In several decades, we have achieved a role reversal where the "common property" has become the "homestead property" and the developers have been the "protected homeowner". What use to be our legislators have now become their legislators. No one is paying attention to our demands, complaints, cries of anguish, and abuse suffered at the hands of our homeowner association except a precious few legislators who are already worn out from being pulled in two different directions.

We are escalating to a war zone that if more legislators do not start paying closer attention to homeowner complaints and reversing this role, we are going to have a major meltdown. Whatever happened to the good old days, when most all legislators respected the voter and the homeowner? Why do we have to say "Mother, may I" to get resolutions to our problems? When did we become so disrespected?

I looked up to the Heavens and thanked God for my competitive nature and debate skills and knew in my heart as every judge we have ever been before and every attorney we have litigated against or been in Court with as a result of being sued by the two associations in our community, that not one attorney won fairly.

We know and they know that without the muscle of their judges and their dirty tricks, they would have been beaten. They know it and we know it. CAI attorneys are not particularly smart; they are just capricious, mean-spirited, Grade C debaters, unethical, and crafty, who have a whole industry on their side. The industry they created.

The times we have won various motions have been before the judge engaged in "ex parte" communication with the CAI attorney. Many judges have inquired into my knowledge and mannerism thinking that I was an attorney. The attorneys have tried to capitalize on the fact I am not. The amounts we were suing for have also made it difficult to win.

Once the CAI attorneys realized the judges were taking us seriously, they went into their dirty fighting mode.

One of my best moments, though, was when I debated Jeffrey Ewalt one-on-one in a fair judge's court—Judge Dwight Jefferson—and for thirty (30) minutes experienced what it felt like to fight a fair fight without a bias judge and without ex-parte communication. I told you about that argument in Chapter 14. That wonderful feeling will last me until the day I die.

We said many years ago, legislators and everyone would pay attention to this foreclosure extortion ring when a white person is thrown out of their house because of it.

When we first heard the news in 2001, we could not believe it. An old white lady by the name of Winona Blevins had just been foreclosed. The picture we saw made her the poster woman for HOA foreclosures.

She had the right look. She was sitting at the correct angle and they took the right shots. She was the saddest looking old lady you ever wanted to see who had lost her Texas homestead over $876 in maintenance fees. The attorney for the association, Marc Markel, was the same attorney involved in our homeowner lawsuit. My God, I thought, was he still foreclosing on people's homes?

I called Johnnie to the bedroom to see the news about Ms. Blevins. He was as shocked as I was. We both spoke of how this foreclosure should blow the top off this scam at last after all it has now happened to a white woman.

We felt all of our advocacy work along with the work of other advocates had somehow helped Winona to get the type of attention she needed. There was none of this slacker label, deadbeat label we had gotten. There were no killed stories. While we had heard from Sen. Jerry Patterson regarding legislation to give notice at closing to the HOA's and the fees so that no one else would be foreclosed like we were, they were talking about introducing a Winona Bill to stop the foreclosures or to do something more than just give notice. Sadly, even Winona could not stop the foreclosures for others.

Sen. Jon Lindsay filed a bill, which allowed homeowners to recover the equity in their home if it were auctioned for less than its market value, as was the case with Wenonah; and the Texas Senate overwhelmingly approved the bill. Marian Rosen, Blevins' attorney, welcomed Lindsay's bill and said it was a necessary companion to the Corona legislation. Lindsay bill did not make it; Corona's bill did. His bill allowed a homeowner 90 days after an eviction notice or two years after a foreclosure sale to buy back the home and pay fees of up to 25 percent of the auction price. (Compliments of the Houston Chronicle, May 10, 2001 issue.)

Unfortunately, these are what I call "band aids" for foreclosure cancer treatment and I have already heard of associations that have skirted around the redemption law by waiting until the time expired before taking action to evict the homeowner. There are no band-aid laws passed that the CAI attorneys have not found a way to skirt around.

Six years' ago, an advocate by the name of E.L. died for the cause. He died in St. Joseph's hospital after undergoing a hernia operation. He was the court watcher who moved around on a cane; one of the ones I mentioned in Chapter 11. He was manhandled during one of his court watching events by the bailiffs and ended up in the hospital.

Then there was Phrogge (pronounced froggie) who spent two (2) years in front of the Family Law Center, where the monthly foreclosures took place. A courageous woman who slept on a cot outside in all the weather for two (2) years to get rid of the corrupt judges that the building she slept in front of contained. She successfully removed all of them during the next election.

Then I thought about my family and me. An innocent black family who came to Texas looking for a new life and naively moved into one of the most racist communities in the State of Texas. A community that unknown to us had in place the blueprints of one of the most efficient and prolific foreclosure filing machines in the State of Texas. Texas being one of several states engaged in a foreclosure racket that will eventually rock the country. This extortion scam, second only to the S & L scandal.

The only differences between Winona Blevins and us were she was older and white. The pain and suffering was there for us too and we had children who were a part of our miserable situation.

We were called "slackers" and "dead beats"; she was the poor "elderly Widow". We left two (2) days after Christmas in 1995 and left before we were physically taken out, although that was Johnnie's choice, not mine.

I wanted to stay. I thought seeing a black woman being dragged from her home might have presented a good story.

According to news accounts, "the association sold Blevins' home at public auction without her knowledge, then had constables evict her with no notice. "'They took everything. They said I could take one change of clothing, one. In addition, they took everything else. Everything,'" she remembers."

Further account stated, "Her friends and neighbors were outraged and challenged the homeowners association at an angry meeting. Then local newspapers picked up the story, and Blevins got an attorney and brought a lawsuit."

Other glaring differences in her story and ours were her ability to get her neighbors outraged enough to challenge the homeowners association, newspapers to pick up the story without it being killed as in our case and to get an attorney.

What a difference six (6) years had made since our foreclosure. It was not a "let's blame the homeowner" scenario anymore but a real concern for the loss of the homeowner's homestead.

Legislation was quickly drafted for Winona with her name firmly affixed to it, a limousine ride to Austin, a special seat in the balcony of the house while they attempted to pass a bill in her name and the attorney that had started the whole thing had placed himself into the background to soften the foreclosure edges a bit. No one publicly acknowledged our earlier loss as they often do in a copycat crime. We were all but forgotten.

Since the journey we have taken to stop homestead foreclosures is a journey we were involuntarily forced into, we seek no notoriety. It is our goal to stop permanently homeowner association and property owner association actual foreclosures and prolific foreclosure filings geared to extort excessive money from homeowners.

Many advocates are sidetracked seeking to carry the baton across the finish line with their name on it but does it really matter who gets the credit for finally stopping the abuse, as it is really a task that all advocates had something to do with. We must all work together.

Then another hitch appeared that had also hit us when the buyer of Winona's property refused to give up the house unless he was paid $50,000. In our parallel case, the association purchased the house for $184.92 but failed and refused to pay the monthly payments on the house and HUD tried to convince us the house was really still ours. It was made clear in Winona's case that no, she did not still own the house. She had been evicted. The man who purchased her house, Danny Hilal, as it turned out had experienced foreclosure himself. He had been sued six (6) times for foreclosure. He was "sued for back taxes every year since 1992; more than 30 times in all. And he's defended himself against charges of professional malpractice twice."

This time it looked like we were looking at what was inside the pot instead of worrying about the outside of it. Every now and then, the ridiculousness of foreclosing on one's homestead property rises to the top of the pot and spills over for all to see. Such instances as people being forbidden from flying their flags, putting up a mailbox that is not agreeable to the board and that type of nonsense does not say much for our intelligence level.

A story that could not be contained burst at the seams in all the newspapers. For several months, you could hardly pick up a paper and not see Winona's sad face peering at you from it. It broke our hearts to see it and you truly felt sorry for this woman.

Her circumstances proved that there could be a situation that goes beyond the inflexible state of the HOA's board members who are more stringent than the IRS.

Winona stated she was unaware of the impending foreclosure because they had been sending mail to her husband who was deceased. She tossed his mail because he was deceased and apparently, the foreclosure notice was among the mail.

The association being the insensitive entity it is and having lost all of its working-with-your neighbor spirit, turned the issue over to their attorney who tacked on their legal fees and recommended foreclosure.

Blevins home was paid for which certainly made her foreclosure more enticing to the HOA's attorney.

This time the HOA had pushed too far and foreclosed the wrong person. While we were foreclosed for a silly reason, "because we would not have moved unless we were foreclosed", the extortion machine is colorblind. It really does not matter what color you are, what age you are, what your financial background is or how expensive or less expensive your home is. The key factors in whether or not you are chosen for foreclosure lies more in whether or not you have equity in your home and if so, how much equity. It matters more on how likely are you to be able to defend yourself in a lawsuit and thus that is why many senior citizens, certain ethnic groups such as black, Vietnamese and Hispanics get chosen and then the neighborhood is important and whether or not you can get to the board and convince them of your worth.

Many, many, many emails arrived here in Texas from all over the world regarding Winona Blevins. Her ordeal is still remembered to this day. They truly picked on the wrong lady this time.

It is not clear to me what was accomplished for the homeowners at large because of Winona's temporary misfortune, though, because while the newspaper gave the impression that HOA foreclosures were no longer possible, that was not the case. The HOA's can still foreclose on one's homestead in the State of Texas, even though we have Homestead

Protection under Article 16, Section 50 of the Texas Constitution and thus the hoax.

Overall, Winona had a good payday. She got her house back, new furniture from Gallery Furniture and $300,000. She was away from her home for one (1) year and her furniture was damaged while being removed from her house. This is a perfect example of what can happen when homeowners get angry and say enough is enough. There should be anger, though, for everyone abused, not just 82-year-old white widows.

Moreover, the LORD appeared unto Abram, and said, unto thy seed will I give this land: and there builded he an altar unto the LORD, who appeared unto him. Gen. 12:7 Land has always been important to us, as it is a gift from God. The Texas Constitution, Article 16, Section 50, in the State of Texas, gave our homestead protection to us. In other states, we also have constitutional rights. Yes, in each state and the advocates in those states know how we lost those rights. I, along with other advocates in this state of Texas, know how we lost it here.

While our distracters have tried to complicate it, steal it away from us, justify their use of it, pay for it, abuse it, use it, camouflage it, and anything else they can think of, I have always remained focus on our homestead rights. Inwood. Inwood. Inwood. Inwood. Stolen. Stolen. Stolen. Stolen. I have even tried to make it very simple, called "How our rights were stolen 101". It looks like this:

On the land	CLOSING
Developer's Contractual Liens	Homestead Rights
Inwood vs. Harris	guaranteed by Art. 16,
	Sec. 50 of the Texas
	Constitution (prior to on the land)

It is very important that advocates take the lead in each state and work for the benefit of the homeowners with their legislators in a manner that is not abusive, arrogant or not creative. Not all of us can be leaders. Not all of us can be followers. I have found in being an advocate since 1990 that there are advocates masquerading as advocates. I have worked for years to make something happen for homeowners and have finally made a breakthrough with God's divine help only, only to have an "advocate" I have known for years to make a call behind my back to the legislator who was kind enough to ask the Attorney General Greg Abbott our question from the group The Texas Homeowner's Advocate Group. The call she made was to make the statement, "this question is not enough. We need more." "It is not just the foreclosures." "What about conflict of interest?"

I thought what nerve. What has anyone else done to get us this close to some answers? Why is it that you get such knives in your back from other advocates when you are trying to do something constructive? Why is it that the advocates who have done nothing but made it harder for other advocates to get anything accomplish, have the worse comments to make? Why do they sit back and do nothing and wait until you do something and then maliciously tear apart everything you try to do to help homeowners? The old saying "if you are not part of the solution, you are part of the problem", applied here too.

Representative Fred Hill on June 9, 2004, only two days after being asked by me as President of The Texas Homeowner's Advocate Group, stepped up to the plate as facilitator and requested the Attorney General answer our question: "Whether the placement of a one-party foreclosable contractual lien on the land by the developer that supersede the homestead rights created in Article 16, Section 50 of the Texas Constitution violate the Texas Homestead Act?" (Request No. RQ-0236-GA)

While my circle of advocates, some of which may not know what person to support or stand behind, I am quite sure the CAI will not have any problem declaring who they will be behind as one of the carbon copies of the letter to The Honorable Fred Hill from the Attorney General's office was Ms. Camellia Belcher, PCAM, Executive Director, Community Associations Institute of Texas, Austin Chapter.

If I were a betting person, I would bet that every chapter in Texas responded to our question with an Amicus Curiae. The list also contained Director of Consumers Union Southwest Regional Office, County Clerks Legislative Committee, Director of Public Citizen, Executive Director of Texas Association of Mortgage Brokers, President of the Texas Association of Realtors, General Counsel for the Texas Bankers Association, myself, Executive Vice President of the Texas Land Title Association, President of the Texas Neighborhoods Together and Governor's Appointment Director. There was one other copy to the President of American Veterans in Domestic

Defense. While I could not figure the relevance of their association with our question, I certainly could figure out the relevance of everyone else on the list, some of whom I pray are on our side.

Before I wrote the brief, I prayed for God to inspire me and give me the right words to bring an understanding to the readers of it. Following is what I wrote:

R. Q. – 0236- GA

OFFICE OF THE ATTORNEY GENERAL
The Honorable Greg Abbott

THE QUESTION:
_____

"Whether the placement of one-party foreclosable contractual liens on the land by the developer that supersede the homestead rights created in Article XVI, Section 50 of the Texas Constitution violate the Texas Homestead Act?"

BRIEF OF

THE TEXAS HOMEOWNER'S ADVOCATE GROUP

Submitted by:
(Mrs) Harvella Jones
President
Post Office Box 420925
Houston, Texas 77242
(XXX) XXX-XXXX
(713) 639-4991 24/7
(XXX) XXX-XXXX FAX

TABLE OF CONTENTS

INDEX OF AUTHORITIES

STATEMENT OF JURISDICTION

Section 402.042 of the Government Code provides that the Attorney General shall issue an opinion not later than the 180th day after the date that an opinion request is received. TEX. GOV'T CODE ANN. 402.042(c)(2) (Vernon 1998). Request was received from The Honorable Fred Hill, Chair, Committee on Local Government Ways and Means, Texas House of Representatives, on June 9, 2004, setting a due date for the Attorney General's opinion of December 6, 2004.

"Whether the placement of one-party foreclosable contractual liens on the land by the developer that supersede the homestead rights created in Article XVI, Section 50 of the Texas Constitution violate the Texas Homestead Act?"

INFORMATION SURROUNDING THE QUESTION

"Whether the placement of one-party foreclosable contractual liens on the land by the developer that supersede the homestead rights created in Article XVI, Section 50 of the Texas Constitution violate the Texas Homestead Act?"

1. Inwood North Homeowners' Ass'n v. Harris 736 S.W. 2d 632 (Tex. 1987) created "contractual liens" that supersede future homeowners' homestead protection and was not created by the legislators or the voters of this state. (Exhibit A)

2. Prior to Inwood, homeowners had active homestead protection at the closing table due to Article XVI, Section 50, Homestead Act, Texas Constitution.

3. Complaints from homeowners have escalated concerning lost homestead rights throughout the State of Texas.

4. The Texas Homeowner's Advocate group is recommending "repeal" of the Inwood law since it is full of legal errors and not in compliance with Article 16, Sec. 50 of the Texas Constitution Homestead Law.

5. The Texas Supreme Court in 1987 gave the developers and their lien holders (if any) a higher homestead protection right than the Texas Constitution allowed..

6. The "contractual lien" was created by three Texas Supreme Court justices, with two other justices dissenting.

7. This unconstitutional placement of the contractual lien on the land prior to a homeowner's homestead designation at closing, affects every current and potential homeowner in this state.

8. When these homesteads are foreclosed, the title to the property is clouded, and the homesteads are held in trust. (Exhibit B)

STANDARD OF REVIEW

1. The Texas Supreme Court made an error in 1987, when it reversed the judgment of the court of appeals and allowed the homeowner association to foreclose on the homeowners' homesteads in spite of homestead protection to collect the maintenance fees due. (Inwood vs. Harris 736 S.W.2d 633 (Tex. 1987). There was no vendor's lien present and the Court recognized that, (Inwood, 634), yet the Supreme Court "created" foreclosure law when they "created" a one-party contract lien. (Inwood, 632) The Texas Constitution has never been amended to allow the judicial body to create law, only to "interpret" it. (The Texas Constitution, Art. 17, Sect. 1, Art. 5, Sect. 31)

2. The Texas Homeowner's Advocate Group on behalf of the thousands of current and potential homeowners who have no voice, and who are subject to loss of homestead rights due to the timing and formation of one-party pre-arranged, pre-existing contractual liens placed on land by commercial developers and their lien holders (if any), asked The Honorable Fred Hill to ask our Attorney General a question. The Honorable Greg Abbott complied, for which we are appreciative, and assigned our question to RQ-0236-GA.

LEGAL ARGUMENT

POINT ONE:

The Texas Constitution has never been amended to allow foreclosable "contractual liens" as one of the foreclosure "exceptions" to Article 16, Section 50, Homestead Act.

LAW IN SUPPORT:

The Texas Constitution, Article 16, Section 50; Article 17, Section 1

ARGUMENT:

Let the document speak for itself:

The Texas Constitution

Article 16 - GENERAL PROVISIONS

Section 50 - HOMESTEAD; PROTECTION FROM FORCED SALE; MORTGAGES, TRUST DEEDS, AND LIENS

(a) The homestead of a family, or of a single adult person, shall be, and is hereby protected from forced sale, for the payment of all debts except for:
(1) the purchase money thereof, or a part of such purchase money;
(2) the taxes due thereon;
(3) an owelty of partition imposed against the entirety of the property by a court order or by a written agreement of the parties to the partition, including a debt of one spouse in favor of the other spouse resulting from a division or an award of a family homestead in a divorce proceeding;
(4) the refinance of a lien against a homestead, including a federal tax lien resulting from the tax debt of both spouses, if the homestead is a family homestead, or from the tax debt of the owner;

150

(5) work and material used in constructing new improvements thereon, if contracted for in writing, or work and material used to repair or renovate existing improvements thereon if:

(A) the work and material are contracted for in writing, with the consent of both spouses, in the case of a family homestead, given in the same manner as is required in making a sale and conveyance of the homestead;

(B) the contract for the work and material is not executed by the owner or the owner's spouse before the fifth day after the owner makes written application for any extension of credit for the work and material, unless the work and material are necessary to complete immediate repairs to conditions on the homestead property that materially affect the health or safety of the owner or person residing in the homestead and the owner of the homestead acknowledges such in writing;

(C) the contract for the work and material expressly provides that the owner may rescind the contract without penalty or charge within three days after the execution of the contract by all parties, unless the work and material are necessary to complete immediate repairs to conditions on the homestead property that materially affect the health or safety of the owner or person residing in the homestead and the owner of the homestead acknowledges such in writing; and

(D) the contract for the work and material is executed by the owner and the owner's spouse only at the office of a third-party lender making an extension of credit for the work and material, an attorney at law, or a title company;

(6) an extension of credit that:

(A) is secured by a voluntary lien on the homestead created under a written agreement with the consent of each owner and each owner's spouse;

(B) is of a principal amount that when added to the aggregate total of the outstanding principal balances of all other indebtedness secured by valid encumbrances of record against the homestead does not exceed 80 percent of the fair market value of the homestead on the date the extension of credit is made;

(C) is without recourse for personal liability against each owner and the spouse of each owner, unless the owner or spouse obtained the extension of credit by actual fraud;

(D) is secured by a lien that may be foreclosed upon only by a court order;

(E) does not require the owner or the owner's spouse to pay, in addition to any interest, fees to any person that are necessary to originate, evaluate, maintain, record, insure, or service the extension of credit that exceed, in the aggregate, three percent of the original principal amount of the extension of credit;

(F) is not a form of open-end account that may be debited from time to time or under which credit may be extended from time to time unless the open-end account is a home equity line of credit;

(G) is payable in advance without penalty or other charge;

(H) is not secured by any additional real or personal property other than the homestead;

(I) is not secured by homestead property designated for agricultural use as provided by statutes governing property tax, unless such homestead property is used primarily for the production of milk;

(J) may not be accelerated because of a decrease in the market value of the homestead or because of the owner's default under other indebtedness not secured by a prior valid encumbrance against the homestead;

(K) is the only debt secured by the homestead at the time the extension of credit is made unless the other debt was made for a purpose described by Subsections (a)(1)-(a)(5) or Subsection (a)(8) of this section;

(L) is scheduled to be repaid:

(i) in substantially equal successive periodic installments, not more often than every 14 days and not less often than monthly, beginning no later than two months from the date the extension of credit is made, each of which equals or exceeds the amount of accrued interest as of the date of the scheduled installment; or

(ii) if the extension of credit is a home equity line of credit, in periodic payments described under Subsection (t)(8) of this section;

(M) is closed not before:

(i) the 12th day after the later of the date that the owner of the homestead submits an application to the lender for the extension of credit or the date that the lender provides the owner a copy of the notice prescribed by Subsection (g) of this section;

(ii) one business day after the date that the owner of the homestead receives a final itemized disclosure of the actual fees, points, interest, costs, and charges that will be charged at closing. If a bona fide emergency or another good cause exists and the lender obtains the written consent of the owner, the lender may provide the documentation to the owner or the lender may modify previously provided documentation on the date of closing; and

(iii) the first anniversary of the closing date of any other extension of credit described by Subsection (a)(6) of this section secured by the same homestead property, except a refinance described by Paragraph (Q)(x)(f) of this subdivision;

(N) is closed only at the office of the lender, an attorney at law, or a title company;

(O) permits a lender to contract for and receive any fixed or variable rate of interest authorized under statute;

(P) is made by one of the following that has not been found by a federal regulatory agency to have engaged in the practice of refusing to make loans because the applicants for the loans reside or the property proposed to secure the loans is located in a certain area:

(i) a bank, savings and loan association, savings bank, or credit union doing business under the laws of this state or the United States;

(ii) a federally chartered lending instrumentality or a person approved as a mortgagee by the United States government to make federally insured loans;
(iii) a person licensed to make regulated loans, as provided by statute of this state;
(iv) a person who sold the homestead property to the current owner and who provided all or part of the financing for the purchase;
(v) a person who is related to the homestead property owner within the second degree of affinity or consanguinity; or
(vi) a person regulated by this state as a mortgage broker; and
(Q) is made on the condition that:
(i) the owner of the homestead is not required to apply the proceeds of the extension of credit to repay another debt except debt secured by the homestead or debt to another lender;
(ii) the owner of the homestead not assign wages as security for the extension of credit;
(iii) the owner of the homestead not sign any instrument in which blanks are left to be filled in;
(iv) the owner of the homestead not sign a confession of judgment or power of attorney to the lender or to a third person to confess judgment or to appear for the owner in a judicial proceeding;
(v) the lender, at the time the extension of credit is made, provide the owner of the homestead a copy of all documents signed by the owner related to the extension of credit;
(vi) the security instruments securing the extension of credit contain a disclosure that the extension of credit is the type of credit defined by Section 50(a)(6), Article XVI, Texas Constitution;
(vii) within a reasonable time after termination and full payment of the extension of credit, the lender cancel and return the promissory note to the owner of the homestead and give the owner, in record able form, a release of the lien securing the extension of credit or a copy of an endorsement and assignment of the lien to a lender that is refinancing the extension of credit;
(viii) the owner of the homestead and any spouse of the owner may, within three days after the extension of credit is made, rescind the extension of credit without penalty or charge;
(ix) the owner of the homestead and the lender sign a written acknowledgment as to the fair market value of the homestead property on the date the extension of credit is made;
(x) except as provided by Subparagraph (xi) of this paragraph, the lender or any holder of the note for the extension of credit shall forfeit all principal and interest of the extension of credit if the lender or holder fails to comply with the lender's or holder's obligations under the extension of credit and fails to correct the failure to comply not later than the 60th day after the date the lender or holder is notified by the borrower of the lender's failure to comply by:

(a) paying to the owner an amount equal to any overcharge paid by the owner under or related to the extension of credit if the owner has paid an amount that exceeds an amount stated in the applicable Paragraph (E), (G), or (O) of this subdivision;

(b) sending the owner a written acknowledgement that the lien is valid only in the amount that the extension of credit does not exceed the percentage described by Paragraph (B) of this subdivision, if applicable, or is not secured by property described under Paragraph (H) or (I) of this subdivision, if applicable;

(c) sending the owner a written notice modifying any other amount, percentage, term, or other provision prohibited by this section to a permitted amount, percentage, term, or other provision and adjusting the account of the borrower to ensure that the borrower is not required to pay more than an amount permitted by this section and is not subject to any other term or provision prohibited by this section;

(d) delivering the required documents to the borrower if the lender fails to comply with Subparagraph (v) of this paragraph or obtaining the appropriate signatures if the lender fails to comply with Subparagraph (ix) of this paragraph;

(e) sending the owner a written acknowledgement, if the failure to comply is prohibited by Paragraph (K) of this subdivision, that the accrual of interest and all of the owner's obligations under the extension of credit are abated while any prior lien prohibited under Paragraph (K) remains secured by the homestead; or

(f) if the failure to comply cannot be cured under Subparagraphs (x)(a)(e) of this paragraph, curing the failure to comply by a refund or credit to the owner of $1,000 and offering the owner the right to refinance the extension of credit with the lender or holder for the remaining term of the loan at no cost to the owner on the same terms, including interest, as the original extension of credit with any modifications necessary to comply with this section or on terms on which the owner and the lender or holder otherwise agree that comply with this section; and

(xi) the lender or any holder of the note for the extension of credit shall forfeit all principal and interest of the extension of credit if the extension of credit is made by a person other than a person described under Paragraph (P) of this subdivision or if the lien was not created under a written agreement with the consent of each owner and each owner's spouse, unless each owner and each owner's spouse who did not initially consent subsequently consents;

(7) a reverse mortgage; or

(8) the conversion and refinance of a personal property lien secured by a manufactured home to a lien on real property, including the refinance of the purchase price of the manufactured home, the cost of installing the manufactured home on the real property, and the refinance of the purchase price of the real property.

(b) An owner or claimant of the property claimed as homestead may not sell or abandon the homestead without the consent of each owner and the spouse of each owner, given in such manner as may be prescribed by law.

(c) No mortgage, trust deed, or other lien on the homestead shall ever be valid unless it secures a debt described by this section, whether such mortgage, trust deed, or other lien, shall have been created by the owner alone, or together with his or her spouse, in case the owner is married. All pretended sales of the homestead involving any condition of defeasance shall be void.

(d) A purchaser or lender for value without actual knowledge may conclusively rely on an affidavit that designates other property as the homestead of the affiant and that states that the property to be conveyed or encumbered is not the homestead of the affiant.

(e) A refinance of debt secured by a homestead and described by any subsection under Subsections (a)(1)-(a)(5) that includes the advance of additional funds may not be secured by a valid lien against the homestead unless:

(1) the refinance of the debt is an extension of credit described by Subsection (a)(6) of this section; or

(2) the advance of all the additional funds is for reasonable costs necessary to refinance such debt or for a purpose described by Subsection (a)(2), (a)(3), or (a)(5) of this section.

(f) A refinance of debt secured by the homestead, any portion of which is an extension of credit described by Subsection (a)(6) of this section, may not be secured by a valid lien against the homestead unless the refinance of the debt is an extension of credit described by Subsection (a)(6) or (a)(7) of this section.

(g) An extension of credit described by Subsection (a)(6) of this section may be secured by a valid lien against homestead property if the extension of credit is not closed before the 12th day after the lender provides the owner with the following written notice on a separate instrument:

"NOTICE CONCERNING EXTENSIONS OF CREDIT DEFINED BY SECTION 50(a)(6), ARTICLE XVI, TEXAS CONSTITUTION:

"SECTION 50(a)(6), ARTICLE XVI, OF THE TEXAS CONSTITUTION ALLOWS CERTAIN LOANS TO BE SECURED AGAINST THE EQUITY IN YOUR HOME. SUCH LOANS ARE COMMONLY KNOWN AS EQUITY LOANS. IF YOU DO NOT REPAY THE LOAN OR IF YOU FAIL TO MEET THE TERMS OF THE LOAN, THE LENDER MAY FORECLOSE AND SELL YOUR HOME. THE CONSTITUTION PROVIDES THAT:

"(A) THE LOAN MUST BE VOLUNTARILY CREATED WITH THE CONSENT OF EACH OWNER OF YOUR HOME AND EACH OWNER'S SPOUSE;

"(B) THE PRINCIPAL LOAN AMOUNT AT THE TIME THE LOAN IS MADE MUST NOT EXCEED AN AMOUNT THAT, WHEN ADDED TO THE PRINCIPAL BALANCES OF ALL OTHER LIENS AGAINST YOUR HOME, IS MORE THAN 80 PERCENT OF THE FAIR MARKET VALUE OF YOUR HOME;

"(C) THE LOAN MUST BE WITHOUT RECOURSE FOR PERSONAL LIABILITY AGAINST YOU AND YOUR SPOUSE UNLESS YOU OR YOUR SPOUSE OBTAINED THIS EXTENSION OF CREDIT BY ACTUAL FRAUD;

"(D) THE LIEN SECURING THE LOAN MAY BE FORECLOSED UPON ONLY WITH A COURT ORDER;

"(E) FEES AND CHARGES TO MAKE THE LOAN MAY NOT EXCEED 3 PERCENT OF THE LOAN AMOUNT;

"(F) THE LOAN MAY NOT BE AN OPEN-END ACCOUNT THAT MAY BE DEBITED FROM TIME TO TIME OR UNDER WHICH CREDIT MAY BE EXTENDED FROM TIME TO TIME UNLESS IT IS A HOME EQUITY LINE OF CREDIT;

"(G) YOU MAY PREPAY THE LOAN WITHOUT PENALTY OR CHARGE;

"(H) NO ADDITIONAL COLLATERAL MAY BE SECURITY FOR THE LOAN;

"(I) THE LOAN MAY NOT BE SECURED BY AGRICULTURAL HOMESTEAD PROPERTY, UNLESS THE AGRICULTURAL HOMESTEAD PROPERTY IS USED PRIMARILY FOR THE PRODUCTION OF MILK;

"(J) YOU ARE NOT REQUIRED TO REPAY THE LOAN EARLIER THAN AGREED SOLELY BECAUSE THE FAIR MARKET VALUE OF YOUR HOME DECREASES OR BECAUSE YOU DEFAULT ON ANOTHER LOAN THAT IS NOT SECURED BY YOUR HOME;

"(K) ONLY ONE LOAN DESCRIBED BY SECTION 50(a)(6), ARTICLE XVI, OF THE TEXAS CONSTITUTION MAY BE SECURED WITH YOUR HOME AT ANY GIVEN TIME;

"(L) THE LOAN MUST BE SCHEDULED TO BE REPAID IN PAYMENTS THAT EQUAL OR EXCEED THE AMOUNT OF ACCRUED INTEREST FOR EACH PAYMENT PERIOD;

"(M) THE LOAN MAY NOT CLOSE BEFORE 12 DAYS AFTER YOU SUBMIT A WRITTEN APPLICATION TO THE LENDER OR BEFORE 12 DAYS AFTER YOU RECEIVE THIS NOTICE, WHICHEVER DATE IS LATER; AND IF YOUR HOME WAS SECURITY FOR THE SAME TYPE OF LOAN WITHIN THE PAST YEAR, A NEW LOAN SECURED BY THE SAME PROPERTY MAY NOT CLOSE BEFORE ONE YEAR HAS PASSED FROM THE CLOSING DATE OF THE OTHER LOAN;

"(N) THE LOAN MAY CLOSE ONLY AT THE OFFICE OF THE LENDER, TITLE COMPANY, OR AN ATTORNEY AT LAW;

"(O) THE LENDER MAY CHARGE ANY FIXED OR VARIABLE RATE OF INTEREST AUTHORIZED BY STATUTE;

"(P) ONLY A LAWFULLY AUTHORIZED LENDER MAY MAKE LOANS DESCRIBED BY SECTION 50(a)(6), ARTICLE XVI, OF THE TEXAS CONSTITUTION;

"(Q) LOANS DESCRIBED BY SECTION 50(a)(6), ARTICLE XVI, OF THE TEXAS CONSTITUTION MUST:

"(1) NOT REQUIRE YOU TO APPLY THE PROCEEDS TO ANOTHER DEBT EXCEPT A DEBT THAT IS SECURED BY YOUR HOME OR OWED TO ANOTHER LENDER;

"(2) NOT REQUIRE THAT YOU ASSIGN WAGES AS SECURITY;

"(3) NOT REQUIRE THAT YOU EXECUTE INSTRUMENTS WHICH HAVE BLANKS LEFT TO BE FILLED IN;

"(4) NOT REQUIRE THAT YOU SIGN A CONFESSION OF JUDGMENT OR

POWER OF ATTORNEY TO ANOTHER PERSON TO CONFESS JUDGMENT OR APPEAR IN A LEGAL PROCEEDING ON YOUR BEHALF;

"(5) PROVIDE THAT YOU RECEIVE A COPY OF ALL DOCUMENTS YOU SIGN AT CLOSING;

"(6) PROVIDE THAT THE SECURITY INSTRUMENTS CONTAIN A DISCLOSURE THAT THIS LOAN IS A LOAN DEFINED BY SECTION 50(a)(6), ARTICLE XVI, OF THE TEXAS CONSTITUTION;

"(7) PROVIDE THAT WHEN THE LOAN IS PAID IN FULL, THE LENDER WILL SIGN AND GIVE YOU A RELEASE OF LIEN OR AN ASSIGNMENT OF THE LIEN, WHICHEVER IS APPROPRIATE;

"(8) PROVIDE THAT YOU MAY, WITHIN 3 DAYS AFTER CLOSING, RESCIND THE LOAN WITHOUT PENALTY OR CHARGE;

"(9) PROVIDE THAT YOU AND THE LENDER ACKNOWLEDGE THE FAIR MARKET VALUE OF YOUR HOME ON THE DATE THE LOAN CLOSES; AND

"(10) PROVIDE THAT THE LENDER WILL FORFEIT ALL PRINCIPAL AND INTEREST IF THE LENDER FAILS TO COMPLY WITH THE LENDER'S OBLIGATIONS UNLESS THE LENDER CURES THE FAILURE TO COMPLY AS PROVIDED BY SECTION 50(a)(6)(Q)(x), ARTICLE XVI, OF THE TEXAS CONSTITUTION; AND "(R) IF THE LOAN IS A HOME EQUITY LINE OF CREDIT:

"(1) YOU MAY REQUEST ADVANCES, REPAY MONEY, AND REBORROW MONEY UNDER THE LINE OF CREDIT;

"(2) EACH ADVANCE UNDER THE LINE OF CREDIT MUST BE IN AN AMOUNT OF AT LEAST $4,000;

"(3) YOU MAY NOT USE A CREDIT CARD, DEBIT CARD, SOLICITATION CHECK, OR SIMILAR DEVICE TO OBTAIN ADVANCES UNDER THE LINE OF CREDIT;

"(4) ANY FEES THE LENDER CHARGES MAY BE CHARGED AND COLLECTED ONLY AT THE TIME THE LINE OF CREDIT IS ESTABLISHED AND THE LENDER MAY NOT CHARGE A FEE IN CONNECTION WITH ANY ADVANCE;

"(5) THE MAXIMUM PRINCIPAL AMOUNT THAT MAY BE EXTENDED, WHEN ADDED TO ALL OTHER DEBTS SECURED BY YOUR HOME, MAY NOT EXCEED 80 PERCENT OF THE FAIR MARKET VALUE OF YOUR HOME ON THE DATE THE LINE OF CREDIT IS ESTABLISHED;

"(6) IF THE PRINCIPAL BALANCE UNDER THE LINE OF CREDIT AT ANY TIME EXCEEDS 50 PERCENT OF THE FAIR MARKET VALUE OF YOUR HOME, AS DETERMINED ON THE DATE THE LINE OF CREDIT IS ESTABLISHED, YOU MAY NOT CONTINUE TO REQUEST ADVANCES UNDER THE LINE OF CREDIT UNTIL THE BALANCE IS LESS THAN 50 PERCENT OF THE FAIR MARKET VALUE; AND

"(7) THE LENDER MAY NOT UNILATERALLY AMEND THE TERMS OF THE LINE OF CREDIT.

"THIS NOTICE IS ONLY A SUMMARY OF YOUR RIGHTS UNDER THE TEXAS CONSTITUTION. YOUR RIGHTS ARE GOVERNED BY SECTION 50, ARTICLE XVI, OF THE TEXAS CONSTITUTION, AND NOT BY THIS NOTICE."

If the discussions with the borrower are conducted primarily in a language other than English, the lender shall, before closing, provide an additional copy of the notice translated into the written language in which the discussions were conducted.

(h) A lender or assignee for value may conclusively rely on the written acknowledgment as to the fair market value of the homestead property made in accordance with Subsection (a)(6)(Q)(ix) of this section if:

(1) the value acknowledged to is the value estimate in an appraisal or evaluation prepared in accordance with a state or federal requirement applicable to an extension of credit under Subsection (a)(6); and

(2) the lender or assignee does not have actual knowledge at the time of the payment of value or advance of funds by the lender or assignee that the fair market value stated in the written acknowledgment was incorrect.

(i) This subsection shall not affect or impair any right of the borrower to recover damages from the lender or assignee under applicable law for wrongful foreclosure. A purchaser for value without actual knowledge may conclusively presume that a lien securing an extension of credit described by Subsection (a)(6) of this section was a valid lien securing the extension of credit with homestead property if:

(1) the security instruments securing the extension of credit contain a disclosure that the extension of credit secured by the lien was the type of credit defined by Section 50(a)(6), Article XVI, Texas Constitution;

(2) the purchaser acquires the title to the property pursuant to or after the foreclosure of the voluntary lien; and

(3) the purchaser is not the lender or assignee under the extension of credit.

(j) Subsection (a)(6) and Subsections (e)-(i) of this section are not severable, and none of those provisions would have been enacted without the others. If any of those provisions are held to be preempted by the laws of the United States, all of those provisions are invalid. This subsection shall not apply to any lien or extension of credit made after January 1, 1998, and before the date any provision under Subsection (a)(6) or Subsections (e)-(i) is held to be preempted.

(k) "Reverse mortgage" means an extension of credit:

(1) that is secured by a voluntary lien on homestead property created by a written agreement with the consent of each owner and each owner's spouse;

(2) that is made to a person who is or whose spouse is 62 years or older;

(3) that is made without recourse for personal liability against each owner and the spouse of each owner;

(4) under which advances are provided to a borrower based on the equity in a borrower's homestead;

(5) that does not permit the lender to reduce the amount or number of advances because of an adjustment in the interest rate if periodic advances are to be made;

(6) that requires no payment of principal or interest until:

(A) all borrowers have died;

(B) the homestead property securing the loan is sold or otherwise transferred;

(C) all borrowers cease occupying the homestead property for a period of longer than 12 consecutive months without prior written approval from the lender; or

(D) the borrower:

(i) defaults on an obligation specified in the loan documents to repair and maintain, pay taxes and assessments on, or insure the homestead property;

(ii) commits actual fraud in connection with the loan; or

(iii) fails to maintain the priority of the lender's lien on the homestead property, after the lender gives notice to the borrower, by promptly discharging any lien that has priority or may obtain priority over the lender's lien within 10 days after the date the borrower receives the notice, unless the borrower:

(a) agrees in writing to the payment of the obligation secured by the lien in a manner acceptable to the lender;

(b) contests in good faith the lien by, or defends against enforcement of the lien in, legal proceedings so as to prevent the enforcement of the lien or forfeiture of any part of the homestead property; or

(c) secures from the holder of the lien an agreement satisfactory to the lender subordinating the lien to all amounts secured by the lender's lien on the homestead property;

(7) that provides that if the lender fails to make loan advances as required in the loan documents and if the lender fails to cure the default as required in the loan documents after notice from the borrower, the lender forfeits all principal and interest of the reverse mortgage, provided, however, that this subdivision does not apply when a governmental agency or instrumentality takes an assignment of the loan in order to cure the default;

(8) that is not made unless the owner of the homestead attests in writing that the owner received counseling regarding the advisability and availability of reverse mortgages and other financial alternatives; (9) that requires the lender, at the time the loan is made, to disclose to the borrower by written notice the specific provisions contained in Subdivision (6) of this subsection under which the borrower is required to repay the loan;

(10) that does not permit the lender to commence foreclosure until the lender gives notice to the borrower, in the manner provided for a notice by mail related to the foreclosure of liens under Subsection (a)(6) of this section, that a ground for foreclosure exists and gives the borrower at least 30 days, or at least 20 days in the event of a default under Subdivision (6)(D)(iii) of this subsection, to:

(A) remedy the condition creating the ground for foreclosure; (B) pay the debt secured by the homestead property from proceeds of the sale of the homestead property by the borrower or from any other sources; or

(C) convey the homestead property to the lender by a deed in lieu of foreclosure; and

(11) that is secured by a lien that may be foreclosed upon only by a court order, if the foreclosure is for a ground other than a ground stated by Subdivision (6)(A) or (B) of this subsection.

(l) Advances made under a reverse mortgage and interest on those advances have priority over a lien filed for record in the real property records in the county where the homestead property is located after the reverse mortgage is filed for record in the real property records of that county.

(m) A reverse mortgage may provide for an interest rate that is fixed or adjustable and may also provide for interest that is contingent on appreciation in the fair market value of the homestead property. Although payment of principal or interest shall not be required under a reverse mortgage until the entire loan becomes due and payable, interest may accrue and be compounded during the term of the loan as provided by the reverse mortgage loan agreement.

(n) A reverse mortgage that is secured by a valid lien against homestead property may be made or acquired without regard to the following provisions of any other law of this state:

(1) a limitation on the purpose and use of future advances or other mortgage proceeds;

(2) a limitation on future advances to a term of years or a limitation on the term of open-end account advances;

(3) a limitation on the term during which future advances take priority over intervening advances;

(4) a requirement that a maximum loan amount be stated in the reverse mortgage loan documents;

(5) a prohibition on balloon payments;

(6) a prohibition on compound interest and interest on interest;

(7) a prohibition on contracting for, charging, or receiving any rate of interest authorized by any law of this state authorizing a lender to contract for a rate of interest; and

(8) a requirement that a percentage of the reverse mortgage proceeds be advanced before the assignment of the reverse mortgage.

(o) For the purposes of determining eligibility under any statute relating to payments, allowances, benefits, or services provided on a means-tested basis by this state, including supplemental security income, low-income energy assistance, property tax relief, medical assistance, and general assistance:

(1) reverse mortgage loan advances made to a borrower are considered proceeds from a loan and not income; and

(2) undisbursed funds under a reverse mortgage loan are considered equity in a borrower's home and not proceeds from a loan.

(p) The advances made on a reverse mortgage loan under which more than one advance is made must be made according to the terms established by the loan documents by one or more of the following methods:

(1) at regular intervals;

(2) at regular intervals in which the amounts advanced may be reduced, for one or more advances, at the request of the borrower; or

(3) at any time by the lender, on behalf of the borrower, if the borrower fails to timely pay any of the following that the borrower is obligated to pay under the loan documents to the extent necessary to protect the lender's interest in or the value of the homestead property:

(A) taxes;

(B) insurance;

(C) costs of repairs or maintenance performed by a person or company that is not an employee of the lender or a person or company that directly or indirectly controls, is controlled by, or is under common control with the lender;

(D) assessments levied against the homestead property; and (E) any lien that has, or may obtain, priority over the lender's lien as it is established in the loan documents.

(q) To the extent that any statutes of this state, including without limitation, Section 41.001 of the Texas Property Code, purport to limit encumbrances that may properly be fixed on homestead property in a manner that does not permit encumbrances for extensions of credit described in Subsection (a)(6) or (a)(7) of this section, the same shall be superseded to the extent that such encumbrances shall be permitted to be fixed upon homestead property in the manner provided for by this amendment. (r) The Supreme Court shall promulgate rules of civil procedure for expedited foreclosure proceedings related to the foreclosure of liens under Subsection (a)(6) of this section and to foreclosure of a reverse mortgage lien that requires a court order.

(s) The Finance Commission of Texas shall appoint a director to conduct research on the availability, quality, and prices of financial services and research the practices of business entities in the state that provide financial services under this section. The director shall collect information and produce reports on lending activity of those making loans under this section. The director shall report his or her findings to the legislature not later than December 1 of each year.

(t) A home equity line of credit is a form of an open-end account that may be debited from time to time, under which credit may be extended from time to time and under which:

(1) the owner requests advances, repays money, and reborrows money;

(2) any single debit or advance is not less than $4,000;

(3) the owner does not use a credit card, debit card, preprinted solicitation check, or similar device to obtain an advance;

(4) any fees described by Subsection (a)(6)(E) of this section are charged and collected only at the time the extension of credit is established and no fee is charged or collected in connection with any debit or advance;

(5) the maximum principal amount that may be extended under the account, when added to the aggregate total of the outstanding principal balances of all indebtedness secured by the homestead on the date the extension of credit is established, does not exceed an amount described under Subsection (a)(6)(B) of this section;

(6) no additional debits or advances are made if the total principal amount outstanding exceeds an amount equal to 50 percent of the fair market value of the homestead as determined on the date the account is established;

(7) the lender or holder may not unilaterally amend the extension of credit; and

(8) repayment is to be made in regular periodic installments, not more often than every 14 days and not less often than monthly, beginning not later than two months from the date the extension of credit is established, and:

(A) during the period during which the owner may request advances, each installment equals or exceeds the amount of accrued interest; and (B) after the period during which the owner may request advances, installments are substantially equal.

(u) The legislature may by statute delegate one or more state agencies the power to interpret Subsections (a)(5)-(a)(7), (e)-(p), and (t), of this section. An act or omission does not violate a provision included in those subsections if the act or omission conforms to an interpretation of the provision that is:

(1) in effect at the time of the act or omission; and

(2) made by a state agency to which the power of interpretation is delegated as provided by this subsection or by an appellate court of this state or the United States. (Amended Nov. 6, 1973, and Nov. 7, 1995; Subsecs. (a)-(d) amended and (e)-(s) added Nov. 4, 1997; Subsecs. (k), (p), and (r) amended Nov. 2, 1999; Subsec. (a) amended Nov. 6, 2001; Subsecs. (a), (f), and (g) amended and (t) and (u) added Sept. 13, 2003.)

The Texas Constitution

Article 17 - MODE OF AMENDING THE CONSTITUTION OF THIS STATE

Section 1 - PROPOSED AMENDMENTS; PUBLICATION; SUBMISSION TO VOTERS; ADOPTION

(a) The Legislature, at any regular session, or at any special session when the matter is included within the purposes for which the session is convened, may propose amendments revising the Constitution, to be voted upon by the qualified voters for statewide offices and propositions, as defined in the Constitution and statutes of this State. The date of the elections shall be specified by the Legislature. The proposal for submission must be approved by a vote of two-thirds of all the members elected to each House, entered by yeas and nays on the journals.

(b) A brief explanatory statement of the nature of a proposed amendment, together with the date of the election and the wording of the proposition as it is to appear on the ballot, shall be published twice in each newspaper in the State which meets requirements set by the Legislature for the publication of official notices of offices and departments of the state government. The explanatory statement shall be prepared by the Secretary of State and shall be approved by the Attorney General. The Secretary of State shall send a full and complete copy of the proposed amendment or amendments to each county clerk who shall post the same in a public place in the courthouse at least 30 days prior to the election on said amendment. The first notice shall be published not more than 60 days nor less than 50 days before the date of the election, and the second notice shall be published on the same day in the succeeding week. The Legislature shall fix the standards for the rate of charge for the publication, which may not be higher than the newspaper's published national rate for advertising per column inch.

(c) The election shall be held in accordance with procedures prescribed by the Legislature, and the returning officer in each county shall make returns to the Secretary of State of the number of legal votes cast at the election for and against each amendment. If it appears from the returns that a majority of the votes cast have been cast in favor of an amendment, it shall become a part of this Constitution, and proclamation thereof shall be made by the Governor. (Amended Nov. 7, 1972, and Nov. 2, 1999.)

POINT TWO:

The Texas Supreme Court does not have the jurisdiction to "create" law, only to "interpret" it.

LAW IN SUPPORT:

The Texas Constitution, Article 5, Section 31

ARGUMENT:

The Texas Constitution, Article 5, Section 31, has not granted the Texas Supreme Court any law making authority. The Texas Supreme Court "created" foreclosable "contractual liens" pertaining to homeowner association maintenance fees in the Inwood vs. Harris case, 736 S.W.2d 632 (Tex. 1987). Following is the Texas Constitution statute pertaining to the Supreme Court's rule-making authority and as you can see, there is none given. Let the document speak for itself once again.

The Texas Constitution

Article 5 - JUDICIAL DEPARTMENT

Section 31 - COURT ADMINISTRATION; RULE-MAKING AUTHORITY; ACTION ON MOTION FOR REHEARING

(a) The Supreme Court is responsible for the efficient administration of the judicial branch and shall promulgate rules of administration not inconsistent with the laws of the state as may be necessary for the efficient and uniform administration of justice in the various courts. (b) The Supreme Court shall promulgate rules of civil procedure for all courts not inconsistent with the laws of the state as may be necessary for the efficient and uniform administration of justice in the various courts. (c) The legislature may delegate to the Supreme Court or Court of Criminal Appeals the power to promulgate such other rules as may be prescribed by law or this

164

Constitution, subject to such limitations and procedures as may be provided by law.

(d) Notwithstanding Section 1, Article II, of this constitution and any other provision of this constitution, if the Supreme Court does not act on a motion for rehearing before the 180ᵗʰ day after the date on which the motion is filed, the motion is denied. (Added Nov. 5, 1985; Subsec. (d) added Nov. 4, 1997.)

POINT THREE:

The Contractual Lien affirmed by the Texas Supreme Court is a pre-existing right that amended the Texas Constitution Homestead Act, Article 16, Section 50.

LAW IN SUPPORT:

The Texas Constitution, Article 16, Section 50; Article 17, Section 1

ARGUMENT:

Inwood states at 632 under #4 Homestead 93, that "homestead rights may not be construed so as to avoid or destroy pre-existing rights. Vernon's Ann. Texas Const. Art. 16, 50". The homeowners' voices are silent in this case law because it was a default judgment. How can a homeowner ever supersede a developer's "pre-existing right" to place "contractual liens" that run with the land? Trying to supersede a developer's "pre-existing right" is like trying to supersede God's creation of man. It cannot be done. Is this what Article 16, Section 50, of the Texas Constitution is trying to protect—the developer's "pre-existing right"? Our forefathers did not envision common property protection taking precedent over our private property homestead rights.

Inwood's declaration of covenants and restrictions referred to the assessments, interest and costs of collection as "a charge on the land and shall be secured by a continuing Vendor's Lien upon the Lot against which

165

such assessments or charges are made." (Inwood at 633) The Supreme Court, however, knew it was not a vendor's lien when it stated, "while we recognize that no vendor's lien was present, we disagree with the result reached by the court of appeals." (Inwood at 634) The Supreme Court initially denied Inwood their foreclosure but after rehearing granted the foreclosure based upon a "contract" theory and "the homeowners had constructive notice of the lien and foreclosure provisions in the declarations, they are bound by them." (Inwood at 635) The Texas Constitution, as stated earlier, has never been amended to permit "contractual" lien foreclosure exceptions nor have "constructive notice" been tied in with expressly permitted foreclosable liens in the Texas Constitution.

The Texas Supreme Court found "the lien in the present case to be superior, and worthy of protection against the homestead claim," yet there is nothing in the present case of Inwood that coincides with the Texas Constitution.

POINT FOUR:

There are no true "contracts" on the land that pre-exist prior to a homeowner's closing.

LAW IN SUPPORT:

The Texas Constitution, Article 16, Section 50

ARGUMENT:

It is unquestioned that an owner of land may contract with respect to their property as they see fit, provided the contracts do not contravene public policy. Well, the "contracts" in Inwood do contravene public policy as they are not expressly permitted in the Texas Constitution, under Article 16, Section 50. In the words of dissenting Justices Mauzy and Gonzales,

166

"A review of the history of the homestead exemption in Texas makes the matter as clear and bright as the Texas sky at night; the public policy of this State has been and is to protect homestead property from creditors' claims." (Inwood at 637-38)

The timing of the contract should have been at closing when the real "parties" are available to form a "contract". Of course, if this were the case, the homeowner would be able to designate his homestead and protect his or her property from a homeowner association foreclosure. It appears as though Inwood was set up and supported by a "cottage industry" that has literally "stolen" homeowner's homestead rights from them. There is no legal basis present to support the loss of homeowner's homestead rights in Texas.

Inwood is extremely concise that a "contractual lien depends only on evidence apparent from language of agreement that parties intended to create a lien." The "contractual lien" language eliminates any other name being assigned to it such as vendor's lien, which the Texas Constitution would support, tax, equity loan, or loan money, all of which the Texas Constitution would support. (Inwood at 634)

A "contract" is "an agreement between two or more persons which creates an obligation to do or not to do a particular thing. Its essentials are competent parties, subject matter, a legal consideration, mutuality of agreement, and mutuality of obligation." (Black's Law Dictionary, (1990), page 322) The only "contract" that exists in Inwood is the one created between the developer and its lien holder (if any). The future homeowner had not arrived in the picture yet and, therefore, could not have been part of this "first" contract that the Supreme Court upheld in Inwood. The five

(5) prongs indicated by Blacks's Law Dictionary, (1990), page 322) for the essential parts of a contract have simply not been met.

Additionally, when Inwood states "a covenant runs with the land when it touches and concerns lands, relates to thing in existence or specifically binds parties and their assigns, is intended by original parties to run with land, and when successor to burden has notice," when Inwood indicates "successor" under Covenants 53, this is when the buyer of the property is actually tied into the original contract according to "Inwood" law. (Inwood vs. Harris, p. 632) Also, the "successor" to burden, meaning the contract, has notice. Of course, Inwood is not speaking of "actual" notice but "constructive" notice, meaning it could be filed in a courthouse and you not know it. But according to Inwood that would not matter, it is your burden to know it is there. Every conceivable way of shutting you down from your homestead rights has taken place in Inwood. It is cleverly written as said before but not constitutional and is in violation of the Texas Constitution. There is absolutely nothing in the Texas Constitution to support losing your homestead rights over "constructive" notice and pre-existing rights of the developer of homestead property.

The current evolution of foreclosure filings supports the theory that Inwood was never to actually foreclose on many houses, but to use it as a scare tactic to collect maintenance fees, attorney fees, late fees, interests, and fines for deed restriction violations. Some of the biggest supporters of Inwood have now become the greatest benefactor as a result of its foreclosing ability. This "extortion" of our homestead rights started with Inwood North Homeowner Association in the Houston area and if you check out the website www.hoadata.org you will find out the "in the present case" (Inwood at 636-37) has spread throughout Harris County and while this particular website deals mainly with Harris county, there is evidence that this problem has moved around the state of Texas and getting worse. Members of The Texas Homeowner's Advocate Group get emails from all over the state regarding various homeowner association problems.

A "lien" is "a claim, encumbrance, or charge on property for payment of some debt, obligation or duty." "Qualified right of property which a creditor has in or over specific property of his debtor, as security for the debt or charge or for performance of some act. Right or claim against some interest in property created by law as an incident of contract." (Black's Law Dictionary, (1990), page 922)

This all sounds good but the only problem with this is that the "parties" mentioned in this lien situation, as it would or should be in Inwood to avoid being unconstitutional, is not the homeowner association and the homeowner but the developer and its lien holder (if any) as exists in the "pre-existing" situation in Inwood. Inwood is a very cleverly put together piece of law that was put together by Atty. Lou Burton and supported by other homeowner associations, developers, management companies, community associations attorneys and other special interests groups. It continues to be supported by the same group of organizations and special interests groups but that should not discouraged any legislator from upholding the Texas Constitution when it has been so badly damaged by this "weak law".

POINT FIVE:

The original "parties" referenced in Inwood vs. Harris are not expressly permitted in the Texas Constitution, Article 16, Section 50, Homestead Law,

169

as having the right to form a "contract" of any kind in order to supersede homeowner's homestead rights and "binding upon all parties acquiring rights to any of the property therein". (Inwood at 633)

LAW IN SUPPORT:

The Texas Constitution, Article 16, Section 50, Inwood vs. Harris, 736 S.W.2d 632 (Tex. 1987)

ARGUMENT:

There is no legal language or express permission in The Texas Constitution, Article 16, Section 50, Homestead Act, that gives developers and their lien holders (if any) the legal right to create "contractual liens" binding other "parties" who are actually the potential buyers/homeowners of the property they have tied into these "contractual liens".

The "parties" consist of two stages....when Inwood speak of "this court must consider the assessment provisions and lien as a whole and must not overthrow the clear and explicit intentions of the parties." (Inwood at 634) It is referring to the 1st set of parties—the developer and their lien holders (if any). These parties' properties are not protected by the Texas Homestead Act. The property only becomes protected when the "successor" or future homebuyer purchases the property. The Homestead Act protection is for the homebuyer.

When Inwood states at 635, "In Texas, a covenant runs with the land when it touches and concerns the land; relates to a thing in existence or specifically binds the parties and their assigns; is intended by the original parties to run with the land; and when the successor to the burden has notice," the "successor" is the potential buyer/homeowner that is protected through

Article 16, Section 50, Homestead Act, of the Texas Constitution, but in Inwood is given a second-generation contractual obligation with empty lien attachments that have not accrued yet because the property has not been bought and damages have not occurred. It is a potential lien for a potential buyer and a forced contract, all contradicting the Texas Constitution, Article 16, Section 50 Homestead Law. One of these explanations, one must understand.

Unfortunate for the developer, in Texas, they must come through the Texas Constitution, Article 16, Section 50, Homestead Act, to usurp our homestead rights.

In Inwood at 633, "The declaration provided that all the lots within the subdivision were impressed with certain covenants and restrictions and that such would run with the land and be binding upon all parties acquiring rights to any of the property therein." This statement was intended to destroy any and all homestead rights of all current and future homeowners in the State of Texas forever, in spite of the fact we have homestead protection under Article 16, Section 50, of the Texas Constitution.

In Inwood at 634, "Creation of a contractual lien depends only on evidence apparent from the language of the agreement that the parties intended to create a lien." "…. this court must consider the assessment provisions and lien as a whole and must not overthrow the clear and explicit intentions of the parties." "….It seems clear from the language used in the agreement that the owner intended to provide for such liens, and we would be remiss in not conforming this decision to such an intent. With this decision made we turn to the crux of this case; the effect of Texas homestead law on the lien in question." As you can see, without a doubt, the 1st parties—the developers and their lien holders (if any), took top priority over the homeowners-- the intended recipient of homestead protection in the Texas Homestead Act--but the Texas homestead law was the acknowledged "crux of the case".

In Inwood, at 635, further "cut and paste" took place to create a preexisting claim on the potential homestead, by stating, "The Declaration of Covenants evidences the intent of the original parties that the covenant run with the land, and the covenant specifically binds the parties, their successors and assigns. Because the property in question was conveyed in a succession of fee simple estates, the requirement of privity is satisfied..... Consequently, the covenant in question satisfies the requirements of a covenant running with the land. Furthermore, the deeds signed by each of the homeowners made reference to the assessments that would be due, thus each of the homeowners had notice of what their obligations were, and a purchaser with constructive notice of restrictive covenants becomes bound by them.... Moreover, a purchaser is bound by the terms of instruments in his chain of title....Therefore, as the homeowners had constructive notice of the lien and foreclosure provisions in the declarations, they are bound by them." The preceding statements sum it up in a nutshell as to what the "original parties" did to take away the home buyers homestead rights all done in opposition to the Texas Constitution, Article 16, Section 50, Homestead Act.

The Homestead Act, Article 16, Section 50, does not permit "original parties" consisting of developers and their lien holders (if any) to make foreclosure exceptions nor to supersede homestead protection given Texas homeowners.

While the "original parties" created bogus homestead rights that superseded those intended by our Homestead Act, Article 16, Section 50 of the Texas Constitution, it also pulled future buyers/homeowners into the pre-existing "contractual lien" formation for the express purpose of superseding the legal homestead rights of every voter and/or homeowner in this state.

In Inwood at 635, "The record discloses that the liens were contracted for several years before the homeowners took possession of their houses. Because the restrictions were placed on the land before it became the homestead of the parties, and because the restrictions contain valid contractual liens which run with the land, the homeowners were subject to the liens in question and an (at 636) order of foreclosure would have been proper...." According to Inwood, homeowners have no preexisting rights when it comes to the "contractual liens" and is wrong to try to seek protection are now prevented from doing so.

CONCLUSION

The bottom line is this is a homestead issue in which unconstitutional contracts creating "empty" pre-existing liens placed on land by developers and their lien holders (if any) have usurped Texas homeowners' homestead rights guaranteed to them by Article 16, Section 50 of the Texas Constitution. A crucial key to this homestead issue is the timing of the lien placement because when it was placed determines if the buyer/homeowner can protect their newly purchased property as the Homestead Act so intended. Thus, this case revolves around when the lien attached on the property. If it occurred simultaneously to or after the homeowners took title, there is authority which would deem the homestead right superior. (Inwood at 635)

However, in Inwood, new prongs were created so that a homeowner's homestead right could be nullified (Inwood at 635) such as evidenced in the following Inwood terminology:

"'On the other hand, if the lien attached prior to the claimed homestead right and the lien is an obligation that would run with the land, there would be a right to foreclose.

In Texas, a covenant runs with the land when it touches and concerns the land; relates to a thing in existence or specifically binds the parties and their assigns; is intended by the original parties to run with the land; and when the successor to the burden has notice.'" (Inwood at 635)

However, in the haste to destroy the homeowner's homestead rights, the "glitch" that occurred failed to patch the hole created in the Homestead Act, Article 16, Section 50.

Since the "original parties" which consist of the developers and their lien holders (if any), both of whom are not homestead protected, could not "fix" the hole created in the homestead glitch situation, (because it is impossible to amend it without going through the legislators and the voters). The "original parties" also decided to add another prong to the contractual lien formation by adding if the successor (buyer/homeowner) to the burden has notice. (Inwood at 635) The notice, and here is a real insidious kicker, is "constructive" or actual notice binds you to the developer's contract even though the Homestead Act, Article 16, Section 50, does not have a "constructive" notice exception for foreclosures.

"Constructive Notice" is defined in Black's Law Dictionary as "information or knowledge of a fact imputed by law to a person (although he may not actually have it), because he could have discovered the fact by proper diligence, and his situation was such as to cast upon him the duty of inquiring into it." "Constructive "'notice'" includes implied actual notice and inquiry notice." (p. 1062)

"Actual notice according to Black's Law Dictionary has been defined as notice expressly and actually given, and brought home to the party directly. (p. 1061)

The evidence in Inwood points to a high-level creation of "contractual liens" to pass the "pre-existing test" to circumvent our homestead rights. It is a situation where the Texas homeowners (past, present and future) have and will be circled by the wagons created by the developers and their lien holders (if any) in which their homestead rights will never again resurface,

175

unless….. Perhaps the following from Inwood explains it better: "It does not seem likely that a true vendor's lien exists in the present case because the assessment charges were not part of the purchase price of the property. Furthermore, there is no deed of trust which would have acknowledged the prior lien." "Much more probable is its existence as a contractual lien, as several older decisions hold that a contractual lien will be enforced regardless of the fact that it was improperly designated as a "vendor's lien." (Inwood at 634)

The laws of this state, did not and do not support homeowner association homestead foreclosures. As a general rule, a homestead is protected against all those who live in that homestead. The only debts which may be collected by foreclosure on the homestead are constitutionally enumerated instances cited in Article XVI, Sec. 50 of the Texas Constitution. (Inwood at 634). There are no "true" vendor's lien nor are the assessment fees part of the purchase price, even though it is commonly thought referencing the declarations that contain the maintenance fees is "constructive notice", the Supreme Court was well aware that "The declarations in question provided that the assessments "'shall be secured by a continuing vendor's lien'" "It does not seem likely that a true vendor's lien exists in the present case because the assessment charges were not part of the purchase price of the property. Furthermore, there is no deed of trust which would have acknowledged the prior lien." (Inwood at 634) Even with that knowledge, three Texas Supreme Court justices against the dissent of two other justices went against The Texas Constitution, Article 16, Section 50.

Our homestead protection is special and we want to preserve and uphold it. We do not take the loss of it casually. Our homestead protection has been intertwined with unconstitutional lien formation, unconstitutional contract formation and developer rights. It must be separated from it and restored to its original purpose. The Texas

Constitution, Article 16, Section 50, Homestead Act, is not just something to dust off and revere when it is beneficial to one's own cause such as equity loans and such but it must be upheld and respected for the purpose for which it was originally created and the true parties it was intended for— the Texas homeowners.

It is time to consider the argument of the dissenting justices in Inwood-Justice Mauzy and Justice Gonzales. They stood up for the Texas Constitution, Article 16, Section 50.

Their dissenting argument was legally correct in accordance with the Texas Constitution, Article 16, Section 50. In Inwood, at 640, they stated in dissent, "The court herein debates whether the purported lien is contractual in nature or rather, a covenant that runs with the land, and has found the duty to pay assessments at Inwood North is a covenant that runs with the land. Irrespective of whether the purported lien for assessments is a covenant or is contractual in nature, if foreclosure of a homestead is the remedy for failure to pay those assessments, then the purported lien must meet constitutional muster. When clearly violative of the Constitution, the lien is void.

This court long has recognized that a lien against the homestead cannot be made valid by agreement between the parties." Furthermore, dissenting Justice Mauzy joined by Justice Gonzalez, respectfully dissented and gives great insight into what happened in the Inwood decision, when he states, at 637, "the court herein has created a remedy in the name of "public policy:" in direct contravention of the Constitution of this State. I would affirm the judgments of the trial court and the court of appeals, which refused to allow the homeowners' association to foreclose on homestead property in order to collect past due neighborhood assessments." (This finally answers a puzzling conclusion to a search of the Inwood records that led to no foreclosure permission up to and including the Texas Supreme Court first hearing but then there was another hearing and the words "granted" stamped on the face of the document, with no paperwork left in the public records to explain the sudden decision to reverse and grant foreclosure rights.)

Additionally, dissenting Justices Mauzy and Gonzalez reminds us in Inwood at 637 that "(c) No mortgage, trust deed, or other lien on the homestead shall ever be valid unless it secures a debt described by this section, whether such mortgage, trust deed, or other lien, shall have been created by the owner alone, or together with his or her spouse, in case the owner is married. All pretended sales of the homestead involving any condition of defeasance shall be void.

Justices Mauzy and Gonzalez stated, "The Constitution specifies the types of indebtedness for which there may be a valid lien; liens for any other purpose are invalid. (Inwood at 637) "Applying the exceptions to the instant cause, maintenance assessments do not constitute part of the property's purchase money; are not taxes, and are not monies for labor and materials for the construction of improvements on the land. Thus, pursuant to the Constitution, homestead property may not be the subject of a forced sale for sums owing for maintenance assessments." (Realizing that the dissenting Justices are right on point, there has been increased activity noted by advocates that the industry during every Texas session has tried to introduce legislation to change the classification for maintenance fees to "taxes" so as to legally qualify for foreclosure exception in the Texas Constitution, Article 16, Section 50.)

Justices Mauzy and Gonzalez educate us in Inwood at 638 by stating "The homestead exemption itself is a Texas creation; the earliest homestead exemption law was the Statute of January 26, 1839." "The drafters of this State's first Constitution, "'determined to safeguard the homestead by putting it beyond the reach of legislators as well as creditors by incorporating an exemption provision in the constitution.'" Subsequent amendments have been legally changed in accordance with the amendment laws of the Texas Constitution.

Both dissenting Justices pointed out in Inwood, at 639, that "since the passage of the 1876 Constitution to date, only one amendment to Article XVI, section 50 has been proposed by either the House of Representatives or the Senate, and that amendment was adopted in 1973 and remains the law. The 1973 amendment included "single adult" persons as a class whose homesteads are protected.[fn4] The protective mantle of the Constitution has guarded homestead property in this State since 1845; since 1876 the extent of that protection has been clear; i.e., no lien other than one for taxes, purchase money, or labor and materials for home improvements is valid. (Of course, there have been amendments since Inwood but none allowing the foreclosure exceptions witnessed in Inwood.)

The court's reliance herein on other jurisdictions is misplaced. Florida's constitution allows foreclosure under the same three circumstances as in Texas; i.e., for payment of taxes, purchase money, and improvements. However, the Texas Constitution, unlike its Florida counterpart, contains the additional proviso that no "'other lien on the homestead shall ever be valid.'" TEX. CONST. Art. XVI, §§ 50. The difference results in a major distinction. In Florida, the constitutional prohibition against the forced sale of homestead property is a prohibition against the use of process for that purpose; it does not invalidate the debt or the lien but, under certain circumstances, merely takes priority over the debt or lien. By contrast, in Texas, a lien other than one of the three enumerated in the Constitution is invalid. TEX. CONST. Art. XVI, §§ 50.

This court also relies on the decisions of Arkansas, Alabama and Mississippi for the proposition that a lien for assessments is valid. In upholding a lien for property assessments, the Supreme Court of Arkansas, found that the language in the property's declarations providing for assessments was "'equally as strong and specific as a mortgage provision extending the lien thereof to future advances, and we can see no reason why the language employed should not be considered as creating a continuing lien on the property for future assessments.'" However, the Constitution of Arkansas, unlike the Constitution of this State, does not prohibit "'any other lien'" against the homestead, the Alabama district court did not reach the issue of whether homestead property could be foreclosed for failure to pay assessments; the property therein was investment property. Lastly, in Mississippi, homesteads are not constitutionally protected; rather, homestead protections are creatures of the legislature. Further, Mississippi's Code specifically provides that property may be subject to forced sale for "nonpayment of taxes or assessments."

The court herein debates whether the purported lien is contractual in nature or rather, a covenant that runs with the land, and has found the duty to pay assessments at Inwood North is a covenant that runs with the land. Irrespective of whether the purported lien for assessments is a covenant or is contractual in nature, if foreclosure of a homestead is the remedy for failure to pay those assessments, then the purported lien must meet constitutional muster. When clearly violative of the Constitution, the lien is void.(Inwood at 641)

....This court contends that the lien attached prior to the property acquiring homestead character. If the purported lien attached at all, it did so simultaneously with the property's purchase. When a lien arises simultaneously in time to the impression of homestead character on the land, then the homestead character of the property is superior. Further, even when an abstract of judgment has been filed, recorded and indexed, the purchaser's intent, formed at the time the property was acquired, to use it as homestead, "render[s] the property exempt from the judgment lien. Even if a lien to pay assessments runs with the land, the judgment ordering foreclosure arises after the property has acquired homestead status. Thus, a judgment lien attaching after the property has been designated homestead is invalid. The Constitution declares no other lien "'shall ever be valid.'" TEX. CONST. Art. XVI, §§ 50. "'What cannot 'ever be valid,' is never valid, and what is never valid, is always void.'" The public policy of this State since before statehood has been to construe the constitutional homestead provision liberally in favor of the exemption and against forced sale. For this court to allow foreclosure for past due maintenance assessments is to create judicially a fourth exception to Article XVI, §§ 50 of the Constitution, which this court is not empowered to do.... The developer, or the association, is a general creditor who, pursuant to Article XVI, section 50 of the Constitution and section 41.001of the Property Code, must stand in line along with Mastercard, Montgomery Ward and the local plumber for payment of sums due and owing. The developer and/or the homeowners' association have no superior right in homestead property for property assessments. To hold otherwise is an abrogation of the Constitution of this State.

If the Constitution is to be amended to destroy or weaken an individual's homestead exemption, it should be done as prescribed by the

Constitution in article XVII, section 1. What is required is passage of a (Inwood at Page 642) proposed amendment by at least 100 affirmative votes of the members of the House of Representatives and at least twenty-one affirmative votes of the members of the Senate, and a majority vote of all the people of this State who choose to vote at a public election held for that purpose. TEX. CONST. Art. XVII, §§ 1 (1845, amended 1972). A strict construction of our Constitution requires this result. I would require no less."

The final paragraph of Inwood at 642, along with a personal homestead loss in 1995 of the writer of this brief gave birth to the Texas Homeowner's Advocate Group which vow to be advocates for homeowners. In the words of dissenting Justices Gonzalez and Mauzy, Texas first homeowner advocates, who tried to protect our homestead rights:

(Inwood at 642) "As a final note, it is unfortunate that this court has no procedures to appoint counsel to permit or require the strenuous advocacy necessary to protect the constitutional protection heretofore provided to homesteads. The rule announced today by the majority affects the homestead protection against forced sale of every person in this State. This is not merely a private dispute between two litigants regarding the collection of a private debt. This court should, at the very least, provide for a pauper's funeral if it insists on burying the body of constitutional protection against forced sale of homesteads. In effect, this case has been tried ex parte. The named defendant-debtors, although served, never appeared nor answered. They made no appearance or answer in the court of appeals. No one appeared before this court to assert the constitutional protection we all were taught in law school years, yea decades ago. This sacred constitutional protection should not be sacrificed on the altar of economic gain for the few at the expense of the multitude without at least the semblance of due process. If our constitutional rights and liberties are to be taken from us one at a time, let us at least have the common courtesy to give those heretofore precious and cherished rights and liberties a respectful hearing before they are snatched from us and succeeding generations, as yet unborn, who have no voice and no advocate."

Exhibit B is attached to this brief to illustrate a personal foreclosure homestead loss of the writer that occurred in 1995 and the status of the house today. Inwood foreclosures are not setup to transfer a good title on any foreclosed house.

A special thank you is owed dissenting Justices Mauzy and Gonzalez for their passionate attempt to save homeowners' constitutional homestead rights in 1987 and for their strong legal argument that should have been listened to and obeyed in 1987. Now seventeen (17) years' later, this legal dispute is being presented once again in the form of a legal question to the Honorable Attorney General of this precious and great state of Texas. This time, we pray the Constitution will be upheld so that homeowners' homestead rights will be restored.

Therefore, on behalf of "every person in this State", The Texas

Homeowner's Advocate Group, humbly and respectfully ask the Honorable

Attorney General of the State of Texas for his opinion on this legal question:

"*Whether the placement of one-party foreclosable contractual liens on the land by the developer that supersede the homestead rights created in Article XVI, Section 50 of the Texas Constitution violate the Texas Homestead Act?*"

Respectfully submitted,

(Mrs) Harvella Jones
President
Post Office Box 420925
Houston, Texas 77242
(XXX) XXX-XXXX
(713) 639-4991 24/7
(XXX) XXX-XXXX FAX

R. Q. – 0236- GA

OFFICE OF THE ATTORNEY GENERAL
The Honorable Greg Abbott

CERTIFICATE OF SERVICE

I certify that a true and correct copy of the brief was sent to the Attorney General's office and the Honorable Fred Hill's office.

The Honorable Greg Abbott
Attorney General
c/o Ms. Nancy Fuller, Chair
Opinions Committee
Texas Attorney General's Office
P. O. Box 12448

The Honorable Fred Hill
 Chair, Committee on Local
Government Ways and Means
Texas House of Representatives
Post Office Box 2910
Austin, Texas 78768-2910 Austin,
TX 78701

Submitted by:
(Mrs) Harvella Jones
President
Post Office Box 420925
Houston, Texas 77242
(XXX) XXX-XXXX
(713) 639-4991 24/7
(XXX) XXX-XXXX FAX

R. Q. - 0236- GA

OFFICE OF THE ATTORNEY GENERAL
The Honorable Greg Abbott

EXHIBIT

Inwood vs. Harris 736 S.W. 2d 632 (Tex. 1987) ....
Exhibit A - - http://www.healylaw.com/cases/inwood.htm Real
   Property Account of foreclosed property by an HOA ....
Exhibit B - http://www.hcad.org/cgi-
bin/AV/AVDetail.asp?taxyear=2004&acct=1076900000057

What is the real purpose of a homeowner association (HOA) or a Property Owner's Association (POA)? What would our neighborhood really be like if we did not have them?

When I first heard of an "association", I remember thinking what is that? Closing did not shed any light on the genre of associations in the neighborhood, its function or if there was in fact an association. There was mystery in the reveal, which did not take place until after we bought the homestead and the annual bill arrived in our mailbox and then we had to educate ourselves as to what it all meant to be billed annually by an "association".

The fat lady hasn't sung yet; but if there were some betting going on, it would be my guess that from a homeowner's perspective, the HOA would have to go. Individuals that want a volunteer workforce to execute their foreclosure hammer, love HOA's and work out presentation packages to be delivered orally and in written form to whomever and wherever necessary.

As I did a little soul searching to get the real answer to my question directed to myself, Do I really think HOA's/POA's are necessary?, my truthful answer was no. Why, not, Harvella? I questioned myself further. They are not necessary because why do we need an organization in our neighborhoods to tell us how to live and then put a price on it?

My gut feeling is the proponents of HOA/POA lifestyle know in their heart that these associations are not necessary but it is an enormous fund raising industry and a good thing for them, so why should they give it up is what they feel.

Here is why they must and will eventually have to relinquish their hold over homeowners' homestead and property rights:

All HOA's and POA's in Texas were formed by allowing the developer of the land to create "contracts" that in turn create the homeowner associations and property owner associations.

These "contracts" called "contractual liens" were given "foreclosure" ower in 1987 when a case law sanctioned by three Texas Supreme Court Justices granted Inwood North Homeowner Association the right to foreclose on a few homeowners in their community who had failed to pay their maintenance fees. These homeowners never showed up in Court to defend their rights and the judgment against them was default.

When the Texas Supreme Court allowed the foreclosures, the Court inadvertently "blocked" homeowner's former homestead protection through Article 16, Section 50 of the Texas Constitution as well as "forced" every homeowner in the State of Texas to be a "mandatory" member of a homeowner association and a property owner's association, whether they want to be or not.

Earlier I spoke of how Johnnie and I lost our $5,000,000 default judgment against our lien holder Union Planters Mortgage Company for their failure to respond to our lawsuit. Yet our default judgment was thrown out and subsequently the lien holder was allowed to "dismiss" the lawsuit, all because Judge Hughes did not want to "ruin their careers".

On the other hand, it has always been a mystery to us, as to why not "ruining" someone's career was more important than "ruining" someone's guaranteed constitutional homestead rights that would lead to egregious repetitive foreclosure filings resulting in great monetary loss to the homeowner as well as possible homestead loss and credit loss. This type of action being repeated time and time again on other homeowners.

Two favorite legal maneuvers of CAI attorneys is "res judicata" and "collateral estoppel" both having the genre of repetitive filings that punish you for filing more than one lawsuit against homeowner associations and other promoters of this abuse of the system against homeowners. While the homeowner is punished for using the judicial system in more than one case and his or her claim is labeled with these words "res judicata" and "collateral estoppel", the CAI attorney with his client on the other hand reaps the spoils of the system by getting summary judgment and dismissed rulings from a homeowner's fallout from being accused of repetitive filings for the same defendant and the same cause of action. The district courts are always complaining about being overworked and under funded while we seek

187

justice; when in fact, they would benefit if they would sanction association attorneys for frivolous filings when they file case after case against the same homeowner.

Therefore, at any rate, when the Texas Supreme Court, forced homeowners into these HOA's and POA's unknown to the homeowner, it created a "hoax" regarding the Texas Constitution Homestead Law.

It is my opinion that the "real" reason why pro homeowner bills demanding repeal of foreclosure power do not pass is a HOA and POA creation that set the tone for the living standards in planned communities. Since management companies and CAI attorneys are appended to HOA's and POA's, the foundation of these associations must be in place in order to add the peripheral management companies, CAI attorneys and the core service which include relevant lawn services, swimming pool services, and so forth.

When homeowners find out and struggle with associations for their rights and lose and move out or want to move out, where are they to go? Developers are snatching up every piece of real estate they can get their hands on to set up these planned communities. Homeowners who want to be free to choose how to live on their property are being forced into areas outside of the planned communities and this is often nonrestrictive property that does not have infrastructure in place or modern-day utilities in place.

Where there is no HOA or POA or dead deed restrictions, a CAI attorney will go into that neighborhood and resurrect the deed restrictions with the amen corner of the HOA volunteers. You may ask well how can they go into a neighborhood and resurrect a dead deed restriction that has the potential to foreclose? Obviously, you have never met a CAI attorney. While homeowner advocates would rather eat a Texas tree roach than be in the same room as a CAI attorney, boards and other special interest groups find them rather refreshing, comforting, knowledgeable, intelligent and the answer to their prayers regarding a "slacker", "deadbeat" and a "neighbor from hell".

The CAI attorney presents his or her self as the total package for your association problems and they are usually well-dressed salespersons. Why not? It is our money that keeps them going to the best tailors, living in the best homes, probably not in a planned community or if so, do you think they are going to live by the rules they create? Homeowners have raised the standard of living for CAI attorneys and we are a savings plan and or bank account for our board neighbors. If I had $1.00 for every association out there that has ran off with association funds, I would be a rich woman. Why do you think they get so mad when you ask for financial reports? It took a lawsuit for us to get our association records. In fact, I am confident that what I discovered in association minutes is why the associations use a form of "shorthand" in their minutes by removing the things you would be interested in into a private meeting inside the meeting and those minutes are not available for the homeowner's eyes.

You see when the CAI attorneys make an error; they correct it nation-wide. They are unified. They are all on the same page. They have successfully distracted legislators for years with their repetitive messages against the homeowner, the majority of whom are not a part of the CAI, as the CAI would have you believe.

Stopping the foreclosure power is a two-prong attack as far as the CAI attorney is concerned, because if you kill the foreclosure power, you also kill the homeowner association mandatory membership.

The CAI attorney along with the board members wants so badly to keep homeowners under their control, under their thumb, and in their view. It appears we have enough sense to buy property but not enough sense to take care of it. We need the team to tell us what to do and how to do it. It is by far the dumbest, most ridiculous system I have ever incurred.

The team has successfully mixed apples with oranges and by that I mean, condominiums and single-family homes are treated with the same speech. How can the homeowner association advocates go to a hearing and tell legislators, they must foreclose on a condominium and a single family home because if they do not have that power, they might end up next door to a purple house? Now let us just look at that argument for a minute. Since homeowner advocates only get a few minutes to speak in comparison to a half hour or so for the homeowner association advocates, we don't have enough time to bring to a halt a cut-and-paste statement geared to sell fear to the legislators.

Condominiums are connected at the hip and while you should not be able to foreclose on them either, they do share utilities and other amenities single-family homes do not share. Single families on the other hand, do not share walls, and roach highways (plumbing), etc., so why do legislators think it is appropriate to listen to a long-winded argument from a self-serving CAI pro homeowner association attorney about needing associations to control a single-family homeowner's ability to make decisions about his or her home?

I have often thought these hearings were shams, particularly when I looked into the eyes of legislators and saw boredom, lack of respect, impatience, and fear. Yes, fear. Fear that maybe your speech is going to convince some honest legislator on the panel that you really do have a point and you are making it to the degree you are going to walk away with a member of the panel converted.

Veteran speakers know to take their winter jackets with them or dress in layers or when you leave, you may want to go to the nearest emergency facility for a chest x-ray. The meeting rooms where the hearings are held are colder than an operating room. Of course, these rooms are a form of operating room. By the time you leave, you have lost control of your bowels, bladders, and you feel comatose. When you enter the room, you feel hopeful; when you leave, you feel used and abused. The first time Johnnie and I testified, we were sort of body pressed out of the room and left in the hallway wondering what that was all about. The anti homeowner speakers were still in the room with the legislators, however, and the bill we testified for never made it out of committee, so I will let you figure it out.

The process kind of work like this—you get your three-minute due process speech so you allow them to safely enter their car but you really have not accomplished anything.

We must start going to these hearings with data and prepare for solid counterattack. Advocates must have a strategy but more importantly, we need a real friend in our legislative mist. We need a real soldier for the cause. I would run but I do not have the money; however, maybe someone will sponsor me. Many have asked me to run for office but I have been too busy trying to get personal justice and publicly help homeowners to follow that dream; but it does take money and so far, those who have money, while not on the same page as me, have managed to accomplish a few things.

One of the words that HOA's and POA's fear the most is "regulation". They want to talk about anything but the "R" word. Associations have been called all kinds of things, including quasigovernments and non-profit corporations. I am not sure how these nonprofit corporations that are registered with the State and incorporated could possibly be not regulated.

I believe they are regulated when it comes to benefiting from not having to pay tax or claim a profit; but unregulated when it comes to being held accountable for their ruthless behavior to their homeowner members. It just depends upon what side of their face they want to show, to whom and for what purpose, that particular day.

The Articles of Incorporation holds much information about your HOA/POA. It will tell you the purpose and power of the association. It will tell you how to dissolve it. It will tell you how to amend it.

I will probably always struggle with how my board neighbor can tell me when to remove my Christmas lights. When to remove my trash can. When to weed my plant beds. When to remove dead grass from the sidewalk and street. When to pull grass from expansion joints. When to remove an oil spill from the driveway. These are just a few of the new and improved association concerns. Let us face if, if you are being paid to "spot violations", then you are going to spot violations. If you do not see a normal violation, such as cars blocking the sidewalk, then you will create a violation, one that a homeowner cannot avoid.

Additionally, if you do not do these things, they threaten to do them for you, bill you and then foreclose on you if you do not comply. The attorney will, of course, tack on his exorbitant fee, which will make it more difficult to pay the fee.

Associations have taken the basic concept of foreclosing on your home for maintenance fees a bit further than originally intended by the Texas Supreme Court to this new level of association interference. This is when the non-regulated side of the Texas Corporation comes into play because no matter whom you complain to, email, call, fax, visit, or write, no one seems to want to help you in your complaint against the treatment.

What people think an association can do, they cannot do. Those items would include stopping a neighbor from playing loud music, stop your neighbor from accumulating multiple cars in their driveway that impede you walking down the sidewalk, really high grass that is attracting pests to your side of the yard, such as snakes, rats, and such.

New neighbors with very little "common" property wonder what they are paying for when it seems that the only thing they are paying for is gas for the volunteer board members' drive-bys to make sure you have pulled the weeds from your expansion joints, or removed the offensive mat still laying in your driveway. These petty annoyances pull in big bucks for the CAI attorneys.

Without an association to annoy the neighbors, how could the CAI attorneys assess their attorney fees? They need an association to support the fees they render for the alleged deed restriction violations.

Of course, when we go to the hearings to tell somebody about being abused, we do not come across quite as cool, calm and collected as the CAI attorneys and their association representatives. We are often tense, stressed, poorly dressed, hungry, sick, irritated and that is just one homeowner speaking. Think how the rest of the homeowner's feel and look when they are trying to present their entire abuse in two to three minutes while looking at the faces of bored, disgusted, grown people you elected gazing at you as though you are the latest freak show with low intelligence and poor manners.

It is fascinating how they can make you feel like you are the intruder in the room, the troublemaker, the pain in the backside. Sometimes we cry while telling our story. Or we are extremely angry. We seldom get to ask or answer questions, though, and I find that particularly troubling. I wonder if they know the answer or are afraid to ask us questions for fear of what they will learn or be reminded of.

Once we find a "friend" among the legislators, he or she is such a rare specimen sometimes we want to abuse him or her by complaining too much or demanding too much. It is not our intent to run this legislator away, we are just so happy to have someone who can make it better, listen or appear to be helping us.

I am sure it has dawned on our legislators that why would so many CAI attorneys, homeowner association board members, developers and other special interests groups show up in a small room with a well organized campaign to kick the wind out of a homeowner's testimony if it were just all about property values, purple houses and slackers.

It is about money. It is about creating creative "violations" nationwide to ensure that homeowners are going to be forced to violate something that will cost them money. It is "easier to get through an eye of a needle" than it is to avoid violating a deed restriction. My goodness the first week after we closed on our newly built home (yes, we moved into another planned community), we received a letter from the Management Company regarding the lawn needing to be cut. Since we had not moved in yet, we thought the letter a bit premature. This from a community in the country. Therefore, you cannot run, you cannot hide, HOA's and POA's are everywhere. I am currently investigating an Annual Meeting in my community in which I was "removed" from the board. I thought I was in "friendly territory" but evil board activity is everywhere. I made a vow to myself when I left Kingwood, Texas, that I would stay informed as to what is going on in my neighborhood. I do not and will not ever support my neighbors being foreclosed by a homeowner association and I will never support my neighbors being harassed by micro management techniques. I believe in a nice neighborhood too but I believe my neighbors are entitled to enjoy their homes. I was part of the Architectural Control Committee to help facilitate the request of my neighbors when they want to make a change to the outside of their homes. Oh, and the letter I got from my HOA, I filed and smiled and cut my lawn when I got ready. I will never be intimated by an HOA again nor will I ever lose one from a foreclosure again.

God brought my family and me to Texas for a reason; perhaps it was to assist in permanently stopping HOA/POA foreclosures. May God use me to do his will.

Now, once you have been nailed with the "violation" and lettered, you might as well get prepared for the foreclosure "extortion" letter that will grab your Christmas money from you, or your bonus, or your Child's college money, or whatever you are saving that extra money for. Wherever you are going to get it from, get ready to give it to the association or you will be foreclosed.

Many anti homeowner speakers tell the legislators, there are very few actual foreclosures. They are right; there are very few actual foreclosures from the association because usually a person in trouble with the association is also in trouble with their lien holder, so the lien holder forecloses and not the association. Our foreclosure was among the few that actually occurred for maintenance fees and attorney fees only. We did not get our house back as Winona Blevins did. In addition, I have talked about already in this book how the purpose of the foreclosure filing is to "extort" money from the homeowner not to foreclose. Foreclosure filings are tools to get money from the homeowner; therefore, the industry can also say they are not actually foreclosing but what they do not disclose is how often they are "filing" foreclosure liens to "extort" money from homeowners.

The association is set up not to perform a real service to the homeowner as everything the association say they do is really a duplicate service that is actually done by the city you are in. Kingwood, for example, was annexed to Houston, so the associations in Kingwood are actually redundant and unnecessary. Developers have used "Texas has no zoning, so we are necessary" for so long, I believe they actually believe that garbage.

Another fundraiser in the association is the architectural review committee. Oh, that is a good one. That is when you want to do what you want to do with the house you are paying for but cannot because your board neighbor think he knows more about your property than you do. The only way you can have that luxury that use to be for every homeowner is to be rich or well to do.

The proponents of associations love to make you think that they are doing the best for homeowners and the neighborhood. They want you to think we cannot do without homeowner associations because without them and their ability to foreclose, the entire community would deteriorate and you will have a bunch of minority drug dealers selling from their garage.

They have given associations a life bigger and grander (in their opinion) than Jesus walking on water. They are just the greatest salespersons around because they have convinced legislators they must exist or the industry will not exist. Something must be in place to keep people in line in their own homes. It is as though the planned community is an outdoor prison only you pay for your own cell, which is your home and the board are the prison guards.

Associations are the best thing for the CAI attorneys since little Jimmy's first kiss. Where else can C average attorneys for which Texas has more than an abundance of, get to write their own check from your checkbook and not be put in jail for doing so? It is done with the blessing of the legislators.

Let us further dissect associations. What other special interest groups are standing back and watching homeowners suffer when they know this concept of homeowner associations owning "actual" homes cloud the titles and cannot be legally accomplished if the association chooses not to cooperate, such as what happened in my case.

The banking industry, for whatever reason, decided more than a decade ago to stop escrowing maintenance fees, leaving that task to the associations to collect the fees. This practice may be making a comeback.

Homeowners think associations are the only bad person, when the management company works at the behest of the board of the association. Nothing happens unless the board tells the management company to make it happen. If the board did not tell their attorney or turned the attorney loose on the homeowners, there would be no foreclosure actions. The CAI

Attorney is allowed to come to the association board meeting to "sell" their services by creating an open checkbook.

Attorneys, management companies and all companies or individuals affiliated with the association are working for the board and that is where the homeowner comes in. Remove your bad boards. Vote in neighbors that share your beliefs as to how your community should be run to be on your board.

Having said that, now let us get to the real world on that subject. Do you know it is easier to say get rid of the board but when you try to do it, it is almost impossible? I have always wondered why volunteer board members are so hard to remove if they are not being paid for the job. Many board members retort it is because they want to keep the neighborhood nice. What an interesting statement.

Let me see, we have sense enough to find the location, pick the house and pay for it; but we do not have enough sense to take care of our neighborhood, we need another neighbor to tell us what to do with our lawn, our weeds, our oil spots, our everything.

Here is what the association is not revealing to its mandatory members. They are not telling you property values are more likely to drop with an association than rise with one, because of the reputation associations have due to their Gestapo way of dealing with issues in their neighborhoods. There are rumors that some banks are refusing to finance homes in HOA communities because of the problems with foreclosures and what happens if a home is taken over by an association.

Associations do not present a positive image and it is time to stop that nonsense.

Associations also cannot take a clear title when they have purchased the home at auction. Do you know why? Because the insurance is in the name of the person you foreclosed on and the title and in order to get it transferred to the association, you need the cooperation of the association through his attorney to get the title and the insurance converted. If the CAI attorney refuses to cooperate, then you have a bigger mess than you did before the foreclosure; because now you do not have a home to live in but you may still end up footing the bill or another foreclosure if the auction buyer does not pay for the house.

The banking industry is aware of this glitch. The real estate industry is aware of this glitch. I have already pointed out to you my former domicile at 2026 Oak Shores Drive, Kingwood, Texas 77339, where it is still sitting since December 5, 1995, with a cloudy title in the name of a trustee Carol Nagel. Barrett, Burke, Wilson, Castle, Daffin & Frappier, LLP foreclosed but did "not make sure Leader Federal Bank (LFB) was clean on this foreclosure." How many more houses in this state do you think have the same disease?

Mortgage brokers do not want this industry destroyed either because they are recycling or selling our homes like hotcakes. The housing industry is healthy. It is healthy because the realtors, associations, management companies, CAI attorneys, title companies, HUD and bankers are all on the same page as far as actual notice to the homeowner regarding recurring maintenance fees, homeowner association contractual liens and the foreclosure power the association has.

The housing industry is more concerned with selling houses than they are with the rights of the buyer. They do not want to chance a lost sale by disclosing to the buyer what will really happen to the sale if they disclosed the foreclosure power of the association or if they disclosed the micro-management that takes place in the community by the association that goes beyond normal regulation. Would you have bought your house if you knew it had a "contractual lien" already on it? …..and it is foreclosable? When I bought in Kingwood, Texas, I would have not bought there, had I known. What has changed for me is I am not losing any more houses to HOA foreclosures.

The industry knows no potential buyer in their right mind would consummate an agreement to purchase a home in a planned community with the insane strict controls that are the norm in today's community living if they knew the truth at closing. The violations are set up to fail. The more violations, the more money yielded to the CAI attorneys. Actual notice should be uniformly set-up by the industry.

My husband and I knowingly consummated another deal in an HOA because somebody has to go onto the front line to fight and what better team than warriors who know how to fight the fight. It did not hurt the fact we love the property as well. We also filed a signed affidavit before closing that alerts anyone looking at our recorded documents that we were forced into the homeowner association and did not willingly become a part of the homeowner association and are voluntary members but willing to pay the maintenance fees.

So they would rather withhold deed restriction documents at closing, force you to agree to mandatory membership in an HOA or a POA whether you want to or not or you do not get the property you want. As well as conveniently fail to disclose the HOA or POA you just became aware of, maybe, can also foreclose on you if you do not mow your lawn when the board says you should, or any other minuscule violation their CAI attorney can dream of.

The housing industry as it stands now in the year of our Lord 2004 is a corrupt octopus system undermined by flawed checks and balances that protect the industry while destroying the homeowner.

The homeowner, once he or she has closed on their purchase of a home, suddenly find their selves in the middle of one of the housing industry's biggest scams—theft of constitutional homestead property rights through bogus case laws and legislative deal making with the industry special interest groups.

When I first entered this maze in 1990, I truly thought no one knew what was going on but the association and their attorneys, it was not until five years' later, when I was foreclosed, that I realized that everyone knew what was going on or it would not have continued. As I have said before, it is a well-oiled machine and everyone but the homeowner is benefiting from this cottage industry.

Now the next big ticket item on an association's hit list is the subject of architectural changes you want to make and the process used to get those changes approved. First, who are the individuals approving these changes? The elected board should be the only individuals handling this sensitive subject. If you are not getting your architectural changes approved, start showing up at your meetings and find out who is on this committee and if there are problems being approved, vote out who is controlling the architectural committee.

What I am telling you, associations are operated like a small government insofar as having the ability to vote out the perpetrators of ill will and discontent. If you are not happy with the drive-by's, the failed attempts to get your architectural requests approved, raised maintenance fees, or whatever the issue is, you have the right to vote that person or persons off the board and vote in the individuals who will serve your community more humanely.

You must be flexible in your thinking process about what can and cannot happen in your community if you do not do something about it. Nothing will change if you do not want it to change.

Maintenance fees can be lowered and money given back to you at the end of the year if you have a surplus. Remember these are supposed to be non-profit corporations. Why do they need a hugh surplus that draws interest? Temptation to steal must be removed. You do not put someone on your board or allow them to stay if they are having personal financial issues or you are going to be missing some money. When you try to report it to the District Attorney, a legislator, or whoever, you guessed it, it is an unregulated entity and they cannot help you or if they can, like a legislator, it will take a while and you may have an acute situation.

Associations are about control. We are talking about multi million dollar corporations in some communities, which are ran by management companies, put in place by the developer. You know the developer is a greedy something. What ever happened to the company that built your home and left the community for good, leaving you the right to enjoy it your own way? Why is it necessary to own the ground the house is built on, running oil pipes as well as covenants through it? The oil pipes we cannot help; the covenants we can.

At closing you pay your large sum of money to own your precious home; and then when you think you know all the occupants of your home, you find out you have another resident in your home—the association.

The developer can only suggest what he or she would like to happen after he finishes building. He or she needs to be completely done and gone and allow you to live in your own house without his or her periscope peeking through your house looking for violations.

It reminds me of one of the CAI attorney's favorite statement; it is like getting "two bites of the apple".

So the concept of associations is flawed. They serve no real purpose for the homeowner. They were created for a source of income for the attorneys that created them and a few board members that think the homeowners' money is their private bank account to do what they want with it.

The "services" portrayed by the CAI attorneys during session testimony as crucial is usually condominium services which may be crucial in some instances as opposed to single-family services. How can a community with county roads, city lights and police protection, as well as garbage collection that you pay one-on-one yourself be upset if you do not have an association live and well in your community? How can a community with one or two swimming pools go bankrupt if you do not get 100% collection? The biggest ticket items are usually swimming pool upkeep and grass cutting.

Many of these services have been corrupted when board members secure contracts for their friends or family members. Usually if you look close enough, there is a family member lurking somewhere in the association makeup. They may be on the Architectural Review Committee. They maybe cutting the common property. They may be servicing the pool. They may be doing a lot of service rendering because they are related to the board member.

The bottom line is associations are not necessary and are not needed. They are intimidating and have outlived their usefulness. It is truly time to get back to the real world and allow people to make their own decision as to whether or not they want to be a mandatory member of an HOA but without foreclosure power.

You do not need an association to enforce the deed restrictions. CAI attorneys have brainwashed homeowners and volunteer board members long enough. Any homeowner can take his or her complaint to the county they are a part of and file a complaint in the Justice of the Peace Court and injunction may be filed against the offender who is generally fined. I would not be surprised if the CAI attorney made a visit to the county officials and convinced them their association package was the real deal and the association would solve all the cities' financial and maintenance problems.

CAI attorneys are always thinking outside the box as to how far they can spread and how deep they can get into our pockets. Wake up, fellow homeowners; it is time to make a change. It is time to take action, It is time to stop being apathetic.

It is time to file class-action lawsuits across this nation. All of us have constitutional issues because of the contracts we are supposed to have willingly signed. The contracts that the developer created and placed on our property or the rights that were legislatively taken away from us by our legislators. If our legislators have stolen our rights, as they have done in Arizona, then homeowners need to revolt in a high-tech manner by massive media coverage, legislative contact through fax machines, mail, phones, computers and personal visits. In places like Texas, we need to do the same thing. One or two advocates cannot resolve the enormous crime scene that is evolving throughout this country. Planned communities are popping up faster than killer beehives. It is going to take the power of God to change it because it is the largest scam I have seen since the S & L scandal.

Tort reform is a political tool that will benefit the industry but does nothing for the truly injured and truly damaged.

The CAI attorneys accused Johnnie and me of filing many lawsuits and they called us "vexatious litigants". However, when they filed their repetitive boilerplate lawsuits in which the only thing that changed was the name, address, HOA name and amount, it was interesting that the court did not cite abuse as Judge Lynn N. Hughes in the Federal Court accused us.

One of the complaints Tort Reformers try to sell everyone is how expensive it is driving up insurance costs for doctors who are forced to stop practicing, while the underbelly of this argument is to stop Joe Brown, average citizen, from winning a big lawsuit against any industry.

Tort reform, unfortunately, has not trickled down to CAI attorneys to affect them for their multiple filings against the same homeowner year, after year, after year. When will it reach the CAI attorneys? Why has it not already?

Most of our lawsuits were filed during the resurgence of tort reform politicking and as we accumulated lawsuit filings, we became the target of more and more labeling for filing our lawsuits for justice. You might say we received the fall out from tort reform advocates pressing the flesh for medical reform.

CAI attorneys would love you to roll over when being sued. They do not want a fight. They want you to be scared and apathetic.

Apathy is one of the worst characteristics one can have. If we as voters, homeowners, and citizens do not start speaking up and actively participating in protecting our rights, we are not going to have any. We are still the most important element in change. We can still make a difference. We must never give in to the belief that we have no power.

We must stop, however, relying on our neighbor to speak for us. We must move out of the shadow of our neighbors and help them fight for our rights. If we cannot attend public protest hearings, then we must call from our home and register a complaint, least our legislators think we have no complaint. We must write, email, fax or visit our legislators' offices to let them know what we want them to do for us. We must do this on an as needed basis and not wait every two (2) or four (4) years to register a complaint by voting, and rely totally on that process; because as we all learned in the year 2000 and 2004, sometimes that does not work either.

I add apathy to one of humanity's greatest civil sins. If we as a people were more actively involved, we would not constantly be running behind our rights. Our history is replete with struggles to hold onto our rights and whenever we become lax, we lose.

Should we depend upon the honesty of our legislators to do the right thing without our monitoring their activity? Of course not. I recall thinking when my husband and I first started our litigations to save our Kingwood home that I would get justice in the courtroom and that if I presented the facts, we would win. It was extremely disappointing to go in and out of court and learn the awful truth of where justice stands. It hedges on how fair your judge is. I recall the judge who signed the summary judgment against us, which started the foreclosure proceedings saying, "I am going to give it to the one who is owed the money!" The judge was Eugene Chambers, aka the "sleeping judge". He was a former librarian and has since died.

I also recall Judge David West, who gave us some good advice, "keep it simple", referring to explaining your case in court. However, he too allowed the homeowner association's attorney Jeffrey Ewalt to slip through the vice we had created around the association and him by granting Ewalt a last-minute summary judgment on the eve of our trial scheduled for the next day. So much for due process. If we survived that shock, we can survive anything.

We are also asking the readers of this book to checkout the group's website www.stoptexashoaforeclosures.com often, as it will keep you upto-date about what the group is trying to accomplish regarding our property and homestead rights. There is also, a national on-line petition at http://www.petitiononline.com/homeback/petition.html that would be to the benefit of everyone to sign. Even if you are like my former neighbor, the one across the street from me who did not want to become involved, you will benefit from signing this petition.

This book was written to spread the word regarding our constitutional homestead rights, to warn homeowners about what happens to your homestead rights at closing, to educate and encourage homeowners to stay strong in your fight to take back your property and homestead rights (never give up until you take back what is yours) and to tell you what happens when you do not become involved. Chapter 21 is the brief that was submitted to the Attorney General's office July 20, 2004. Read it from beginning to end and you will never again be in the dark as to how and why we lost our homestead rights; and thus right now, why the homestead act is a hoax. However, we are praying that the hoax is a temporary situation and that soon and very soon, our Constitutional rights across the land, not only here in Texas, but throughout this country, will be reinstated through pro homeowner legislation sponsored by legislators who are as passionate about our Constitution as advocates are. Remember the power to do something is in your hands too! No one wants to help you, if you do not want to help yourself. If you are one to hide behind your neighbor and not become involved, stop it! It is because of our apathetic nature that has allowed this foreclosure cancer to spread so far across this country. Our constitutional rights are precious and worthy to be defended!

We kept up with our judges and followed their fate. Judge West has since resigned under the cloud of some other controversy. One of our best judges, though, was Dwight Jefferson and to him we say, thank you and God bless you and your family. When we sued the association that foreclosed and the clerk's office placed the case back in the same court that it had originally been in--Court 215, we were astounded as to how this could have happened but it worked out for us. Judge Eugene Chambers had gone back to the Law Library and has since passed away. However, who was this new judge? The new judge turned out to be Judge Dwight Jefferson who proved to be a judge of decency, integrity, ethical and listened to both sides before making a decision

The bottom line in all of this is please actively participate in the legislative process, whether it is in your neighborhood association or in your local, state or national government. When it is time to vote, vote (even if it sometimes does not work the way you want it to). When it is time to go to a homeowner association meeting, go. When an elected official is not doing their job, spread the word and fire him or her next election.

We live in a high-tech society. We are computer literate. Participate in the on-line polls and communication concerning things that matter to us as a people. Start your own lists, your own groups, your own polls. Or join the groups that are already out there and be a positive force. Participate! What I am saying, is be an active part and do not put your personal life way ahead of your civil duties or you will truly regret it and make it so much harder for others to correct.

As you can see from my experience, you may or may not get justice. Sometimes it hinges on a kind judge and let us face it, how many of those are around. You must take charge of your own destiny or you will lose that control. Remember, years ago, during World War II, many people did not speak out when they noticed what was happening to their neighbors around them and eventually the tyranny reached them. We must not fail to help a neighbor in their fight for justice and we must not fail to speak out on malfeasance that represses our constitutional right to make choices regarding our property and homestead rights.

Having been an activist for more than a decade now, I think I am qualified to say, this foreclosure issue and other related homeowner problems would have been fixed a long time ago, but some of us advocates are not truly advocates under the skin. We are "wolves in sheep's clothing". When we have private sessions with legislators and sell out, how is this helping homeowners? When we could donate time, money and energy to the homeowner's cause, we choose not to. We are not as fervent in our defense of homeowners' rights as the CAI is in their fervent fight for the homeowner association rights. We have pockets of anger in a few but we need thousands of angry homeowners to push fast forward this movement or we need most all of our legislators to care about the thousand of homeowners out there who do not know what is going on because the news media has not done an efficient job in telling our side of the story and they owe it to their readers to educate them.

While we are trying to decide if we want to help do something about this problem as homeowners and other individuals that could help us out, the CAI are becoming more and more intertwined in our business. Their rules have started to seep into our homes. Some associations are telling their buyers what kind of draperies to hang when they say the color showing on the outside has to be the same color. They are in our kitchen when they tell us what kind of garbage disposal we should have.

CAI attorneys have changed the way we live and where we live. The ABCs A Basic Course for Community Associations they put together has given a legal face to unconstitutional laws throughout the State of Texas and probably in other states called something else.

We must stop tearing each other up in our advocate groups. We must start supporting other advocates in our groups and elsewhere. We must stick together as one to form a stronger bond to fight the enemy—CAI.

CAI has created a College of Community Association Lawyers (CCAL) It was created in 1994. They are giving management companies awards. They have setup deed restriction models for training purposes and write all the deed restrictions we are "governed" by. They have gone outside

215

the constitution through the developers to "control" our lives through the management of our homes.

CAI attorneys have captured the attention of legislators making them believe it is okay to violate the Constitution across the country. It is our job to turn that trend around and breath new life into our Constitutions, after all, they were written to protect us.

Deed restrictions are living plans for HOA's that run our lives. At closing, they sometimes appear and sometimes they do not, so many of us are not aware what happens at closing to our property rights. After the excitement dies down and we get into our first altercation with the HOA, which may be a letter in the mail regarding cutting your lawn even if you have not moved in yet, we begin to realize what we have moved into. It is like buying a car from a fantastic salesperson but when something is wrong with the car, you end up in a rude service area.

Homeowners, do not wait until you have a personal problem with your HOA; support the effort now to get back your property rights. It is not vogue to be able to foreclose on someone's home. While you may think that is only reserved for your next-door neighbor with two many cars in his driveway, or the one with the oil stain in his driveway, or the one with the high grass, it is also for you. While deed restrictions are a "cleansing tool" for HOA neighborhoods targeting specific individuals, they are also used against anyone and everyone if necessary. No one is exempt. Some homeowners have reported, though, some deed restrictions that still carry a "no black's clause". We must stop looking for ways to take away our neighbor's freedom and controlling our neighbors and realize that we are in a country of freedom in which many people have died so that we would have these freedoms.

Homeowner Associations have done much to take away these hard fought for freedoms and have many of us in servitude. It is important to pay attention to the oppression rolling across the United States in the name of Homeowner Association property value control and so forth before a new form of civil war erupt in our communities.

Start thinking about why CAI attorneys do not want to stop foreclosures. Let us set aside the usual argument—property values, slackers, and that completely bogus argument about the community falling apart if a few people do not pay their fees and now let us look at the real reason not to stop the foreclosures--the Benjamin's (the money). Some of these associations are multi-million dollar operations. Okay, let us put on our thinking caps. How much money does it take to cut the common ground— the esplanades? How much money does it take to keep up the pool? Do you actually have a pool? Look around what common property do you have in your neighborhood? Do you pay for your own garbage collection?

When you ask for a financial report, is your board getting mad? Is it possible they could be using the money for their own personal agenda? Are the people they are hiring, their relatives? Can you vote for your President, Vice President, Treasurer or Secretary? Or has that now been moved to the board members and they make the decision to vote for these officers? Remember: Control is an important key to keep the money.

The CAI reworks its plans as needed. Years ago, when I moved here in 1988, the members of the association, the homeowners, could vote for the President, Vice President, Secretary and Treasurer. Now it is in the hands of the Board Members. Control, it is all about control.

Homeowners, wake up! When are you going to get mad? When are you going to stop being apathetic? When are you going to start making demands from your legislators? When are you going to return the CAI attorney back to the backside of the ambulance?

Remember do not let any one say you do not count. We do count! We are important! We can make a difference! We must, all of us, uphold our rights, our constitution and not be deceived!

If the homeowners in Inwood had spoken up for their rights and fought back, we would not have lost our homestead rights in Texas. We really cannot expect the one man or woman that we put in office to handle all our problems and do the right thing all the time for us. We must monitor our elected officials if we do not, we will lose. Would you give someone your checkbook, walk away, and expect all your money to be there when you return?

It was my dream that by the time this book was published, the Texas Homestead would be up and running again for the thousands of homeowners who live or anticipate living in planned communities throughout the state of Texas and that other states would have restored their Constitutional laws to their homeowners. This book will also benefit homeowners in other states as they work to restore their property and homestead rights. All you need to do is substitute what you call your "contract" and place it in the scenario presented in the brief because the basic principle is the same. Your "contract" may have been created by the developer or legislatively created.

Whatever or however it is created, there is a common fabric in what is and has happened to our Constitutional right to make decisions about our property. This is the year of our Lord 2004. It is up to us to fix it! You know the truth now. You know your rights have been taken from you. You know how they were taken from you! You may have to educate your legislator but make sure you educate your legislator and tell others to do so. Help your neighbor and you will be helped. Do not wait until you are embroiled in a life or death struggle to save your property. Act now, while you are thinking well.

There is such passion for abortion rights and gay rights. People worry about their weight, the war, religion, and so forth; but when it comes to our property and homestead rights, there does not seem to be as much interest or compassion unless you read about some poor old person that has lost their home. Let us not wait until we are jarred from our chair to save our rights. No elected official should get a blank check on our rights. We must take control of our rights and monitor any politician that we put into office. This is our right, handed down to us from our forefathers who wrote all of these wonderful Constitutions for us to make sure they stay protected. Do not settle for less. If we do not start protecting our Constitutions, and believe it, we are rapidly moving close to this time frame, we are going to wake up one day with our local association board standing over us in our bedroom with the key they made at closing and fining us for sleeping too long and not opening our blinds early enough!

Do not laugh! You did not think years' ago that a board would be telling you to remove the grass from your expansion joints or your home would be foreclosed? Or remove the mat from your driveway? Right?

Atty. General Greg Abbott finally responded to our question RQ0236-GA, "Whether the placement of one-party foreclosable contractual liens on land by a developer that supersede the homestead rights created in article XVI, section 50 of the Texas Constitution violates the Texas Homestead Act," three (3) days after his December 6th deadline. The issue being "real-time" contracts vs. "developer" contracts.

He basically protected the foreclosing industry and I personally challenge his love for our Texas Constitution.

It was mainly a regurgitation of the underlying Inwood vs. Harris case law and facts we were already aware of. He summarized stating "A property owner may encumber real property with a covenant running with the land, which, depending on the particular instruments and circumstances involved, may be enforced by foreclosure without violating subsequent purchasers' constitutional and statutory homestead rights."

However, it was a personal relief for me that he did open the door to seeking legislative help in changing the foreclosure issue. His complete opinion may be read on website www.stoptexashoaforeclosures.com Check our website regularly to stay updated. Stay tuned! Stay blessed! Stay educated!

CASES

Inwood North Homeowners' Ass'n. v. Harris
736 S.W. 2d 632 (Tex. 1987)

Geneva Brooks, et al v. Northglen Association
Cause 02-0492
Texas Supreme Court

Woodland Hills Trail Association vs. Johnnie Jones and wife, Harvella
Cause No. 91-48229
270th Judicial District Court, Harris County, Texas
Reversed and Remanded
Association Attorney Michael Treece

Woodland Hills Trail Association vs. Johnnie Jones and Harvella Jones
Cause No. 91-48229
152nd Judicial District Court, Harris County, Texas
Judge Harvey Brown
Association Attorney Jeffrey Ewalt

Johnnie Jones and Harvella Jones, Appellants v. Woodland Hills Trail
Association, Appellee
No. 01-92-00963-CV
Association Attorney Jeffrey Ewalt

North Woodland Hills Village Community Association vs. Johnnie Jones and
Harvella Jones Cause 92-23162
215th District Court
Judge Eugene Chambers
Association Attorney Jeffrey Ewalt

Jones, Johnnie and Jones, Harvella, Appellant vs. North Woodland Hills
Village Community Association, Appellee
Cause 14-93-00545-CV
14th Court of Appeals
Association Attorney Jeffrey Ewalt

Johnnie Jones and Harvella Jones v. North Woodland Hills Community
Association
Cause No. 94-8927
Supreme Court of the United States
Association Attorney Jeffrey Ewalt

Johnnie Jones and Harvella Jones vs. North Woodland Hills Village
Community Association
Cause 95-02085

215th District Court
Judge Dwight Jefferson
Association Attorney Jeffrey Ewalt

Johnnie Jones and Wife Harvella Jones vs. Jeffrey H. Ewalt and Ewalt & Dickinson
Cause 95-01886
269th Judicial District
Judge David West
Defendant Attorney: David Dickinson

Geneva Kirk Brooks et al vs. Northglen Association
Cause 02-0492
Texas Supreme Court

Johnnie Jones, et al vs. Leader Federal Bank for Savings
Cause 96-022132
295th Judicial District
Judge Tracy Christopher
Leader Federal Bank for Savings Attorney Ronald G. Mitchell, Kathleen Marie Vossler and Stephen C. Porter

Jones, et al v. Leader Federal Bank, et al (Injunction)
Cause 96-CV-1385
Southern District of Texas (Houston)
Judge Vanessa D. Gilmore
Leader Federal Bank for Savings Attorney Ronald G. Mitchell

Jones, et al v. The State of Texas
Cause 96-CV-1621
Southern District of Texas (Houston)
Judge Vanessa D. Gilmore
The State of Texas Attorney Dan Morales, Attorney Jorge Vega, Attorney Laquita A. Hamilton, Attorney Toni Hunter and Attorney G. Stewart Whitehead

Jones, et al v. Smith, et al
Cause 96-CV-4368
Southern District of Texas (Houston)
Judge Nancy F. Atlas
Appellees' Attorney: Blake Brodersen for Shearn Smith and David West; David B. Dickinson for Jeffrey H. Ewalt and self

Johnnie Jones; Harvella Jones v. Shearn Smith; David West; Jeffrey H. Ewalt; David B. Dickinson

Cause 97-20403
Appellees' Attorney: Blake Brodersen for Shearn Smith and David West;
David B. Dickinson for Jeffrey H. Ewalt and self

Jones, et al v. Union Planters
Cause 98-CV-818
Southern District of Texas (Houston)
Judge Lynn N. Hughes
Attorney Ronald G. Mitchell, Attorney David Kirkendall

REFERENCES

The Bible

Winona Blevins' information Courtesy of ABC 13, Eyewitness News' Article, "Purchaser of elderly widow's home reportedly owes back taxes by Tom Abrahams

ABC 20/20 – Problems with Homeowners' Associations

Houston Chronicle, May 10, 2001 Article

DOCUMENTS

CLOSED

NO. 554467 #2

NOTICES MAILED

JOHNNIE JONES & MARVELLA JONES	)	COUNTY CIVIL COURT
0175087	)	
Plaintiff	)	817=88=0313
	)	
VS.	)	NO. 2
	)	
ROYCE HOMES, INC.	)	
	)	
Defendant	)	HARRIS COUNTY, TEXAS

JUDGMENT

On the ___10th___ day of ___May___, 1990, the parties appeared and announced ready for trial, and submitted the matters in controversy, as well of fact as of law, to the court without the intervention of a jury. The court heard the evidence and the argument of counsel and is of the opinion that judgment should be rendered for the plaintiff. It is therefore ordered, adjudged and decreed that the plaintiff, ___Johnnie and Marvella Jones___, do have and recover of the defendant, ___Royce Homes, Inc.___, the sum of $2,500, with interest thereon at the rate of ___10___ per cent per annum, together with his court costs, miscellaneous expenses incurred due to this cause, attorney fees, and that he have his execution; that the defendant, ___Royce Homes, Inc.___ go hence with his costs without day.

MAY 3 0 1990

Signed and rendered this _____ day of _____, 1990.

Judge Presiding
County Civil Court, Harris County, Texas

CHAPTER 2

Court of Appeals

First District of Texas

COPY OF JUDGMENT

JOHNIE JONES AND HARVELLA JONES, APPELLANTS	Appeal from the 270th District Court of Harris County, Texas. (Tr. Ct. No. 91-48229). Panel consists of Justices Bass, Dunn, and Wilson.
NO. 01-92-00963-CV V.	
WOODLAND HILLS TRAIL ASSOCIATION, APPELLEE	

     The cause heard today by the Court is an appeal from the judgment rendered and entered by the court below on May 27, 1992. After hearing the cause on the record of the court below and inspecting the same, it is the opinion of this Court that there was error in the judgment. It is therefore CONSIDERED, ADJUDGED, AND ORDERED that the judgment of the court below be reversed and the cause remanded.

     It is further ORDERED that the appellee, WOODLAND HILLS TRAIL ASSOCIATION pay all costs incurred by reason of this appeal.

     It is further ORDERED that this decision be certified below for observance.

     Judgment rendered by panel consisting of Justices Bass, Dunn, and Wilson.

Judgment entered   APR - 1 1993   _____

CHAPTER 3

In The

Court of Appeals

For The

First District of Texas

NO. 01-92-00963-CV

JOHNNIE JONES AND HARVELLA JONES, Appellants

V.

WOODLAND HILLS TRAIL ASSOCIATION, Appellee

On Appeal from the 270th District Court
Harris County, Texas
Trial Court Cause No. 91-48229

OPINION

The appellants, Johnnie and Harvella Jones, appeal by writ of error from the trial court's award of a default judgment in favor of the appellee, Woodland Hills Trail Association ("Woodland Hills"), on Woodland Hill's action for collection of annual maintenance assessments and foreclosure of its lien securing the payments, and appeal the court's denial of the Joneses' motion for new trial. We reverse the judgment and remand the cause to the trial court.

The Joneses are owners of property in a residential development of Harris County known as Woodland Hills Village. Prior to their purchase of the property, a

"Declaration of Covenants, Conditions and Restrictions" applicable to each section of the development was recorded in the official public records of real property of Harris County, Texas. The declaration provides:

> Declarant hereby declares that all of the properties described above [of which the Jones' property is one] . . . shall be held, sold and conveyed subject to the following easements, restrictions, covenants, and conditions, which are for the purpose of protecting the value and desirability of, and which shall run with, the real property and be binding on all parties having any right, title or interest in the described properties or any part thereof, their heirs, successors and assigns, and shall inure to the benefit of each owner thereof.

Article IV of the declaration provides for a covenant for maintenance assessments including the creation of a continuing lien and personal obligation to pay the assessments, and grants Woodland Hills the right to "bring an action at law against the Owner personally obligated to pay the same, or foreclose the lien against the property."

On September 17, 1991, Woodland Hills sued the Joneses for unpaid annual maintenance assessments and for foreclosure of its lien securing payment of the assessments. A default judgment was entered May 27, 1992, after the Joneses failed to file an answer or appear for trial. The judgment awarded Woodland Hills $229.21 plus costs, attorney's fees, and pre- and postjudgment interest. The judgment further ordered that the lien on the Joneses' lot be foreclosed. The Joneses' motion for new trial was denied after a hearing on July 27, 1992.

The Joneses bring this pro se writ of error, alleging 15 points of error. A direct attack on a judgment by writ of error must: (1) be brought within six months after the judgment was signed, (2) by a party to the suit, (3) who did not participate in the actual trial, (4) and the error complained of must be apparent from the face of the

232

record. *DSC Fin. Corp. v. Moffit*, 815 S.W.2d 551 (Tex. 1990). The Joneses have met these requirements.

In their tenth point of error, the Joneses contend they were not served.

Woodland Hill's sworn motion to retain, which is contained in the record, states the trial court granted Woodland Hill's motion for substituted service, alias citations were issued, and the Joneses were served. However, no return is contained in the record before us. Woodland Hills does not respond in its brief to the Joneses' claim of lack of service.

There are no presumptions in favor of valid issuance, service, and return of citation in the face of a writ of error attack on a default judgment. *Uvalde Country Club v. Martin Linen Supply Co., Inc.*, 690 S.W.2d 884, 885 (Tex. 1985). Further, in a direct attack by writ of error on a default judgment, no presumption exists simply because, as in the present case, the judgment recites that proper service was issued. Strict compliance with the rules requiring service of process must be affirmatively shown by the transcript unless the defendant voluntarily appeared before judgment was rendered. *Stephenson v. Corporate Servs., Inc.*, 650 S.W.2d 181, 183 (Tex. App.--Tyler 1983, writ ref'd n.r.e.); *see also McKanna v. Edgar*, 388 S.W.2d 927, 929 (Tex. 1965).

There is a specific rule requiring the return to be filed in the case before default judgment is granted, and therefore error is apparent on the face of the record when a proper officer's return is absent from the court's file. *See* Tex. R. Civ. P. 107; *United States ex rel. Adm'r of Small Business Admin. v. Charter Bank*, 694 S.W.2d 16, 18 (Tex. App.--Corpus Christi 1985, no writ).

Jeff Ewolt 780-4135

...ment in 1985   44.05 / Lot
   "   "   1986   68.00 / Lot

...ings were called for June 25, 1985 and August 27
...but had to be continued because of lack of a
...rum. Next meeting October 1, 1985
...the Oct. 1 meeting proxy votes were declared to
...ufficient for a quorum

...s Count
...   304   Against 4

...

CHAPTER 3

234

WOODLAND HILLS
TRAIL ASSOCIATION

SPECIAL MEETING OCTOBER 1, 1985

The Woodland Hills Trail Association held a third special meeting on October 1, 1985 at 7:00 p.m. at the Village Green. Members present were Sheila and Bill Miller, Jack and Janice Douglas, Jane Hagest, Lou Milano, Dwayne Fontenot, Barbara Adams and Stephanie Wentzel. Also in attendance were John Tonachek of Kingwood Trails, and Dick Boughton of Houston Management Services. Eight residents attended.

Sheila Miller called the meeting to order and announced that the purpose of the special meeting was to gain enough votes by proxy or members in attendance to raise the base annual assessment. Discussion among the board members and residents followed as to the necessity of the increase in the assessment and the responsibilities of the board in serving the community.

A vote was taken. Sheila Miller tentatively announced that the assessment increase had passed. The official tally of the votes was _____ for and _____ against.

Lou Milano moved that we adjourn the meeting. Janice Douglas seconded. Motion carried.

CHAPTER 3

Kingwood, Texas 77339

Defendant's Exhibit 7

CAUSE NO. ~~92-23162~~ 91-48229

WOODLAND HILLS TRAIL	§	IN THE DISTRICT COURT OF
ASSOCIATION,	§	
Plaintiff	§	
vs.	§	HARRIS COUNTY, T E X A S
	§	
JOHNNIE JONES and	§	
HARVELLA JONES,	§	
Defendants	§	152ND JUDICIAL DISTRICT

FINAL JUDGMENT

On the 29th day of March, 1995, the above entitled and numbered cause was duly called for trial on the merits. Plaintiff *WOODLAND HILLS TRAIL ASSOCIATION* appeared with its attorney of record and announced ready for trial; Defendants *JOHNNIE JONES and HARVELLA JONES* appeared pro se and announced ready for trial. A jury was not demanded by either party and the case proceeded to trial before the Court. The Court, after hearing and considering the testimony, together with the pleadings on file, the evidence presented into the record and the argument of counsel, is of the opinion and finds that Plaintiff is entitled to judgment against Defendants as requested.

IT IS THEREFORE, ORDERED, ADJUDGED and DECREED that Plaintiff *WOODLAND HILLS TRAIL ASSOCIATION* have and recover of and from Defendants *JOHNNIE JONES and HARVELLA JONES* the sum of TWO HUNDRED NINETY-EIGHT AND 24/100 DOLLARS ($298.24) for past due assessments.

IT IS FURTHER ORDERED, ADJUDGED and DECREED, that Plaintiff *WOODLAND HILLS TRAIL ASSOCIATION* have and recover of and from Defendants *JOHNNIE JONES and HARVELLA JONES* the sum of NINE THOUSAND AND 00/100 DOLLARS ($9,000.00) as a reasonable attorney's fee; and that Defendants *JOHNNIE JONES and HARVELLA JONES* have and recover of and from the Plaintiff *WOODLAND HILLS TRAIL ASSOCIATION* the

CHAPTER 3

236

sum of TWO THOUSAND FOUR HUNDRED AND SIXTY-EIGHT AND 50/100 DOLLARS ($2,468.50) as reasonable fee, including expenses, which sum is to be offset against the fees awarded to Plaintiff *WOODLAND HILLS TRAIL ASSOCIATION.*

IT IS FURTHER ORDERED, ADJUDGED and DECREED that Plaintiff *WOODLAND HILLS TRAIL ASSOCIATION* has a valid lien upon that certain real property described as:

> Lot 57, Block 37, of Woodland Hill, Section Five (5), according to the map or plat thereof recorded at Volume 217, Page 83 of the Map Records of Harris County, Texas, and having a common address of 2026 Oak Shores Dr., Kingwood, Harris County, Texas 77339.

Said lien is provided under the Declaration of Covenants, Conditions and Restrictions (the "Declaration") for Woodland Hills, Section Five (5), which Declaration is recorded in the Official Public Records of Real Property of Harris County, Texas. Plaintiff's lien upon Defendants' property is hereby foreclosed in accordance with the express provisions of the Declaration. Further, an Order of Sale shall issue to any Sheriff or Constable within the State of Texas, to seize and sell the above described property the same as in a mortgage or deed of trust lien in satisfaction of this Judgment. The Sheriff or other Officer executing the Order of Sale shall place the purchaser of the above described property in possession within thirty (30) days after the date of sale. The Order of Sale shall have all the force and effect of a Writ of Possession between the parties in this action and any person claiming under the Defendants by any right acquired pending this action. In the event that proceeds from the Sale do not fully satisfy the Judgment, said Sheriff or other Officer shall attempt to levy upon any non-exempt assets of Defendants as in ordinary executions.

IT IS FURTHER ORDERED, ADJUDGED AND DECLARED that the Declaration of Covenants, Conditions and Restrictions for Woodland Hills Section Five (5), as recorded under County Clerk's File No. D684522 and refiled under County Clerk's File No. E086798 of the Real Property Records of Harris County, Texas, do not entitle Defendants, as a matter of right, to pay the annual maintenance assessments provided for therein on a monthly basis.

IT IS FURTHER ORDERED, that all sums awarded Plaintiff, as offset by the sum awarded Defendant, shall bear interest at the rate of ten percent (10%) per annum from the date of judgment until paid in full.

IT IS FURTHER ORDERED, ADJUDGED AND DECREED that all costs of Court expended or incurred in this cause by Plaintiff are hereby adjudged against Defendants. All writs and processes for the enforcement and collection of this judgment shall issue to Plaintiff as necessary.

All relief not expressly granted herein is denied.

SIGNED this the 25th day of August , 1995.

_____
Judge Presiding

APPROVED:

EWALT & DICKINSON

_____
Jeffrey H. Ewalt   TSB #06752700
14614 Falling Creek, Suite 206
Houston, Texas 77068
(713) 444-9250
(713) 444-2404 - FAX
Attorneys for Plaintiff

NO. 91-48229

WOODLAND HILLS TRAIL ASSOCIATION	IN THE DISTRICT COURT OF
Plaintiff	
VS.	HARRIS COUNTY, TEXAS
JOHNNIE JONES and HARVELLA JONES	
Defendants	152 JUDICIAL DISTRICT

ORDER GRANTING DEFENDANTS' MOTION TO COMPEL ANSWERS TO INTERROGATORIES AND TO COMPEL RESPONSES TO REQUEST FOR PRODUCTION

On the 3rd day of December , 1993, came on to be considered Defendant's Motion to compel plaintiff to answer defendants' second set of interrogatories to plaintiff and to compel responses to request for production and the plaintiff's response thereto, and it appearing to the Court that the motion should be GRANTED;

IT IS, THEREFORE, ORDERED that the plaintiff WOODLAND HILLS TRAIL ASSOCIATION respond completely and in good faith to Defendants' Written Interrogatories and production requests no later than December 13, 1993 .

IT IS FURTHER ORDERED that defendant will not be held liable for attorney fees and any other expenses incurred by Plaintiff in regard to the Motion to Compel.

SIGNED this 3rd day of December , 1993.

JUDGE PRESIDING

CHAPTER 3

239

C 5283

NO. _____

IN THE

SUPREME COURT OF TEXAS

INWOOD NORTH HOMEOWNERS' ASSOCIATION, INC.,

Petitioner,

vs.

CHARLIE HARRIS, ET AL,

Respondents,

GRANTED

Pt. #3

Appealed from
the Court of Appeals for the First Supreme
Judicial District of Texas

No. 01-85-00595-CV

SET FOR ORAL ARGUMENT
ON WEDNESDAY Feb. 18
AT 9:00 A.M.

APPLICATION FOR WRIT OF ERROR
OF
INWOOD NORTH HOMEOWNERS' ASSOCIATION, INC.

BURTON & ASSOCIATES, P.C.

By: _____
LOU W. BURTON
Texas Bar Card No. 03479225
5301 Hollister, Suite 490
Houston, Texas 77040
(713) 462-3838

ATTORNEYS FOR PETITIONER,
INWOOD NORTH HOMEOWNERS'
ASSOCIATION, INC.

CHAPTER 4

Jones
vs
State of Texas

491. 1121

240

CRAIG A. WASHINGTON
EIGHTEENTH DISTRICT
TEXAS

1711 LONGWORTH BUILDING
WASHINGTON, DC 20515-4318
(202) 225-3816

MAJORITY WHIP AT LARGE

VICE CHAIRMAN
DEMOCRATIC STUDY GROUP
EXECUTIVE COMMITTEE

Congress of the United States
House of Representatives
Washington, DC 20515-4318

MEMBER:
COMMITTEE ON
ENERGY AND COMMERCE
SUBCOMMITTEE:
ENERGY AND POWER
HEALTH AND THE ENVIRONMENT

COMMITTEE ON
THE JUDICIARY
SUBCOMMITTEE:
CIVIL AND CONSTITUTIONAL RIGHTS
CRIME AND CRIMINAL JUSTICE

COMMITTEE ON
GOVERNMENT OPERATIONS
SUBCOMMITTEE:
ENVIRONMENT, ENERGY AND NATURAL RESOURCES
HUMAN RESOURCES AND INTERGOVERNMENTAL RELATIO

February 9, 1994

Mr. Johnnie Jones
P.O. Box 2431
New Caney, TX 77357-2431

Dear Mr. Jones:

Thank you for your inquiry and your patience. Please pardon the long delay in responding.

Your understanding of the Homestead Act is correct in that a foreclosure can only be affected due to failure to make payments of mortgage, home repair loans, or taxes. There are no exceptions. You should rest assured that nonpayment of assessment fees does not constitute grounds for foreclosure.

Enclosed you will find additional information regarding the Homestead Act. I hope you find it helpful.

Thank you for the opportunity to be of service. Should you have any questions, or require additional assistance in the future, please do not hesitate to contact me.

Sincerely,

Craig A. Washington
Member

CAW:TNA

CHAPTER 6

NO. 9223162

NORTH WOODLAND HILLS VILLAGE COMMUNITY ASSOCIATION	)	IN THE DISTRICT COURT OF
	)	
Plaintiff	)	
	)	
VS.	)	HARRIS COUNTY, TEXAS
	)	
JOHNNIE JONES and HARVELLA JONES	)	
	)	
Defendants	)	215TH JUDICIAL DISTRICT

ORDER

On the 28th day of December, 1992, the Court heard the motion of Defendants Johnnie and Harvella Jones for an order to Compel Plaintiff to answer Defendants' First Set of Interrogatories to Plaintiff, to Produce Request for Production No. 2, and Examination of Plaintiff's Books and Records, in the above-entitled and numbered cause.

The motion was duly presented to the Court, and the Court is of the opinion that the motion should be granted.

IT IS, THEREFORE, ORDERED, ADJUDGED, AND DECREED that the motion to Compel Plaintiff to answer Defendants' First Set of Interrogatories Nos. 3, 4, 5, 6, 7, 8, 9, 11, 12, 13, 14, 15, 16, 17, 18, 19, 23, 24, 25, 26, 27 and 28 to Plaintiff, to Produce Request for Production No. 2, and to provide the time and date Plaintiff's Books and Records may be inspected at Plaintiff's attorney's office in this cause be granted in its entirety and that this be done within fifteen (15) days from the date of receipt of this order. IT IS FURTHER ORDERED that

CHAPTER 7

242

defendant will not be held liable for Attorney fees and any other expenses incurred by Plaintiff in regard to the above-entitled cause.

Signed December 29th, 1992

Eugene C Chambers
Judge Eugene Chambers

243

TAMARA HENSARLING PAUL
Attorney At Law
116 South Avenue C
P.O. BOX 1383
Humble, Texas 77347-1383

713) 548-5000   *Fax (713) 446-5237*

March 12, 1993

<u>Via Messenger</u>

Mr. Jeffrey H. Ewalt
5718 Westheimer, Suite 1600
Houston, Texas 77057-5794

Re: Cause No. 92-23162
        Northwoodland Hills Village C.A.
        vs.
        Johnnie Jones and Harvella Jones

Dear Mr. Ewalt:

Enclosed are file folders containing information you requested regarding the Jones case. The following file folders are enclosed:

1.   Correspondence to Community Residents

2.   Minutes from the years 1973, 1974, 1975,1976, 1977, 1978, 1979, 1980, 1981, 1982, 1983, 1984, 1985, 1986, 1987, 1988

3.   Minutes from the years 1989, 1990, 1991, 1992

4.   Annual Meeting

5.   Annual Meeting Ballots for the years 1990, 1991, 1992

6.   Correspondence General

If you have any questions concerning the above referenced, please do not hesitate to call.

Very truly yours,

Tamara Paul

Tamara Hensarling Paul
(bkd)

CHAPTER 9   000145

244

NORTH WOODLAND HILLS
VILLAGE COMMUNITY ASSOCIATION

SEptember 10,1990

Members Present:

Dee Price
Shirley Baum
Ken Baum
Mary Lou McIver
John Clifton
Bob Pringle
Constance Phillips
John Tomocheck

The meeting was called to order by President Dee Price,
at 7:30 PM.

The minutes of August 13,1990 were approved as ammended
on a motion by Ken Baum and seconded by John Clifton.

Pool Report---Russell Duplechain said there were no problems
at this time. The pool is closed and will reopen May 1991,
but will continue to be maintained during this time.

Financial Report---Dee Price passed out financial statement for August 1990. John Rood went over the financial
audit.

Deed Restrictions---President Dee Price said we needed to
address the subject of gazebos,trailers, boats and RV's.
Steve McFadden submitted the following guidelines for gazebos;
    All gazebos shall be of wood construction and have six (6)
sides. All sides are to be of open-air construction, none
are to be enclosed. Size shall be limited to a maximum
diameter of ten (10) feetand a maximum height of ten (10)
feet above ground level. A motion was made by Ken Baum to
adopt Steve's guidelines and seconded by John Clifton.
Motion carried.

CHAPTER 9

P. O. Box 5050
Kingwood, Texas 77339

A motion was made by Shirley Baum stating homeowners must provide written request for permission to store vehicles semipermanately. The motion was seconded by John Clifton and carried.

Public Comments---2135 Fir Springs---
Mrs. Hart built a gazebo and a shed higher than 8 ft. Because her yard slopes and floods. She called a member, but doesn't remember who, and they told her to make it attractive. Dee and Steve looked at it and it is in harmony. Mrs. Hart was told that this issue would be discussed at the meeting, and she would be notified of the results.

Mrs. Lindsey wants to know where she stands concerning her R.V. She was told that this issue would be discussed at the meeting and she would be notified when an agreement had been reached.

Mr. Haggest ---2119 Fir Springs requested a copy of the deed restrictions.

Architectural Control
2211 Middle Creek roof follow up
Steve McFaddens guidelines on gazebo construction was passed out and voted on under deed restrictions.

Public Safety--- Ken Baum announced there would be a meeting on September 12 at the Elm Grove Community Center.

Parks--- There is a need for more parks. Dee Price made mention of giving one girl's ballfield back to K.S.A. and opening it up to the public.

All proceeds from the Fun Run go to the parks committee.

The duckpond is completed.

K.S.A.---K.S.A, meeting was held at the Episcopal church at 7:00p.m. on Sept. 20. There is a meeting on the third Thursday every month.

Old Business---F.I.S.T.
A motion was made by John Clifton to donate 1000.00 to F.I.S.T. and was seconded by mary Lou McIver. The motion failed. A motion was made by Shirley Baum to donate 500.00 to F.I.S.T. and was seconded by Mary Lou McIver. The motion carried.

New Business---Notice must be out by Fri. Sept. 14 for the annual meeting. The meeting will be held at the Woodland Hills cafet at 7:30 pm on Oct.8.A regular meeting will immediately follow.
A motion to adjourn the meeting was made by Bob Pringle and

seconded by Shirley Baum. The meeting was adjourned at 9:30 pm.

Signed Recording Secretary Mary Lou McIver

INVOICE

Lillian I. Hutchison & Associates

Hutchison Forensic Laboratory and Conference Chambers
Document Examination and Handwriting Identification

(713) 723-8604   FAX (713) 723-8680

9660 Hillcroft, Suite 200G   Houston, Texas 77096
NCNB Banking Center Braes Bayou

Johnnie and Harvella Jones
2026 Oak Shores Dr.
Kingwood, Texas   77330-1724

or *Professional Services Rendered:* Document copies   Case No. 5498-3DI

DATE	DESCRIPTION	AMOUNT
iy 11, 1993	Examination and Comparison of Documents	
	Letter of Opinion	
	2.4 hrs. @ $125.00 per	$300.
	TOTAL	$300.
	4/29/93 Retainer Paid	100.
	BALANCE	$200.
	Agreed total service fee $200.00 BALANCE DUE -----	$100.
	THANK YOU	

PAYMENT IS DUE UPON RECEIPT OF THIS INVOICE

CHAPTER 9

May 7, 1993

Johnnie and Harvella Jones
2026 Oak Shores Dr.
Kingwood, Texas   77339-1724

RE: Letterhead copies   Case No: 5498-3DE

Dear Mr. and Mrs. Jones:

On April 29, 1993, the following documents were submitted to me, in person, for the purpose of examination and comparison to determine the discrepancies in the machine copies of the three documents submitted.

DOCUMENTS UNDER INQUIRY

Q1. A notification on the letterhead of North Woodland Hills Village Community Association of a special meeting to be held June 3, 1980.
     Identified as: "Defendant's Exhibit "F"

Q2. Letter to "Dear Association Member" on the letterhead of North Woodland Hills Village Community Association.
     Subject: Meeting of North Woodland Hills Village Community Association for vote about increased maximum annual assessment.
     Identified also as: "Defendant's Exhibit "F" in the same handwriting as Q1.

Q3. A notice on the letterhead of North Woodland Hills Village Community Association
     Subject: The second special meeting for assessment increase, that was held on July 14, 1980.
     Signature: "Judy Ray Sara Leach"
     Identified as: "Exhibit '7'" in light blue ink at the bottom right corner.

FINDINGS AND CONCLUSION

As a result of this comparison study, based on the three (3) documents supplied, it is the opinion of this examiner that Q1 and Q2 appear to be copies of copies several generations down the line. Each time a document is copied, it loses more and more detail and the overall size of the printed page is distorted.

Hutchison Fort
NCNB Banking Center Bldg

3t 77096

249

The notice dated July 14, 1980 (Q3) appears to be a first generation copy from the original document. The edges of the letters appear to be sharper and clearer than those of Q1 or Q2; also, the alignment is fairly accurate.

The same make and model of typewriter was used for all three notifications. The type is Pica, 10 pitch. It is a well worn typewriter as evidenced by the misalignment of one letter to another. Corresponding letters and words have the same misalignment with the baseline in all three documents.

Other physical evidence: there are two (2) holes at the top of each page (as pages fastened to a file folder) and copy machine evidence of two holes (also at the top) in a previous document from which it was copied. Also, there is evidence of a hole indication in the middle of the left side (suggesting notebook holes) of a previous page from which it was copied.

The top left corner of Q1 and Q2 has a black triangle indicating that the page was copied with the corner turned back. This situation is common when multiple pages are stapled together and are folded back over the staple to expose a particular page to the plate of the copy machine.

The top left corner of Q3 indicates that the original document was stapled to another document before copying. This document, Q3, has been stapled twice to another document since the copying process.

In the event a hearing or trial is scheduled and it becomes necessary to furnish visual evidence of these findings, additional time — at least two weeks — will be needed and all documents returned for such preparation.

All submitted documents are being returned to you with this letter of opinion. If I can be of assistance to you in the future, please do not hesitate to call.

Respectfully submitted,

Lillian Hutchison

Lillian I. Hutchison
Certified and Court Qualified
Document Examiner

LIH:wp
Enclosures as stated

STATE OF TEXAS   )(
                                              AFFIDAVIT
COUNTY OF HARRIS   )(

BEFORE ME, the undersigned official, on this day appeared Lillian I. Hutchison, who is personally known to me, and first being duly sworn according to law upon her oath deposed and said:

My name is Lillian I. Hutchison; I am over 18 years of age, and I practice my profession at 9660 Hillcroft, Suite 200G. I have never been convicted of a crime, and am fully competent to make this affidavit. I am a specialist in the field of Handwriting and a Certified Forensic Document Examiner, who has been duly qualified as an expert document examiner and handwriting analyst in criminal, civil, and probate courts.

"I have personally prepared the forgoing written report of this case and all opinions stated in the FINDINGS AND CONCLUSION section are to be considered as professionally correct and precise as possible."

Lillian I Hutchison
AFFIANT

SUBSCRIBED AND SWORN TO BEFORE ME on the ___12___, day of ___May___, ~~1990~~ 1993

Nikki J. Selby
NOTARY PUBLIC/STATE OF TEXAS
MY COMMISSION EXPIRES: _____

PRINTED NAME OF NOTARY

_____

251

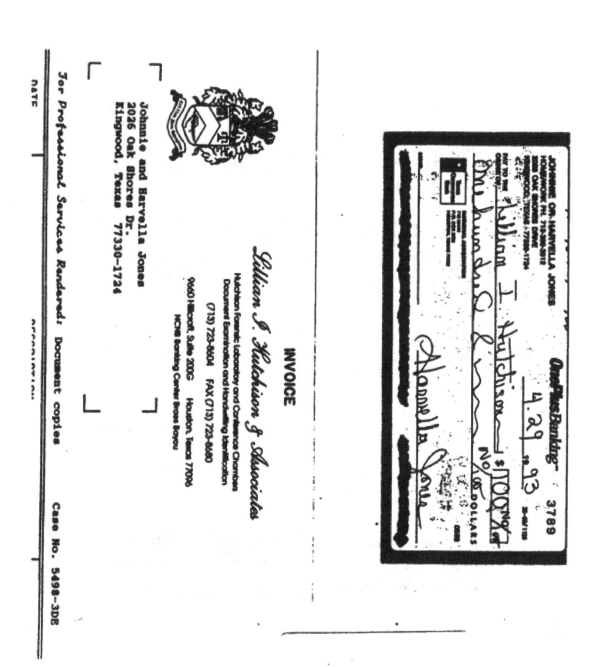

INVOICE

Lillian S. Hutchison & Associates

Hutchison Forensic Laboratory and Conference Chambers
Document Examination and Handwriting Identification

(713) 723-6604   FAX (713) 723-6680

9660 Hillcroft, Suite 200G   Houston, Texas 77006
NCNB Banking Center Brae Bayou

Johnnie and Harvella Jones
2026 Oak Shores Dr.
Kingwood, Texas 77330-1724

For Professional Services Rendered: Document copies   Case No. 5498-3DE

DATE

252

Roberta J. Nunn, B.B.A. & Associates
Certified Document Examiner
8706 Katy Freeway, Suite 105
Houston, Texas 77024

August 8, 1995

Johnnie & Harvella Jones

Re:

Re: Cause No: 95-882985. Johnnie Jones and Wife Harvella Jones vs. North Woodland
Hills Village Community Association.

I. On August 8, 1995, the following documents were delivered to my office. A three page
typewritten copy of the September 10, 1990, Minutes from North Woodland Hills Village
Community Association. Photocopy.

II. *ASSIGNMENT:*

To determine if alterations have been made on page two of the above document noted in
section I.

III. *FINDINGS & CONCLUSIONS:*

Laboratory equipment was used to examine the documents. Spacing was evaluated and
measured. Alignment was examined under stereomicroscopic procedures. Page two shows
alignment balance for the first half of the page. There is a line, indicating the possibility of
another print out, or several paragraphs included.

Alignment grids were superimposed on all three pages. Page one and three, were in
alignment with consistency. Page two shows various mis-alignment. From slanting downward
to sentence structures being spaced midway, out of alignment from the beginning of the sentence
and finishing on lead in alignment.

Based upon reasonable scientific certainty, it is my opinion that page two of the document
noted in section I. has been altered from the original document. This opinion is qualified due to
the fact that the document in question was not the original document. In the event the original
document is provided for examination, this opinion could be altered.

CHAPTER 9

Joseph cont. ...2

In the event this case proceeds to a hearing or trial, I am willing to testify to my findings in a Court of Law. I require at least two weeks for preparation of exhibits and my consultation with the attorney representing the client before appearing in a Court of Law. The consultation with the attorney is required for testimony.

I appreciate your calling me to assist you in this case. It was a pleasant experience meeting you and working with you.

Respectfully submitted,

Roberta J. Hanna C.D.E
Certified Document Examiner

Member: World Association of Document Examiners
National Association of Document Examiners

No. 95-002085

Johnnie Jones and Wife Norvella Jones   215th District Court

vs

North Woodland Hills Village Association   Harris County Texas

STATE OF TEXAS   :   *AFFIDAVIT OF ROBERTA JONES HANNA C.D.E.*
COUNTY OF HARRIS

BEFORE ME. the undersigned Notary Public, on this day personally appeared

ROBERTA JONES HANNA ("Affiant"), who is personally known to me, and being by me first

dully sworn according to law, stated upon her oath as follows:

"My name is Roberta Jones Hanna. I am over eighteen (18) years of age, have not been convicted of any crime and am otherwise competent to make this affidavit. I have read the contents here and every fact stated is within my personal knowledge and true and correct.

My address is 8705 Katy Freeway, Suite 105. Houston, Texas 77024.

I am a member of the World Association of Document Examiners since 1986, and a member of the World Association of Document Examiners since 1987. I have training in the area of forensic questioned document examination, comparison, handwriting, handprinting identification, typeface and have been a consulting document examiner on various types of cases involving questioned documents.

I am Court Qualified and Certified as a Forensic Document Examiner.

I have been retained to examine a three page document, dated September 10, 1990, of the North Woodland Hills Village Community Association meeting report.

I was provided photocopies of the above noted documents. My assignment was to determine if there has been alterations on page two (2), of the document noted above.

Laboratory equipment was used to examine the documents. Based on the document submitted, it is my qualified opinion that the page in question does indeed show alterations.

255

Due to the fact that the document in question was a photocopy, in the event the original document is provided for scientific examination, my opinion could be altered. A more definitive report can then be made. Due to time limitations, I have not examined the originals.

Further, Affiant says not.

_____
Roberta Jones Hanna, Affiant

SWORN TO AND SUBSCRIBED BEFORE ME by Roberta Jones Hanna on this 7TH day of August, 1995, to certify which witness my hand and official seal.

JUNE D. MITCHELL
Notary Public, State of Texas
My Commission Expires
MAY 8, 1998

_____
Notary Public, State of Texas

L
easures
ignmen
other p

A
ignmen
sooren
ha ci

x in s.

FFIDAVIT

oberta Jones Hanna

Roberta J. Hanna C.D.E. & Associates
Certified Document Examiner
8705 Katy Freeway, Suite 105
Houston, Texas 77024

(713) 683-1530   Fax (713) 683-1530

August 10, 1998

Records of Payments to Roberta J. Hanna, Certified Document Examiner from
Harvella Jones
Cause # 95-002085

Number	Date	Amount	Bank
5527	8/8/95	$ 350.00	Texas Commerce
5528	8/9/95	757.00	"
5529	8/16/95	450.00	"
5532	8/23/95	1,170.00	"
Total Paid		$ 2,727.00	

Checks given and "Stop Payment, do not re-present"

5534	8/28/95	$590.75	Statement for completion of examination and Court exhibits.
5533	8/28/95	600.00	Agreed payment before testifying in 215 District Court. Usual fee $ 600.00.
Total amount due		$ 1,190.00	

CHAPTER 9

Roberta J. Hanna C.D.E. & Associates
Certified Document Examiner
8706 Katy Freeway, Suite 106
Houston, Texas 77024

August 24, 1995

Johnnie & Harvella Jones
P.O. Box 2431
New Caney, Texas 77357-2431

Re: Cause No: 95-002085. Johnnie Jones and Wife Harvella Jones vs. North Woodland
      Hills Village Community Association.

STATEMENT FOR FORENSIC DOCUMENT EXAMINATION

Second Phase. Beginning with the examination of original documents on 8/16/95, at the Law
offices of Roberts, Markel & Folger, 24 Greenway Plaza, Suite 2000, Houston, Texas 77046.
Laboratory comparisons and examinations with Photography and findings at this meeting.

13 HOURS AT $ 90.00 HOUR	$ 1,170.00
3 HOURS 8/24/95, COMPLETING EXHIBITS FOR COURT TESTIMONY, AFFIDAVITS AND STATEMENTS, AT $90.00 HOUR	270.00
27 PHOTOCOPIES, INC. ENLARGEMENTS .25 EA.	6.75
2 SCANNER COPIES AT $ 3.50 EA.	7.00
34 POLAROID PRINTS OF DOCUMENTS AT $ 2.00 EA.	68.00
TOTAL	$ 1,261.75
LESS RETAINER OF	450.00
	$ 1,453.75
AMOUNT DUE UPON RECEIPT OF THIS STATEMENT	$ 801.75

Thank you,

Roberta J. Hanna C.D.E.
Certified Document Examiner

CHAPTER 9

Roberta J. Hanna C.D.E & Associates
Certified Document Examiner
8706 Katy Freeway, Suite 106
Houston, Texas 77024

August 24,1995

Johnnie & Harvella Jones
P.O.Box 2431
New Caney, Texas 77357-2431

Re: Cause No: 95-002085. Johnnie Jones and Wife Harvella Jones vs. North Woodland
       Hills Village Community Association.

FINAL STATEMENT FOR FORENSIC DOCUMENT EXAMINATION

STATEMENT OF AUGUST 8, 1995, TOTAL	$ 1,107.00
STATEMENT OF AUGUST 24,1995, TOTAL	1,521.75
TOTAL	$ 2,628.75

LESS AMOUNTS PAID BY JOHNNIE JONES AND WIFE HARVELLA JONES,
PERSONAL CHECKS :

8/9/95	Check no. 5527 retainer for the amount of	$ 350.00
8/9/95	Check no. 5528 Payment for hours above	757.00
8/16/95	Check no. 5529 retainer for the amount of Examination of originals	450.00
8.23/95	Check no. 5532 for hourly charges above on phase 2, of originals examined.	1,170.00
TOTAL AMOUNT PAID		$ 2,727.00

****

TOTAL AMOUNT OF CHARGES	$ 2,628.75
TOTAL AMOUNT PAID	2,727.00
Credit due	$ 98.25

Thank you,

Roberta J. Hanna C.D.E

CHAPTER 9

NO. 95-02085

JOHNNIE JONES AND WIFE MARVELLA JONES)   IN THE DISTRICT COURT OF
)
    Plaintiff   )
)
VS.   )   HARRIS COUNTY, TEXAS
)
NORTH WOODLAND HILLS VILLAGE   )
COMMUNITY ASSOCIATION   )
    Defendant   )   215TH JUDICIAL DISTRICT

ORDER/CONTEMPT OF COURT SANCTIONS

Defendant North Woodland Hills Village Community Association is to produce all the records still missing that were indicated were transmitted to Jeffrey E. Ewalt from Tamara Hensarling Paul in the March 12, 1993 letter:

The following files are still to be produced:

1. Any and all minutes, correspondence, and notes pertaining to Johnnie and Marvella Jones.

2. September 11, 1989 Board of Directors Minutes

3. July 9, 1990 Board of Directors Minutes

4. August 13, 1990 Board of Directors Minutes

5. September 10, 1990 Board of Directors Minutes

6. October 8, 1990 Board of Directors Minutes

7. November 12, 1990 Board of Directors Minutes

8. December 10, 1990 Board of Directors Minutes

9. June 10, 1991 Board of Directors Minutes

10. August 9, 1993 Board of Directors Minutes

11. June 13, 1994 Board of Directors Minutes

12. August 8, 1994 Board of Directors Minutes

13. October 10, 1994 Board of Directors Minutes

CHAPTER 9

14. February 13, 1995 Board of Directors Minutes

15. April 10, 1995 Board of Directors Minutes

16. May 8, 1995 Board of Directors Minutes

17. June 12, 1995 Board of Directors Minutes

18. Original proxies (forms) and notice for 1980 special meetings for inspection

19. Any and all July 14, 1980 minutes covering the increase. (complete)

19. All monthly payment agreements from any and all homeowners (members) from 1985 thru 1995. (Including agreements prior to lawsuits)

20. Frank Sklenka's deed restrictions report that was attached to the February 8, 1993 Board of Directors Minutes.

21. The 316 page exhibit photographed at 25 cents per sheet June 19 and 20, 1995 in Travis McCormick's office.

This production is due _August 7, 1995_. In the alternative, if an extremely plausible explanation is not given as to why the documents have not been produced, severe sanctions will be granted, which will include ~~summary~~ default π is awarded ~~judgment, as well as a~~ sanction of $350.00 ~~Frank~~ as attorney fees for the preparation and hearing of this motion. ~~for the plaintiffs Johnson and Horvellings.~~ The Defendant North Woodland Hills Village Community Association is not entitled to any attorney fees or any other reimbursement as a result of this Motion.

SIGNED this 24th day of July, 1995.

JUDGE PRESIDING

Said amount to be paid w/in 30 days of the signing of this Order.

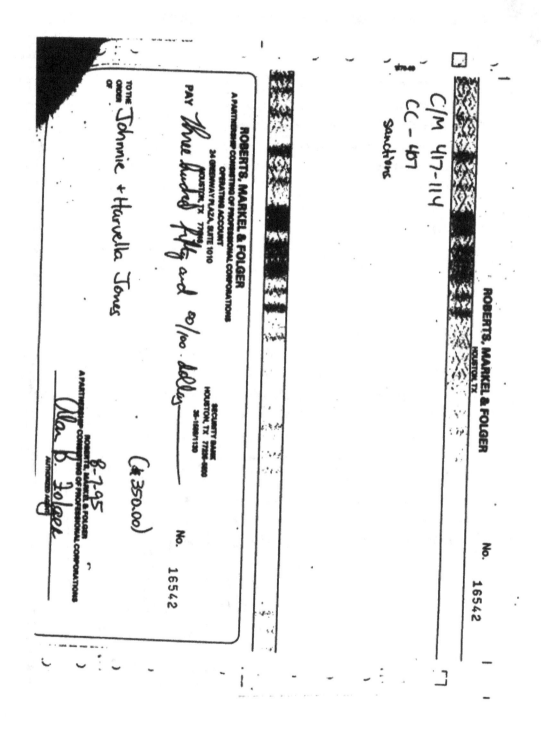

ROBERTS, MARKEL & FOLGER
HOUSTON, TX

No. 16542

C/M 47-1114
CC - 467
Sanctions

ROBERTS, MARKEL & FOLGER
A PARTNERSHIP CONSISTING OF PROFESSIONAL CORPORATIONS
OPERATING ACCOUNT
24 GREENWAY PLAZA, SUITE 1010
HOUSTON, TX 77046

SECURITY BANK
HOUSTON, TX 77258-4600
36-1599/1130

No. 16542

8-7-95

PAY Three hundred Fifty and 80/100 dollars

($ 350.00)

TO THE
ORDER
OF   Johnnie + Harvella Jones

ROBERTS, MARKEL & FOLGER
A PARTNERSHIP CONSISTING OF PROFESSIONAL CORPORATIONS

Alan B. Folger
AUTHORIZED AGENT

EXHIBIT A
ROBERTA J. HANNA
STATEMENT OF ACCOUNT

Johnnie & Harvella Jones

	AMOUNT	BALANCE
⋆ Invoice August 8, 1995	$1107.00	$1107.00
Payment August 9, 1975	350.00	757.00
Payment August 22, 1995	450.00	307.00
Payment August 23, 1995	1170.00	-863.00
Invoice August 24, 1995	1453.75	590.75
Invoice August 24, 1995	600.00	1190.75

AFFIDAVIT

STATE OF TEXAS   ⋆
                       ⋆
COUNTY OF HARRIS   ⋆

BEFORE ME, the undersigned notary public, on this day personally appeared ROBERTA J. HANNA, known to me, who, after being by me duly sworn, stated on her oath that the foregoing and annexed account in favor or Roberta J. Hanna and against Johnnie & Harvella Jones for the sum of $1,190.75 is, within the knowledge of the affiant, just and true, that it is due and unpaid, and that all lawful offsets, payments and credits have been allowed.

Roberta J. Hanna
Roberta J. Hanna, affiant

SWORN TO AND SUBSCRIBED BEFORE ME on 9/24/ , 1998.

Henrietta H. Turner
Notary Public, State of Texas

ρ CHAPTER 9

DOCKET NUMBER 711839

Harvella Jones

V.S.

Roberta J. Hanna

IN THE COUNTY CIVIL COURT

AT LAW NUMBER 4

HARRIS COUNTY, TEXAS

ORDER OF TRANSFER

On ___FEB - 2 1999___ came on to be considered:

    1. ☒ The Court's own motion for recusal.

    2. ☐ An objection filed pursuant to Tex.Govt.Code
        Ann.§74.051.

and it is herby **ORDERED**,

    1. ☒ I voluntarily recuse myself.

    2. ☐ I refuse to recuse myself.

    3. ☐ I am automatically recused.

Signed:___FEB - 2 1999___.

Cynthia Crowe

Judge,
County Civil Court at Law No.

Upon above action, It is **ORDERED** that the above-styled and numbered cause be
transferred from County Civil Court at Law _2_.

Signed: 2/2/99 .

Division Presiding Judge   **CHAPTER 9**

264

J. CURTIS BROWN
CHIEF JUSTICE

PAUL C. MURPHY
SAM ROBERTSON
ROSS A. SEARS
BILL CANNON
JOE L. DRAUGHN
GEORGE T. ELLIS
GARY C. BOWERS
NORMAN R. LEE

JUSTICES

Fourteenth Court of Appeals

1307 San Jacinto, 11th Floor
Houston, Texas 77002

MARY JANE SMART
CLERK

PHONE
713-655-2800

FAX
713-655-2820

May 10, 1994

Ms. Harvella Jones
2026 Oak Shores Drive
Kingwood, TX 77339

Hon. Jeffrey H. Ewalt
5718 Westheimer
Suite 1600
Houston, TX 77057

Case Number: 14-93-00545-CV
Trial Court Case No.: 92-23162

Jones, Johnnie and Jones, Harvella, Appellant
                    vs.
North Woodland Hills Village Community Association, Appellee

Counsel:

This appeal is set for submission in the Fourteenth
Court of Appeals courtroom, at 1307 San Jacinto, ninth floor,
June 7, 1994, at 01:30 o'clock, before Justice Ross A. Sears,
Justice Norman R. Lee, Justice William E. Junell. Oral argument
is permitted from each party who has timely filed a brief and has
timely requested oral argument.

If the case is settled, the clerk should be notified at
once so that the Court can maintain a full docket of cases.
No motion to reschedule, whether agreed or otherwise, will be
granted within one (1) week of the date set without showing a
good cause.

Respectfully yours,

MARY JANE SMART, CLERK

CHAPTER 10

SUPREME COURT OF THE UNITED STATES
OFFICE OF THE CLERK
WASHINGTON, D. C. 20543

April 20, 1995

Johnnie Jones
2026 Oak Shores Drive
Kingwood, TX 77339-1724

     Re: Johnnie Jones and Marvella Jones,
          v. North Woodland Hills Community Association
          No. 94-8927

Dear Mr. Jones:

    The petition for a writ of certiorari in the above
entitled case was docketed in this Court on April 11, 1995
as No. 94-8927.

    A form is enclosed for notifying opposing counsel that
the case was docketed.

                 Very truly yours,

                 William K. Suter, Clerk

                 by

                 Troy D. Cahill
                 Assistant

Enclosures

CHAPTER 10

Cause No. 95-001886

JOHNNIE JONES AND WIFE, HARVELLA JONES	§	IN THE DISTRICT COURT OF
	§	
VS.	§	HARRIS COUNTY, TEXAS
	§	
JEFFREY H. EWALT AND EWALT & DICKINSON	§	269TH JUDICIAL DISTRICT

C

ORDER ON DEFENDANTS' MOTION TO ABATE

On this day, the court considered defendants Jeffery H. Ewalt and Ewalt &
Dickinson's motion to abate. After considering the pleadings, the court

GRANTS the motion and abates plaintiffs' suit until the judgments in both
Cause No. 91-48229, styled Woodland Hills Trail Association v. Johnnie Jones and
Harvella Jones, and Cause No. 92-23162, styled North Woodland Hills Village
Community Association v. Johnnie Jones and Harvella Jones, become final.

SIGNED: _April 17, 1995_

_____
JUDGE PRESIDING

APPROVED AND ENTRY REQUESTED:

EWALT & DICKINSON
14614 Falling Creek Dr., Ste. 206
Houston, TX 77068
[713] 444-9250, telephone
[713] 444-2404, facsimile

_____
David B. Dickinson, SBOT#05833800
Attorney for Defendants

RECORDER'S MEMORANDUM:
This instrument is of poor quality
and not satisfactory for photographic
recordation; and/or alterations were
present at the time of filming

CHAPTER 11

267

Cause No. 95-001886

JOHNNIE JONES AND WIFE, HARVELLA JONES	§ § §	IN THE DISTRICT COURT OF
VS.	§ §	HARRIS COUNTY, TEXAS
JEFFREY H. EWALT AND EWALT & DICKINSON	§ § §	269TH JUDICIAL DISTRICT

ORDER ON PLAINTIFFS' MOTION TO RECUSE
(157TH JUDICIAL DISTRICT ON ASSIGNMENT FOR RECUSAL HEARING)

On the 5th day of May, the court considered plaintiffs' motion to recuse the Honorable David West, presiding judge of the 269th Judicial District Court. After considering the pleadings, the motion, and after hearing on the motion and considering the argument of the parties and counsel and receiving evidence, the court

DENIES the motion to recuse.

SIGNED: _May 5 1995_

_____
JUDGE PRESIDING

APPROVED AND ENTRY REQUESTED:

EWALT & DICKINSON
14614 Falling Creek Dr., Ste. 206
Houston, TX 77068
[713] 444-9250, telephone
[713] 444-2404, facsimile

_____
David B. Dickinson, SBOT#05833800
Attorney for Defendants

CHAPTER 11

Cause No. 95-001886

JOHNNIE JONES AND WIFE, HARVELLA JONES	§ § §	IN THE DISTRICT COURT OF
VS.	§ §	HARRIS COUNTY, TEXAS
JEFFREY H. EWALT AND EWALT & DICKINSON	§ § §	269TH JUDICIAL DISTRICT

AGREED ORDER OF REINSTATEMENT

On this day, at the request of the parties hereto, this cause is reinstated on this Court's Docket.

SIGNED: May 6, 1996

_____
DISTRICT JUDGE PRESIDING

APPROVED:

_____
(JOHNNIE JONES, PRO SE
P.O. Box 2431
New Caney, TX 77357-2431
[713] 952-0926

_____
HARVELLA JONES, PRO SE
P.O. Box 2431
New Caney, TX 77357-2431
[713] 952-0926

EWALT & DICKINSON
14614 Falling Creek Dr., Ste. 206
Houston, TX 77068
[713] 444-9250, telephone
[713] 444-2404, facsimile

_____
David B. Dickinson, SBOT#05833800
Attorney for Defendants

CHAPTER 11

JOHNNIE JONES and Wife HARVELLA JONES	)	IN THE DISTRICT COURT OF
Plaintiff	)	
	)	
VS.	)	HARRIS COUNTY, TEXAS
	)	
JEFFREY H. EWALT and EWALT & DICKINSON	)	
	)	
Defendants	)	269TH JUDICIAL DISTRICT
	)	

ASSESSED

ENTERED

PLAINTIFF'S DEMAND FOR JURY TRIAL

TO THE HONORABLE JUDGE OF THIS COURT:

JOHNNIE JONES and HARVELLA JONES, Plaintiff in the above-entitled and numbered cause, assert their rights under Tex. Const. art. I, 15 and U. S. Const. art. III, 2; and makes a demand for jury trial more than 30 days before the date this case is set for trial, in accordance with Tex.R.Civ.P. 216.

II.

Plaintiffs, JOHNNIE JONES and Wife, HARVELLA JONES, tenders the fee of $10.00 for district court, as required by Tex.R.Civ.P.216. Harris County has a population of over two million, and Plaintiffs add the additional fee of $20.00 for District Court, as required by Tex.Gov't.Code 51.604.

Respectfully submitted,

Johnnie Jones, Pro Se

Harvella Jones, Pro Se
Post Office 42265
Houston, Texas 77242-2265
(713) 952-0926

CHAPTER 11

270

NO. 95-01886

JOHNNIE JONES ANE WIFE, HARVELLA JONES	)))	IN THE DISTRICT COURT OF
Plaintiff	))	
VS.	))	HARRIS COUNTY, TEXAS
JEFFREY H. EWALT AND EWALT & DICKINSON	)))	
Defendant	)	269th JUDICIAL DISTRICT

ORDER ON PLAINTIFF'S MOTION TO COMPEL PRODUCTION

On the ____ day of _____, 1996, the court considered Plaintiffs' Johnnie Jones and Wife Harvella Jones's Motion to Compel Production. After considering the motion, response, and after a hearing on the motion and considering the arguments of counsel, the court

GRANTS the motion, orders the Defendants Jeffrey H. Ewalt and Ewalt & Dickinson to produce the documents to the Plaintiffs Johnnie Jones and Wife Harvella Jones's on or before _____ Aug 5 _____, 1996, and orders the Defendants Jeffrey H. Ewalt and Ewalt & Dickinson to pay the Plaintiffs' Johnnie Jones and Wife Harvella Jones's $_____ for attorney fees incurred in preparing the motion and attending the hearing .

SIGNED this 22 day of ___July___, 1996.

_____
PRESIDING JUDGE

CHAPTER 11

271

Post Office Box 42265
Houston, Texas 77242-2265

Home Phone (713) 952-0936

June 3, 1996

The Honorable David West
Judge, 269th District Court
Harris County District Court
301 Fannin/POB 4651
Houston, Texas 77210

Dear Honorable West:

Subject: Cause- 95-01886
           Johnnie Jones and wife Harvella Jones vs.
           Jeffrey H. Ewalt and Ewalt & Dickinson
           Harris County, Texas
           PLAINTIFF'S MOTION FOR CONTINUANCE AND AFFIDAVIT

Please file the following documents for the above subject cause:

____X____   Plaintiff's Motion for Continuance and Affidavit

                              Very truly yours,

                              Johnnie Jones

                              Harvella Jones
                              Harvella Jones

        cc: David B. Dickinson
             Attorney at Law
             Ewalt & Dickinson
             14614 Falling Creek Ste. 206
             Houston, Texas 77068

                    Not Required

                    Denied
                    WDW
                    6-10-96

Plain   CHAPTER 11

272

Cause No. 95-001886

JOHNNIE JONES AND WIFE, HARVELLA JONES	§ § §	IN THE DISTRICT COURT OF
VS.	§ § §	HARRIS COUNTY, TEXAS
JEFFREY H. EWALT AND EWALT & DICKINSON	§ §	269TH JUDICIAL DISTRICT

SUMMARY JUDGMENT

On September 9, 1996, the court heard defendants Jeffrey H. Ewalt and Dickinson & Ewalt's motion for summary judgment, which was filed in this court at least 21 days before the hearing on the motion. The parties appeared before the court for the hearing on the motion. After considering the pleadings, the motion, the response, and evidence on file, and arguments of counsel, the court grants the motion.

IT IS ORDERED that plaintiffs, Johnnie Jones and Harvella Jones, take nothing by their suit, that defendants, Jeffrey H. Ewalt and Ewalt &Dickinson, recover from plaintiffs, defendants' costs for defending this case, and that execution issue for those costs.

The court denies all relief not granted in this judgment.

SIGNED the _____9_____ day of September, 1996.

_____
JUDGE PRESIDING

CHAPTER 11

Cause No. ___95-01886___

Johnnie Jones
Harvella Jones   ) (IN THE DISTRICT COURTS OF

              vs.   ) (HARRIS COUNTY, TEXAS

Ewalt, Jeffrey H   ) (218th JUDICIAL DISTRICT

ORDER GRANTING MOTION TO RECUSE AND REFERRAL TO
PRESIDING JUDGE OF THE SECOND ADMINISTRATIVE JUDICIAL REGION

On ___Oct. 3, 1996___ came on to be considered a motion filed pursuant to Texas Rules of Civil Procedure 18a.

It is ORDERED that I voluntarily recuse myself and that this case is referred to the Presiding Judge of the Second Administrative Judicial Region for assignment to another Harris County judge pursuant to Texas Rules of Civil Procedure 18a.

Signed ___Oct 3___, 1996.

David West

Judge, _218th_ District Court

CHAPTER 11

ADMCRT01 Revised 4/18/96

274

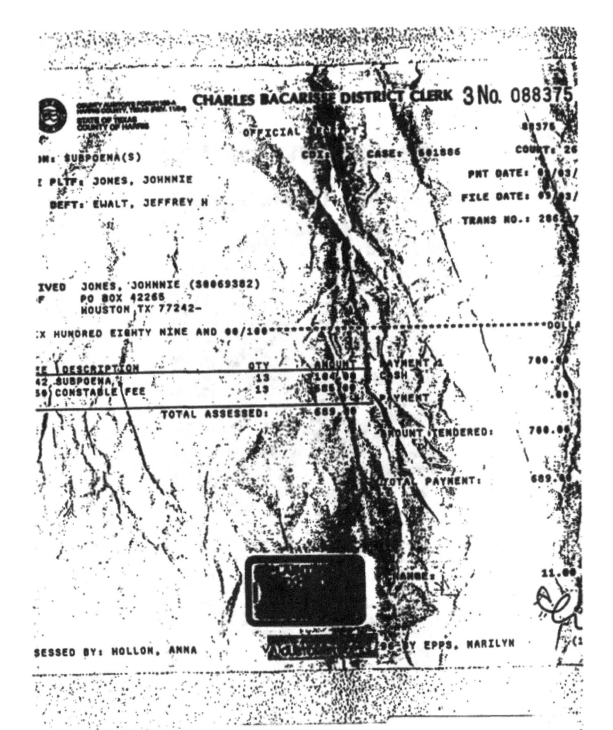

CHARLES BACARISSE DISTRICT CLERK 3 No. 088375

OFFICIAL RECEIPT

ON: SUBPOENA(S)   CDI: CASE: 661886   COUNT: 26

PLTF: JONES, JOHNNIE   PMT DATE: 03/03/

DEFT: EWALT, JEFFREY H   FILE DATE: 03/03/

                                                       TRANS NO.: 286217

IVED   JONES, JOHNNIE (S0069382)
F   PO BOX 42265
        HOUSTON, TX 77242-

:X HUNDRED EIGHTY NINE AND 00/100*********************************DOLLA

E DESCRIPTION	QTY	AMOUNT	PAYMENT		700.00
42 SUBPOENA	13	104.00	CASH		
50 CONSTABLE FEE	13	585.00	PAYMENT		.00
TOTAL ASSESSED:		689.00			

                                    AMOUNT TENDERED: 700.00

                                    TOTAL PAYMENT: 689.00

                                    CHANGE: 11.00

SESSED BY: HOLLON, ANNA   VAG   BY EPPS, MARILYN   (1

CHAPTER 11

By WALTER G. WORKMAN, JR.

More than 120 homeowners ... North Woodland Hills Village Community Association ...

The homeowners also voted in favor of reducing to 20 years from 25 years the time before the North Woodland Hills Village Community Association's declaration may be amended, and reduced the majority required for amendment from 75 to 66 percent.

... was purchased by the North Woodland Hills Community Association at a ... sale last month.

The property was foreclosed by the association after a three-year legal dispute over a $55 increase in the Joneses' assessment, which they say was illegal, and whether they could pay the assessment monthly rather than annually.

... legal battle is far from over.

The Joneses are scheduled to ... in a lawsuit against the North Woodland Hills Village Community Association May 8.

Five
furni CHAPTER 12

276

DATE: __October 18, 1995__

REQUEST FOR WRIT OF EXECUTION,
WRIT OF EXECUTION & ORDER OF SALE
OR WRIT OF POSSESSION

Please process this request to have:

_____ WRIT OF EXECUTION ISSUED

___X___ WRIT OF EXECUTION & ORDER OF SALE ISSUED

_____ WRIT OF POSSESSION ISSUED

Returnable in: _____ 30 days _____ 60 days ___X___ 90 days

Party requesting: ____Plaintiff____

Cause No: __92-23162__   Court: __215th__ Judicial District Court

Style____North Woodland Hills Village Community Association____

vs.___Johnnie Jones and Harvella Jones____

Date of Judgment: ____April 2, 1998____

Amount of Judgment: __$11,023.89 (plus court cost & interest at 10% per annum)__

County to be executed: __Harris__

Judgment Credit, if any: ____0____

Please mail this request to: Ewalt & Dickinson
                                 Law Firm

                                 Jeffrey H. Ewalt   06752700
                                 Attorney   Bar No.

                                 14614 Falling Creek, Sta. 206, Houston, Texas 77068
                                 Address

                                 444-9250
                                 Telephone No.

This request is made in accordance with the time frames set out in Rule 627 T.R.O.P.

Requested By:_____

CHAPTER 12

...dinner and holiday enter-tainment. Businesses in the downtown area will remain open late to accommodate shoppers."

gether," Walsh said.

Lennar, he says, agrees with those goals.

"The new owner sees value in Kingwood and doesn't plan to make any changes," Walsh said. "There is no specific plan by Lennar to do anything different than in the past. We will take the same approach and the same people will be in charge.

As far as Friendswood and its relationship with Kingwood is concerned, Walsh says the change in ownership is not as big an issue as the fact that Kingwood is almost built out.

"In anticipation of Friendswood

...vices must be found elsewhere.

Friendswood Development Company was chartered in 1988 as a wholly owned subsidiary of Humble Oil & Refining Co., now known as Exxon Company, U.S.A. The company employs 145 people.

Friendswood began development of Clear Lake City in 1962, Cypresswood in 1974, Kingwood in 1971, Deerfield Village in 1974 and Copperfield in 1979. Building in Cypresswood was completed in 1989. Deerfield was finished in 1991 and Copperfield in 1994.

More than 15,000 homes have been built in Kingwood to date.

☐ See LENNAR, page 10A

road a bit

but speed ...s will be

...ding the ...up if they ...here the ...mph?

...hief pros-Municipal ...fident they

...ists travel-...is week will ...the front-...tway 8 and

"All traffic will be diverted from the frontage road around the connector on Greens," she says. "This will affect north bound traffic only."

Anita Bostwick says the Sam Houston Tollway and Beltway 8 will not be affected by the speed limit increase.

"Our toll roads are under the jurisdiction of Harris County," she says. "We are doing a study looking into what would be appropriate for the tollway, but any change would have to be approved by Harris County Commissioner's Court."

507-05-2194

Foreclosed home purchased for $448

By WALKER C. WOODING JR.
Reporter

The North Woodland Hills Community Association has foreclosed on the home of Johnnie and Harvella Jones and purchased it for $448 at a constable's sale.

The sale took place last week at the Family Law Center in Houston.

The Joneses bought the property for $75,000 in 1989.

The property was foreclosed by the North Woodland Hills Community Association because the Joneses failed to pay $842 in assessment fees.

John Clifton, association president, who bought the property on behalf of the association, did not respond to requests for comment.

For the past three years, the Joneses have been locked in a legal dispute with the community association over a $55 increase in their assessment fee, which they claim is illegal, and whether they could pay the fee monthly rather than annually.

As a result of the dispute, they began withholding their association fees, and continued to do so despite court rulings that supported the association.

The Joneses have been given 30 days to vacate the home.

They say they will continue to fight.

"We had no notice to these maintenance fees at closing," the Joneses say. "We want homeowners to become aware of how their associations are being run and to read the wording of their declarations."

Dist. 11 State Sen. Jerry Patterson said he plans to introduce legislation that will give full disclosure to a homebuyer on foreclosure possibilities.

"No one should be able to voluntarily foreclose on a home because of maintenance fees without there being some notice of indication on their deed," said Patterson. "If a home can be foreclosed for the failure of paying maintenance fees, the homeowner needs to know that."

battle Moore

stee position

...es filed last ...r Position 6 ...ndent School ...stees, bring-... of challeng-...for the past ...ore.

Ron Webber, ...he Position 6 ...errero, Rami-...s, Dr. Mike ...ilson.

...nbent Lynn ...ditional chal-...final week of ...she will face

Robert Wanatick in the Jan. 30 election.

Early voting is scheduled from Dec. 29 through Jan. 16 from 8 a.m. to 4 p.m. Monday through Friday at the Humble ISD Curriculum and Staff Development Center, 611 Higgins, in Humble.

The candidates (in the order they will appear on the ballot):

Position 6

Natalie Guerrero, 18, Kingwood, student. Guerrero believes trustees should be in touch with student needs, which "can be accomplished only if the students are setting the agenda."

Lyn Reavis, 44, Humble, engineer/business analyst employed

☐ See SIX, page 10A

ELECTION

CHAPTER 12

Kingwood Sun, Wednesday, December 13, 1995
Vol. 54, No. 50

WOODLAND HILLS
COMMUNITY ASSOCIATION

2071

GUARANTY BANK

507-05-2192

RE: EXECUTION / ORDER OF SALE

STYLE: PLAINTIFF _____
DEFENDANT _____

CAUSE NO. 92-23162

CONSTABLE COSTS:

Levy and Return	$
Posting	$ 30.00
Deed/Bill of Sale	$ 12.00
Certified Mail	$ 6.00
Publication	$ 110.00
Miscellaneous	$ 26.92
TOTAL COST OWED	$ 184.92

Please remit costs to Constable Dick Moore at the address
shown above in care of the Writ Division. If there are any
questions, please call 320-32.

Deputy Constable

CHAPTER 12

ORDER ~~PAY OFF BID~~

TO HAND ON THE _9_ DAY OF _November_ A.D., 19 _85_ _1:57_ O'CLOCK _P_.M., AND EXECUTED IN HARRIS COUNTY, TEXA ON THE _5_ DAY OF _December_ A.D., 19 _85_ BY _Sale Held_ _Sold To Humbert Burgos, Plaintiff; And Cost Paid By Plaintiff._

612-00-219.

PRINCIPAL	$	
(PRE-JUDGMENT INTEREST)		
DATE @ _/_/_ TO _/_/_		DATE @ _/_/_ TO _/_/_
INTEREST	$	
(POST-JUDGMENT INTEREST)		
DATE @ _/_/_ TO _/_/_		DATE @ _/_/_ TO _/_/_
INTEREST	$	
ATTORNEY'S FEES	$	
DATE @ _/_/_ TO _/_/_		
INTEREST	$	
DETERMINING IDENTITY		$
TOTAL JUDGMENT		$
WRIT FEE (_HC-5/4870_)	$ _50_.00	
COMMISSION _Paid_	$ _26_.92	
CERTIFIED MAIL & POSTAGE	$ _6_.00	
POSTING	$ _30_.00	
DEED OR BILL OF SALE	$ _15_.00	
CONSTABLE'S TOTAL COST		$
COURT COST	$ _239_.00	
PUBLICATION	$ _110_.00	
MISCELLANEOUS COST	$	
TOTAL COST		$
TOTAL JUDGMENT AND COST		$
AMOUNT COLLECTED (RECEIPT NO. _____)		$
(DATE _____)		

AMOUNT BID OR COLLECTED	TOTAL COST	CREDIT TO JUDGMENT
$ _448_.00	$	$

PAY PLAINTIFF	$	
PAY DEFENDANT (REFUND)	$	
PAY CONSTABLE	$ _74_.92	
PAY PUBLICATION	$ _110_.00	
PAY TAX MASTER	$	
PAY DISTRICT CLERK	$	
TOTAL COLLECTED	$ _184_.92	

CONSTABLE OF
Pct. #4 Harr
6831 Cypress
Spring, Texa
(713) 350-

PLAINTIFF'S NAME _____

C/O _____

ADDRESS _____

DEPUTY _Wayne E. Toom_

CHAPTER 12

WALT & HAILEY
ATTORNEYS AT LAW

_____, Suite 1600, Houston, Texas 77057-5794, Telephone 713/780-4185, Telefax 713/780-4549

North Woodland Hills Village Community Assoc.   Client 00-023:
c/o Mr. Steve McFadden
P.O. Box 5050
Kingwood   TX 77235-5050

                    M A T T E R   S U M M A R Y

002 General - Deed Restrictions

        Invoice No. 0043374   90.79
        Total for Matter $ 90.'

003 General - Collections

        Invoice No. 0043375   264.11
        Total for Matter $ 264.:

001 Suit vs Johnnie & Harvella Jones (2026 Oak Shores)

        Invoice No. 0043376   300.79
        Total for Matter $ 300.'
        Advances Balance   231.00

        Total Due for All Matters $ 655.(

Check No. 1575   6/8/92 $655.69

CHAPTER 13

BUTLER, EWALT & HAILEY
ATTORNEYS AT LAW

718 Westheimer, Suite 1600, Houston, Texas 77087-5794, Telephone 713/780-4135, Telefax 713/780-4549

> North Woodland Hills Village Community Assoc.   Client 00-02339
  c/o Mr. Steve McFadden
  P.O. Box 5050
  Kingwood   TX 77235-5050

M A T T E R   S U M M A R Y

000-001-001 General - Corporate

06/19/92   Invoice No. 0043565   1.75
             Total for Matter
                                                              $ 1.75

000-001-002 General - Deed Restrictions

06/19/92   Invoice No. 0043566   326.85
             Total for Matter
                                                              $ 326.85

000-001-003 General - Collections

06/19/92   Invoice No. 0043567   561.83
             Total for Matter
                                                              $ 561.83

000-003-001 Suit vs Johnnie & Harvella Jones (2026 Oak Shores)

06/19/92   Invoice No. 0043568   26.50
             Total for Matter
                                                              $ 26.50

000-003-003 Suit vs Donald Kadner (2010 Lake Creek Dr.)

6/19/92   Invoice No. 0043569   257.00
             Total for Matter
             Advances Balance   53.00 $ 257.00

00-003-004 Suit vs Janice Wiederhold (2054 Aspen Glade Dr.)

Check No. 1583   6/10/92 $7,124.75

CHAPTER 13

282

JTLER, EWALT & HAILEY
TORREYS AT LAW

18 Westheimer, Suite 1600, Houston, Texas 77057-5794, Telephone 718/780-4188, Telefax 718/780-4549

Client 00-02335

North Woodland Hills Village Community Assoc.
c/o Mr. Steve McFadden
P.O. Box 5050
Kingwood   TX 77005-5050

MATTER SUMMARY

00-001-002 General - Deed Restrictions

4/26/93	Invoice No. 0052112	269.37		
	Total for Matter		$	269.3:

00-002-001 Suit vs Isenmann

4/26/93	Invoice No. 0052114	8.00		
	Total for Matter		$	8.0(

00-003-001 Suit vs Johnnie & Harvella Jones (2026 Oak Shores)

4/26/93	Invoice No. 0052115	2,038.73		
	Total for Matter		$	2,038.73

	Total Due for All Matters		$	2,316.10

1/26/93   Invoice No. 0052113   8.08
          TOTAL for Matter   8.08
                                             ─────────
                                             2,324.18

Check No. 1713   5/10/93 $2,324.18   ──

CHAPTER 13

BUTLER, EWALT & HAILEY
ATTORNEYS AT LAW

5718 Westheimer, Suite 1600, Houston, Texas 77057-5794.

02/24/92   Invoice   40165

North Woodland Hills Village Community Assoc.
c/o Mr. Steve McFadden
P.O. Box 5050
Kingwood   TX 77235-5050

Client No.   00-02339
Matter No.   000-001-001 General - Corporate

FOR LEGAL SERVICES RENDERED THROUGH
02/14/92

Received and reviewed the Complaint Form filed by
Mr. and Mrs. Johnnie Jones (2026 Oak Shores Dr.)
with the Attorney General's office citing numerous
issues concerning the Association's authority to
assess and collect assessments from
residents/owners within Woodland Hills Village.
Reviewed the Declaration of Restrictions for
Woodland Hills Village, Section Three (3) and Five
(5); the Annexation document of Section Five (5);
and, the Aritcles of Incorporation and Bylaws of
the Association in preparation of the required
Response to the complaints of the Jones'. Reviewed
the amounts of the annual assessments levied by
the Association for the years 1974 through 1992 to
confirm that the annual increases in the
assessments are in compliance with the provisions
of the Restrictions. Prepared a letter to Mr.
Steve McFadden to request his review of the
Association's records to verify a membership
meeting in 1980 increasing the 1981 annual
assessment by more than 5% of the 1980 assessment.
Prepared a Response to the Attorney General's
office addressing the complaints of Mr. and Mrs.
Jones. Telephone conference with Mr. Steve
McFadden to discuss the Assessment increase of

000001

CHAPTER 13

OFFICE OF THE ASSISTANT SECRETARY
FOR HOUSING-FEDERAL HOUSING COMMISSIONER

JUN 3 0 1997

Mrs. Harvella Jones
P.O. Box 42265
Houston, TX   77242

Dear Mrs. Jones:

Subject: Hotline Complaint Number FHOO-8519

I am replying to your letter dated June 20, 1997, concerning reinstatement of your complaint.

The complaint handled by this office was filed in 1996 as result of your letter dated February 28, 1996, addressed to the Inspector General HUD HOTLINE OIG. On March 1, 1996 it was received, recorded and became a permanent record in the Office of the Inspector General for Investigation.

On June 11, 1997, @ 4:00PM, you left a 30 seconds message for a member of my staff, Janice Moore, inquiring about the status of your case. This office was unaware of any other correspondence sent to this Department. Ms. Moore conducted a research of records and information surfaced, whereby we closed the case in our report to the Office of Inspector General On May 31, 1996, based on information provided by our Houston Field Office. That enabled us to respond to your complaint, regarding your letter of February 28, 1996. A copy of your original complaint is attached.

This office does not have the authority to assign case numbers nor change subjects for any case relating to the Hotline Complaint System. All of our caseloads are forwarded to us via the Office of Inspector General. However, your letter of June 20, 1997 and other documents have been referred to our Office of Lender Activities and Program Compliance. The contact person is Morris E. Carter, Director. Mr. Carter's number is (202) 708-1515, ext. 101. You should be hearing from Mr. Carter in the near future.

Sincerely,

Helen Stackhouse
Director, Management Control
Staff

Enclosure

CHAPTER 14

U. S. Department of Housing and Urban Development
Washington, D.C. 20410-8000

OFFICE OF THE ASSISTANT SECRETARY
FOR HOUSING-FEDERAL HOUSING COMMISSIONER

JUN 16 1997

Mrs. Harvella Jones
P.O. Box 42265
Houston, TX 77242

Dear Mrs. Jones:

Subject: Hotline Complaint Number FHOO-8519

This is in response to your complaint filed with the United States Department of Housing and Urban Development, Office of Inspector General for Investigation, regarding the problems that you are experiencing with the North Woodland Hills Village Community Association.

We contacted our program staff in the Houston Area Office and were provided with the following information: Woodland Hills Village, Section 5, Protective Covenants specifically refer to both Woodland Hills Trails Association and North Woodland Hills Village Community Association. Your home at 2026 Oak Shores Drive, Kingwood, Texas was endorsed on August 8, 1988. Through the closing procedure, you had actual or effective notice of the fact that there were two Homeowners Associations. In the Houston Area Office jurisdiction, there are large master planned communities. It is not unusual for large developments to be covered by two Homeowners Associations. Each HOA has a separate defined responsibility and collects fees accordingly. Therefore, homeowners are not paying double for the same services.

In Texas, HOA's are very aggressive in collecting fees and offer very limited flexibility when homowners refuse to make timely payments. It is generally known that fees should be paid first, and questions or complaints should be made later. The HOA is a first lien position unless they have agreed to subordinate. Even if they subordinate, they can still foreclose to recover the amount of fees due.

Based on the above research, we have determined that there were no violations of HUD rules or regulations.

CHAPTER 14

This letter concludes our review of this matter. The Office of Inspector General has been notified of our findings.

Thank you for bringing this matter to our attention.

Sincerely,

Helen Stackhouse
Director, Management Control
Staff

FH10-8519

Harvella Jones

Telephone (713) 917-2480

Post Office Box 42285
Houston, Texas 77242-2285

February 23, 1996

Inspector General
HUD HOTLINE, OIG
451 - Seventh Street S.W.
Washington, DC 20410

Dear Sir:

Subject: Suspected Fraudulent Acts by North Woodland Hills Village C.A.
and their attorney Jeffrey H. Ewalt Bar #56752700
(A suspected conspiracy to defraud Johnnie and Harvella Jones
of their house located at 2026 Oak Shores Drive - Kingwood, TX)

On August 4, 1998, my husband and I purchased a house at 2026 Oak Shores Drive,
Kingwood, Texas. It was not disclosed to us at that time that we would be obligated to
pay annual maintenance fees to two associations nor was it disclosed to us that if we did
not pay these fees, our house would be foreclosed by a homeowner's association.

Over the course of a few years, my husband and I became engaged in a nasty dispute with
both associations regarding our alleging they were assessing partially illegal fees. A court
has already verified that one of the associations--Woodland Hills Trails Association--is in
effect assessing a partially illegal fee assessed in 1985 and illegally being carried over from
year to year.

I am writing about the other association--No. Woodland Hills Village Community
Association--that foreclosed on us December 5, 1995 after a culmination of years of
trying to get this association to correct its illegal 1981 maintenance fee increase that they
refused to correct and after years of trying to get them to collect monthly as their
declaration indicates. I have enclosed a copy of their declaration and marked the
appropriate pages for your edification.

The association is in a second-lien position and it is now their responsibility to pay or
extinguish the deficiency they created with our lienholder--Leader Federal Bank, P. O.
Box 1860, Memphis, Tennessee 38101-1860. Our loan number was 8974909, property
address 2026 Oak Shores Drive, Kingwood, TX 77339 and their phone number is 1-800-

CHAPTER 14

Enclosure

322-9903. Ms. Diane Floyd, Collection Dept. or Jerry Hudson have been our main contact 1-800-392-3279 x 2107.

The intent of the association along with their attorney Jeffrey Ewalt was to collect attorney fees which we allege to be unreasonable. Jeffrey Ewalt started off being paid as he billed them but once it got to around $3,900, he switched to a contingency agreement. It is our contention that he has no contract which Texas Law is clear, contingent fees are permissible. However, such agreements must be in writing and must state the method by which the fee is to be determined (State Bar Rules, Art. 10 and 9, Rule 1.04(d); also Gov. C #82.065--contingent fee contracts must be in writing and must be signed by attorney and client. If different percentages are to be paid to the lawyer in the event of settlement, trial, or appeal, those percentages must be stated in the contract.

The association and their attorney Jeffrey Ewalt's intent when they foreclosed was to collect unreasonable fees as I stated before. We posted a $1,000 bond which had accrued interest and that money covered maintenance fees. The attorney refused to work with us to reduce the attorney fees. The association has not expended $12,000 in attorney fees, which is what they contend they have done in their Constable's Sale form (a copy has been included with this letter).

Although, the association and their attorney blocked every path we have taken to save our house and refused to hold off from the foreclosure until our lawsuit against them had been resolved (we were proposing an offset), their claim to foreclose and sell so that they could get their fees has dried up momentarily as they have refused to supply our lienholder with the title they received during the auction in which they bidded and bought the house for $448.00 but actually only paid $184.92. So in addition to our allegation that this association not only conspired with their attorney to defraud us out of our FHA house but also participated in a controlled bid (auction).

Since this association and its attorney are aware the association is in a second-lien position they know their legal obligation is to satisfy the first-lien holder. However, they have made a concerted effort to avoid giving the lienholder the title as they have requested so that they can convert the title in their name. This can be verified with Leader Federal Bank.

It is their (the association and their attorney)'s objective to have our lienholder foreclose on us so that they can then add their fees to the house and recoup. We were informed by the bank that Jeffrey Ewalt told them on January 3, 1996, that he would "pay them when he gets ready or they (you) can continue with foreclosure."

There was absolutely no reason to foreclose on us. Under the law (see the Declaration I have enclosed and marked to enable you to know what the law is for this association), my husband and I were entitled to demand the association comply with the Declaration. We are or were legally obligated to pay the fees raised in compliance with the declaration and had the legal right to challenge fees we alleged to be incorrect. Foreclosing is an alternative plan not a must plan. There is a remedy in the Declaration--you may make monthly payments. I have marked that section also for you in the Declaration.

289

It is our contention they used the foreclosure right they have here in Texas to shut us down and move us out of the neighborhood, so that we would not be able to carry out our lawsuit to force them to correct their maintenance fees and collection policy. With us out of the neighborhood, it would be business as usual for them.

This association along with many the other one in our old village - Woodland Hills Trails Association have for years been running their associations and raising and collecting fees not in compliance with their declarations. The Woodland Hills Trails Association in 1985 raised a fee that was illegally raised (I have enclosed a copy of their declaration and also I have enclosed the court's findings in a Findings of Fact and Conclusion of Law as well as a calculation of the fees--what they have been assessed since 1985 and what they should have been since 1985.) The North Woodland Hills Village Community Association that foreclosed on my husband and I raised their fee in 1981 not in compliance with the declaration. We have a lawsuit pending coming up for trial May 6, 1996, where this hopefully will be resolved as far as the issue of the 1981 fee and the fact they discriminated against us by allowing other Class A members pay monthly but not us and instead moved forward with their foreclosure proceedings.

Texas has not done a good job in protecting its homeowners in these planned communities. In fact, homeowners are virtually unaware that they have no homestead protection and that their home can be swept from underneath their feet by any meanspirited person that wants to do same.

What we have noticed and uncovered, if you will, is that District Court here in Houston, Texas, is kept very busy with numerous homeowner association filings that are being filed by a small nucleus of attorneys, Jeffrey Ewalt included, who help pushed through the law that allows them to foreclose on homesteads here and these attorneys are now benefiting from this law with the court's blessings.

What I find appalling is that the courts don't care about this abuse because they are benefiting from the filings of these lawsuits from a monetary standpoint. So seeking help from this entity has not been fruitful as it appears everyone or most everyone in the court system, the district court, is programmed to chew up and spit out the homeowner whenever one dare enter its doors for justice.

I am, therefore, seeking investigation from you. Because frankly I don't think this Federal Agency is aware of the homeowner association fraud that is taking place in Texas. It is one of our newest cottage industries. It needs to be investigated. Plan and simple, here is how it works, the attorney's seek out the most vulnerable associations that are run by aging, lazy and autocratic people who want to be important so they run for a homeowner's association office. Once they are in they reach out for a hammer--a slick attorney. This scam, this fraud, this circus would not be possible without the help of the board of directors. Once a strong, savvy lawyer who knows the clichés, the holes in the law, (and what better attorney than the ones who represented the legal committee and collectively wrote an amicus curiae and petitioned the Texas Supreme Court and passed a caselaw called Inwood vs. Harris 736 S.W.2d 632 (Tex. 1987) has been chosen, the association is ready for business. The business of refusing to allow annual assessments to be collected monthly. Banks and mortgage companies no long escrow maintenance fees since early

1980's because of the sloppy way in which the associations keep their books, so the associations in Kingwood, Texas and probably in some other communities, refused to collect uniformly monthly maintenance fees. What they do is pick and choose who they will allow to pay monthly and who they won't. That is what we got caught up in.

When the association refuses to collect monthly, basically what that does is force you into a default position if you are having other financial problems. When you default, (remember now you could have paid monthly but they wouldn't let you and if you could have paid monthly, you wouldn't have the acute situation you now have), by now the savvy, district court filing attorney has now come on the scene, oftentimes, they are already on the scene because the homeowner is unable to talk to a live board member and only the attorney is available, which lets you know, your attorney fee clock has already started to tick.

Once you have reached this stage, you can send in payments (they will more than likely be returned), you can show them what they have done wrong (it will be ignored) and you finally realize that you are as close to Nazi Germany as you will ever get because you have lost your rights to your property. Every single foreclosure proceeding gets appropriately $1,200 to $1,500 basic attorney fees attached to the maintenance fees and every knee-jerk reaction you make to try to save your property continues to cause the clock to tick.

If you have a strong fighting spirit, like my husband and I did, you get right up to the foreclosure door and if you have been luck enough to beg and borrow the money, you are now able to talk to the association through its attorney and settle this matter, of course, you also have a very large monthly payment to make whereas before you were not able to negotiate with the association to pay monthly.

We were assessed $12,000 against a $842.00 maintenance fee. Of course, we could not pay that amount, so we lost our house. Our attempt at a TRO (Temporary Restraining Order was a farce as well).

I feel like the man in the movie - the first version - "The Body Snatchers", they are planting pods everywhere or in this case "attorneys trained in the benefits of the Inwood Caselaw" everywhere and our property rights have been violated.

I must go outside the State for true justice in this situation and since FHA has guidelines and they are not being followed here in Texas--there is absolutely no disclosure that you can be foreclosed on by a homeowner's association if you don't pay your maintenance fees. Some of us, my husband and I for one, were not disclosed that you even have to pay annual maintenance fees (I mentioned this earlier).

In summation, foreclosure here in Texas is being abused. It is on an upswing. Have someone investigate the District Court computer system, pull those homeowner association screens, and you will see what I am talking about. I also have a lot of those screens copied and would be more than happy to share them with you if you so desire.

When occasionally a family such as my husband, children and I cannot come up with the money, and is foreclosed on, the association suddenly doesn't know what to do with the house they so dearly wanted. Although there is no Texas law demanding a certain time to file a title, the fact you don't file one in a certain amount of time, shed some light on the initial intent of the foreclosure.

It is a malicious, fraudulent process and it warrants a thorough investigation. I will be more than happy to help you in anyway that I can.

I look forward to a response to this letter and we also enclosed a copy of the actual statements pertaining to the attorney fees actually expended. There were only three responses filed after these bills accrued and Jeffrey Ewalt was on a contingency basis at that time. The statements that were paid enclosed total $3,912.04.

Very truly yours,

Harvella Jones

(Mrs) Harvella Jones

:j:enc.

DISTRICT ATTORNEY'S BUILDING
201 FANNIN, SUITE 200
HOUSTON, TEXAS 77002-1901

JOHN B. HOLMES, JR.
DISTRICT ATTORNEY
HARRIS COUNTY, TEXAS

October 26, 1995

COPY

Mark Markels
Patricia Quinn
Robert, Markel & Folger
24 Greenway Plaza Suite 2000
Houston, TX 77046

Dear Mr. Markels & Ms. Quinn:

This is to advise you that Johnnie and Harvell Jones came to this office complaining that you delivered documents to them in response to a court order that had been tampered with.

Conduct of this nature could constitute a criminal offense under the Texas Penal Code.

In the event that the above mentioned allegations are true and if this matter is not properly resolved, then our office will have no alternative than to refer this complaint to the appropriate police agency for investigation, and then following completion of that investigation, the appropriate action will be taken, including the possibility of filing criminal charges.

To resolved this problem please contact Mr. and Mrs. Jones within ten days from receipt of this letter to set up a time for them to come in to your office and compare their copies of the documents you provided them with to the originals.

Sincerely,

Caroline Dozier Merrill

Caroline Dozier Merrill
Assistant District Attorney
Community Services Section
Central Intake Division
(713) 755-7114

scl
c: Johnnie and Harvell Jones

CHAPTER 14

Judge,
Currently there is
only $150,000.00 plus
interest of $2,554.59
for a total of
152,554.59 in the
Registry. We cannot make
a payment of $201,304.68.

Kathleen Riska
Finance

Doc No. 9

CHAPTER 14

NO. 92-23162

NORTH WOODLAND HILLS VILLAGE COMMUNITY ASSOCIATION	)	IN THE DISTRICT COURT OF
Plaintiff	)	
vs.	)	HARRIS COUNTY, TEXAS
JOHNNIE JONES AND WIFE HARVELLA JONES	)	
Defendant	)	215 JUDICIAL DISTRICT

ORDER TO DETERMINE THE FAIR MARKET VALUE

On the 5 day of March, 1996, came on to be considered Defendant's Motion to Determine the Fair Market Value of the Real Property Lot 57 Block 37, Woodland Hills Village Section 5, as of the date of the foreclosure sale and the Court has determined after testimony; cost of sale and all evidence, the fair market value of the subject Real Property as of the date of the foreclosure sale on December 5, 1995, was determined to be $ 75,000.

IT IS, THEREFORE, ORDERED that the fair market value of the subject Real Property as of the date of the foreclosure sale on December 5, 1995, was $ 75,000.

SIGNED this 5 day of March, 1996.

JUDGE PRESIDING

CHAPTER 14

NO. 92-23162

NORTH WOODLAND HILLS VILLAGE)
COMMUNITY ASSOCIATION)
      IN THE DISTRICT OF HARRIS
      District Clerk
      Plaintiff)

      FEB 0 5 199.

      vs.)
      HARRIS COUNTY, Texas
JOHNNIE JONES and wife)
MARVELLA JONES)
      By_____ Deputy

      Defendant)
      215 JUDICIAL DISTRICT

MOTION TO DETERMINE THE FAIR MARKET VALUE

TO THE HONORABLE JUDGE OF SAID COURT:

    NOW COMES Plaintiff, JOHNNIE JONES and wife, MARVELLA JONES, who files this Motion to Determine the Fair Market Value of the Subject Real Property as of the Date of the Foreclosure Sale pursuant to Texas Property Code 51.005:

I.

    On December 5, 1995, Plaintiff NORTH WOODLAND HILLS VILLAGE COMMUNITY ASSOCIATION foreclosed on the property of the Defendant. Property Description is Lot 57, Block 37, Woodland Hills Village Section 5. The physical address is 2026 Oak Shores Drive, Kingwood, Texas 77339-1724.

II.

    On December 5, 1995, Plaintiff NORTH WOODLAND HILLS VILLAGE COMMUNITY ASSOCIATION purchased the property it foreclosed on at a Constable's Sale, at Court House Door of Harris County, Houston, Texas.

CHAPTER 14

State of Te

III.

Plaintiff NORTH WOODLAND HILLS VILLAGE COMMUNITY ASSOCIATION created a deficiency (the price at which the house was sold is less than the unpaid balance of the indebtedness secured by the real property). Property Code 51.004 (a) (2).

IV.

The purpose of this motion is to determine the fair market value of the real property as of the date of the foreclosure sale.

WHEREFORE, Defendant JOHNNIE JONES and wife HARVELLA JONES pray that the fair market value of the real property as of the date of the foreclosure sale be determined.

Respectfully submitted

Johnnie Jones, pro se

Harvella Jones, pro se
P. O. Box 2431
New Caney, Texas 77357-2431

297

DEC 0 7 1999

OFFICE OF THE ASSISTANT SECRETARY FOR
CONGRESSIONAL AND INTERGOVERNMENTAL RELATIONS

DEC 1 1999

The Honorable Kay Bailey Hutchison
United States Senator
10440 North Central Expressway, Suite 1160
LB 606
Dallas, TX   75231

Dear Senator Hutchison:

Thank you for your letter of November 2, 1999, on behalf of Mr. and Mrs. Johnnie Jones concerning the loss of their home through foreclosure.

I can certainly sympathize with the Jones' situation. However, this Department has no authority to investigate or overturn actions taken by any Court or homeowner associations even though it may affect an FHA-insured mortgage.

With respect to Union Planters Mortgage Corporation filing a claim with HUD due to the default and subsequent foreclosure of the FHA-insured mortgage on the property known as 2026 Oak Shores Drive in Houston, Texas, I offer the following explanation. In 1988, when the Jones' mortgage was originated, HUD entered into an agreement at that time which stated that HUD would insure the FHA-approved mortgage holder against loss should this mortgage go into default and subsequent foreclosure. This agreement remained in effect for the life of the mortgage. Therefore, after Union Planters foreclosed on the mortgage on April 15, 1996, under this agreement, Union Planters was within its rights to file a claim with HUD for any loss incurred in connection with this mortgage and HUD was obligated to pay the claim.

I hope the above information is helpful in responding to your constituents' inquiry. Please contact me if you need further assistance.

Sincerely,

Hal C. DeCell III
Assistant Secretary

CHAPTER 14

R851249

THE STATE OF TEXAS,
COUNTY OF HARRIS } *Know all men by these Presents*

THAT WHEREAS, by virtue of a certain execution and order of sale issued out of the ...

[document body largely illegible]

LOT 27, 28 BLOCK 27, WOODLAND HILLS VILLAGE, SECTION 3, BEING MORE COMMONLY KNOWN AS ... OAK SQUARE DR., KINGWOOD, HARRIS COUNTY, TEXAS.

CHAPTER 16

CHAPTER 16

ANY PROVISIONS HEREIN WHICH RESTRICT THE SALE, RENTAL, OR USE OF THE DESCRIBED REAL PROPERTY BECAUSE OF COLOR, OR RACE, IS INVALID AND UNENFORCEABLE UNDER THE FEDERAL LAW.

A CERTIFIED COPY

ATTEST: APR 0 4 1996
BEVERLY B. KAUFMAN, County Clerk
Harris County, Texas

_____, Deputy
SUSAN L. McPHERSON

Plaintiff's Exhibit 3!

507-72-0944

To have and to hold the above described land and premises unto the said _____
_____

heirs and assigns forever, as fully and as absolutely as I, as Constable, Precinct No. 4, of Harris County, Texas, can
convey by virtue of said order of sale.

In Testimony Whereof, I have hereunto set my hand, this _____ day of
_____, ____.

_____
Constable, Precinct No. 4, of Harris County, Texas

THE STATE OF TEXAS)
COUNTY OF HARRIS)

Before me, _____, a Notary Public
in and for Harris County, Texas, on this day personally appeared Dick Moore, Constable, Precinct No. 4, of Harris
County, Texas, known to me to be the person whose name is subscribed to the foregoing instrument, and
acknowledged to me that he executed the same as Constable, Precinct No. 4, of Harris County, Texas, for the
purposes and consideration, and in the capacity therein expressed.

Given under my hand and seal of office, this _____ day of _____.

_____
Notary Public in and for Harris County, Texas

MAR 29 1996

315

DEED
UNDER ORDER
OF SALE

A CERTIFIED COPY

ATTEST: _____APR 0 4 1996_____
BEVERLY B. KAUFMAN, County Clerk
Harris County, Texas

_____, Deputy
SUSAN L. McPHERSON

300

BARRETT BURKE WILSON
STLE DAFFIN & FRAPPIER, L.L.P.
A RETAINER INCLUDING
PROFESSIONAL CORPORATIONS

ATTORNEYS AND COUNSELORS AT LAW

STEPHEN C. PORTER
ATTORNEY AT LAW
LITIGATION DIVISION

6900 HILLCREST PLAZA DRIVE
SUITE 343
DALLAS, TEXAS 75230
TELEPHONE: 214-386-5040
TELECOPIER: 214-386-5043

March 22, 1996

Johnnie Jones
Hervella Jones
P.O. Box 2431
New Caney, TX 77357

Re: Leader Federal Bank for Savings
      Loan No. 897490-9
      Borrower: Jones
      Property Address: 2026 Oak Shores Drive
                          Kingwood, Texas 77339
      BBWCDF No. 96-0144-F-0052

Dear Borrowers:

As counsel for Leader Federal Bank for Savings, we are responding to your letter of 3/19/96.

The assertions stated in your letter that North Woodland Hills Village Community Association ("the Association") assumed the above indebtedness and that the foreclosure by the Association released you from liability on the loan are incorrect.

The title obtained by the Association by virtue of the constable's deed was acquired subject to the first lien held by Leader and that acquisition of title by the Association did not release you from liability on the above-referenced loan.

In verification of the debt, we are enclosing copies of the Promissory Note and Deed of Trust that you signed on 5/4/88.

Pursuant to the Federal Fair Debt Collection Practices Act , we advise you that this firm is a debt collector attempting to collect the indebtedness referred to in the above paragraphs and any information we obtain from you will be used for that purpose.

Sincerely yours,

Stephen C. Porter

SCP/srw
cc: Denise Neal (via fax 901/578-4880)
      Leader Federal Bank for Savings
      scp\leader\jones.b3

CHAPTER 16

IN THE UNITED STATES DISTRICT COURT
FOR THE SOUTHERN DISTRICT OF TEXAS
HOUSTON DIVISION

MAY 28 1996

MICHAEL N. MILBY, Clerk

JOHNNIE JONES, et ux.
         Plaintiffs

vs.

LEADER FEDERAL BANK FOR SAVINGS, et al.
         Defendants

NO. H-96-1385

ORDER

     Plaintiffs motion to dismiss the above-captioned case is granted, and

     It is Ordered that the above-captioned case is dismissed, without prejudice.

     SIGNED this the 16th day of May, 1996.

_____
United States District Judge

STATE OF TENNESSEE
COUNTY OF SHELBY

Before me the undersigned authority on this day personally appeared Denise Neal, Foreclosure Specialist for and on behalf of Leader Federal Bank for Savings, who, upon being duly sworn did testify and depose that she has read the foregoing answers to interrogatories and that the answers thereto are true and correct.

Denise Neal
DENISE NEAL, FORECLOSURE SPECIALIST
LEADER FEDERAL BANK FOR SAVINGS

Sworn to and subscribed before me, the undersigned authority on this the 2nd day of September, 199_, to which witness my hand and seal of office.

_____
Notary Public, State of Tennessee

_____
Printed Name of Notary
My commission expires: _____

Leader Federal Savings' Answers to Interrogatories Page 10

1

CHAPTER 16

```
T T=CMM' (=CNNNOO1A OPER=INQ    8/19/96 16:17:15 USERID=DNEAL

 l 8974909            UX  D F L I N Q U E N C Y  OWNR n/a 08/16/96  16:16:2)
  F.H.A.          MER/CLS/OFF F/ /97 AGE:  8Y  OM IR: 19.00000 INV: 705
 :( 9)    7,373.79  DUE 12/01/95(    )(11/13) ASSUM:           ACQ:02/01/95
 :E CHRG   294.93  PAYHT          819.31 P: 2026 OAK SHORES DR
 ) CK FEES    .00  L/C AMT         32.77  KINGWOOD TX 77339
 ER FEES     .00  PAYHT + LC      852.08 M:
 T DUE    7,668.72* PRIN BAL    71,583.34
 3PENSE      .00  P&I            464.98  POST OFFICE BOX 2431
 T DUE    7,668.72  DL.O  9 TIME,PAY 12 DAY  NEW CANEY TX 77357
 HNNIE JONES
 RVELLA JONES
                     ── * ADDITIONAL MESSAGES * ────────────────────
 ──────────────────────          AEGIS CODE = ' '
 SSING TELEPHONE NO               CASHIER STOP 5
 ESS PF14 FOR MEMOS  ───────────── * COMMENTS * ─────────────────── ─
 :CH2──────────────────────────── * COMMENTS * ────────────────────
 MTE USR        CONTACT   RESPONSE  REASON        RECALL   'F/B  REMIND
                                                        :              MMDDP6
 10396 GAB (JEFF EWALT WAS TO CALL ASSN TO SEE WHAT THEY WANTED)
             (TO DO.                                          )
 10396 GAB (DO NOT CALL JONES' CALL JEFF EWALT ATTY 713-444-  )
             (9250 AND SEE COMMENTS AS OF THIS DATE.....       )
 10396 GAB TEL BUS HE
```

CHAPTER 16

CHAPTER 16

T=CNVP L=CNMB0016 OPER=IMO   8/19/96 16:17:08 USERID=DMEAL

8974909   OX   D E L I N Q U E N C Y   OWNR n/a 08/16/96 16:16:29)
F.H.A.   PER/CLS/OFF   F/ /97   AGE: BY OM IR: 10.00000 INV: 70')
    9)   7,373.79 DUE 12/01/95(   )(11/13) ASSUM: ACQ:02/01/95
CHRG   294.93 PAYMT   819.31 P: 2026 OAK SHORES DR
CK FEES   .00 L/C AMT   32.77   KINGWOOD TX 77339
R FEES   .00 PAYMT + LC   852.08 M:
DUE   7,668.72 PRIN BAL   71,583.34
ENSE   .00 P&I   644.98   POST OFFICE BOX 2431
DUE   7,668.72 DLQ   9 TIME,PAY 12 DAY   NEW CANEY TX 77357
NIE JONES
ELLA JONES

------------------------ * ADDITIONAL MESSAGES * ------------------------
                                     AEGIS CODE = * *
SING TELEPHONE NO   CASHIER STOP S
SS PF14 FOR MEMOS
------------------------------ * COMMENTS * ------------------------------
#2
TE USR   CONTACT RESPONSE REASON   RECALL   -F/B REMIND
                                                                  MMDDYY
0396 OAB (CAN YOU DO BUT F/C ON PROP AGAIN HE WANTED NAME OF)
         (SOMEONE RATHER THAN JUST A COLLECTOR TO CALL BACK)
         (GAVE CM NAME AND EXT. TAKING JONES PHONE N OFF SYST)
0396 OAB HE TEL OFC
0396 OAB (HE SD HE WAS PUT OUT OF PROP 12/5 HE SD FHA TLD HIM)

```
r T=CNVP L=CNM00016 OPER=1MD    8/19/9A 16:16:59 USERID=DNEAL

                    DX   D E L I N Q U E N C Y   OWNR n/a 08/16/96  16:16:2?)
L 8974909           ----    PCR/CLS/OFF  F/  /97  AGE:  8Y  OM IR: 10.00000 INV: 705
F.H.A.                      PCR/CLS/OFF  F/  /97  AGE:  8Y  OM IR: 10.00000 INV: 705
( 9)      7,373.79  DUC 12/01/95(   )(11/13)  ASSUM:          ACQ:02/01/95
I CHRG      294.V3  PAYMT          819.31 P: 2026 OAK SHORES DR
 CK FEES       .00  L/C AMT         32.77  KINGWOOD TX 77339
ER FEES       .00  PAYMT + LC     452.08 M:
  DUE     7,668.72" PRIN BAL   71,583.34
PENSE         .00  P&I             664.98  POST OFFICE BOX 2431
  DUE     7,668.72  DLQ  9 TIME,PAY 12 DAY  NEW CANEY TX 77357
NNIE JONES
NELLA JONES

------------------------------ * ADDITIONAL MESSAGES * ------------------------------
                                    AEGIS CODE = " "
SING TELEPHONE NO                   CASHIER STOP 5
SS PF14 FOR MEMOS
-------------------------------------* COMMENTS *-----------------------------------
M2
TE  USR         CONTACT  RESPONSE  REASON        RECALL      F/B  REMIND
                ----     ----      ---           --'---      ---------  MMDD96

296 GAB  SHE TEL OFC
0296 GAB (SHE SD WAS F/C ON 12/5 AS PER MEMO SCREEN I CLD RL )
0296 GAB (IN INS AND THEY SD ALL WAS SENT TO F/C I CLD F/C  )
         (AND THEY SD NEVER GOT INFO AND IF THEY DID THEY WLD)
0296 GAB (SEND TO ASSUMP DEPT TO HAVE NAME CHANGED...........)
```

CHAPTER 16

T=CMUP L=CNM80016 OPER=INO   8/19/96 16:17:02 USERID=DNEAL

: 8974909   QX D E L I N Q U E N C Y OWNR n/a 08/16/96 16:16:20)
F.H.A.   PER/CLS/OFF F/ /97 AGE: 8Y OM IR: 10.00000 INV: 70M
(9)   7,373.79 DUE 12/01/95(   )(11/13) ASSUM: ACQ:02/01/95
: CHRG   294.93 PAYMT   819.31 P: 2026 OAK SHORES DR
CK FECS   .00 L/C AMT   32.77   KINGWOOD TX 77339
2R FEES   .00 PAYMT + LC   852.08 M:
  DUE   7,668.72* PRIN BAL   71,583.34
PENSE   .00 P&I   664.98   POST OFFICE BOX 2431
  DUE   7,668.72 DLQ 9 TIME,PAY 12 DAY   NEW CANEY TX 77357
MMIE JONES
VELLA JONES

---------------------------- * ADDITIONAL MESSAGES * ----------------------------
                              AEGIS CODE = * *
SINO TELEPHONE NO   CASHIER STOP 5
38 PF14 FOR MEMOS
M2-------------------------------* COMMENTS *-------------------------------------
ITE USR   CONTACT RESPONSE REASON   RECALL   F/B REMIND
                  ---   ---   ---   __1__   MMDDY6
)296 GAA TEL RES   INCORRECT PH NO.
)296 GAB (PER CM MRS WL HAVE TO KEEP CURRENT UNLESS WOODLAND)
         (HILLS REQUESTS NAME CHANGED DUE TO F/C 12/5/95   )
         (CUST IS STILL RESPONSIBLE FOR PMTS   )
)296 GAB SHE TEL OFC

CHAPTER 16   000050

308

```
NT T=CMVP L=CNN00016 OPER=IHG    8/19/96 16:17:27 USERID=DNEAL.

.J1 8974909              OX  D E L I N Q U E N C Y  OWNR n/a 08/16/96  16:16:20
L F.H.A.                PER/CLS/OFF  F/  /97  AGE:   BY  OM IR: 10.00000 INV: 70S
JE( 9)       7,373.79  DUE 12/01/95(       )(11/13)  ASSUM:            ACQ:02/01/95
NTE CHRG       294.93  PAYMT                819.31 P: 2026 OAK SHORES DR
AD CK FEES       .00   L/C AMT               32.77  KINGWOOD TX 77339
THER FEES        .00   PAYMT + LC           852.08 M:
JT DUE       7,668.72* PRIN BAL          71,583.34
USPENSE          .00   P&I                  664.98   POST OFFICE BOX 2431
ET DUE       7,668.72  DLQ  9 TIME,PAY 12 DAY        NEW CANEY TX 77357
OHNNIE JONES
ARVELLA JONES

------------------------------- * ADDITIONAL MESSAGES * -----------------------------
ISSING TELEPHONE NO                      AEGIS CODE = " "
RESS PF14 FOR MEMOS                      CASHIER STOP 5
COM2--------------------------------# COMMENTS *---------------------------------
DATE  USR           CONTACT   RESPONSE   REASON        RECALL      · F/B  REMIND
                                                                          MMDC96
·12996 GBY (THE INFO CKED W/CARDESTER SHE SD THAT MR SHOULD FAX)  )
            (INFO TO RAYELYNN
·12696 GAF SHE TEL OFC                                            )
·12696 GAF (THIS HOME WAS FORECLOSED ON BY AN ASSOCIATION CO      )
            (SHE WILL SEND US TRANSFER OF TITLE                   )
```

CHAPTER 16

000067

309

```
NT T=CMVP L=CMN80016 OPER=IND    8/19/96 16:17:58 USERID=DNEAL

11 8974909       ____ GX   D E L I N Q U E N C Y   OWNR n/a 08/16/96  16:16:20
  F.H.A.             PER/CLS/OFF  F/  /97  AGE:  8Y  OH IR: 10.00000 INV: 705
E( 9)    7,373.79  DUE 12/01/95(    )(11/13)  ASSUM:            ACQ:02/01/95
TE CHRG    294.93  PAYMT          819.31 P: 2026 OAK SHORES DR
D CK FEES     .00  L/C AMT         32.77    KINGWOOD TX 77339
HER FEES      .00  PAYMT + LC     852.08 M:
T DUE    7,668.72* PRIN BAL    71,583.34
SPENSE        .00  P&I            664.98    POST OFFICE BOX 2431
T DUE    7,668.72  DLQ  9 TIME,PAY 12 DAY   NEW CANEY TX 77357
HMMIE JONES
RVELLA JONES

-------------------------- * ADDITIONAL MESSAGES * ----------------------------
SSING TELEPHONE NO                  AEGIS CODE = " "
:ESS PF14 FOR MEMOS                 CASHIER STOP 5
CM2---------------------------* COMMENTS *------------------------------
ATE  USR          CONTACT   RESPONSE   REASON        RECALL      F/B  RE-IND
                    ---       ---        ---          --1--      ------- MMID96
!1496 GAJ SHE TEL OFC
!1496 GAJ (SD THAT SHE WENT TO SHERIFF'S OFFICE AND HE SD THAT)
          (HE WAS ORDERED NOT TO GIVE HERE DEED.SD SPOKE WITH )
          (AN ATTY WITH FHA AND SD THAT WE CAN DO SOMETHING   )
!1496 GAJ (OTHER THAN GET DEED FROM THEM TO GET THIS PUT IN TH)
```

```
IT T=CNMR L=CNNB0016 OPER=INQ    8/19/96 16:17:56 USERID=DNEAL

I1 0974909        --- QX   D E L I N Q U E N C Y  OWNR n/a 08/16/96 16:16:20
  F.H.A.                   PER/CLS/OFF  F/  /97 AGE:  BY  OH IR: 10.00000 INV: 705
:( 9)      7,373.79  DUE 12/01/95(    )(11/13) ASSUM:             ACQ:02/01/95
'E CHRG      294.93  PAYMT             819.31 P: 2026 OAK SHORES DR
) CK FEES      .00  L/C AMT             32.77   KINGWOOD TX 77339
 ER FEES      .00  PAYMT + LC         852.08 M:
! DUE      7,668.72* PRIM BAL       71,583.34
 SPENSE       .00  P&I                664.98   POST OFFICE BOX 2431
 f DUE     7,668.72  DLQ  9 TIME,PAY 12 DAY    NEW CANEY TX 77357
 ANNIE JONES
 MILLA JONES

--------------------------------- * ADDITIONAL MESSAGES * ---------------------------------
 SSING TELEPHONE NO                AEGIS CODE = " "
 ESS PF14 FOR MEMOS                CASHIER STOP 5
 OM2--------------------------* COMMENTS *------------------------------------------
 ATE  USR        CONTACT   RESPONSE  REASON         RECALL        F/8  REFIND
                                                                        MHED96
 1496 GAJ (OTHER THAN GET DEED FROM THEM TO GET THIS PUT IN TH)
          (E HOMEOWNER'S ASSOC NAME.OV NOTE TO D F            )
 1496 GBF CERT CARD RET
 1396 GAJ SHE TEL OFC
 1396 GAJ (SD THAT HOMEOWNERS'ASSOC FORECLOSED ON PROP AND     )
```

CHAPTER 16

```
8974909                    FORECLOSURE PROCESS NOTES              08/16/96   16:18:20
                                                                                FC E
3HES      MAN F    INV 703/400/261758CHC1    TYPE F.H.A.
26      OAK SHOREE DR    KINGWOOD                  TX 77337    FHNN 703 493-443230
------------------------------- PROCESS NOTES ---------------------------------
1/96   14:58:18 RE3   GAVE ALL FILES TO HM
1/96   13:53:08 GCN   FAXED TO ATY ON  5-30 TO RECORD DEED TO HUD,RCD
                      CONF TODAY,CAROL FNN W/FAX 1ST UNC**FLS GVN TO POS
8/96   09:54:04 GDW   SENT REQ 2 FNN 2 DO FINAL..
9/96   08:41:27 GCN   OV ACTS PYBL BBW INV #17898 $572.49
5/96   10:10:41 GCN   FAXED TO FNN FOR STAT ON FNL..
14/96   08:37:54 GCN   OV ACTS PYBL FNN INV #635492 620.00& INV #72314
                      $45.00
14/96   16:34:03 GDW   SENT REQ 2 FNN 2 DO FINAL MAIN FOR FHA CONVEYANCE.
14/96   13:31:37 OCN   SL HELD TO LEADER 5-7 $76163.40,REO SHEET TO ACTN
                      FNL IN PROCESS..
11/96   07:36:43 GDW   MAILED PAYMENT $494.00 INVOICE #68724 TO FNN.
29/96   16:17:45 BDL   MAST FILE W/ORIG MIC TO BBU...SL.
29/96   12:41:40 GDW   SENT SALE DATE INSPEC REQ 2 FNN.
29/96   11:25:06 GCN   FAXED ATY BID FOR 5-7 SL & REQ SL DATE INSP..
25/96   16:16:53 GDU   RET GEN WARR DEED TO ATTY
25/96   13:03:16 GCD   DEREK HANKINS W/HUD CLD FOR STATUS ON FILE...DN
22/96   15:12:34 OCN   CLD ATY FEES THRU 5-6-96 $372.49 PER SHAE..
'16/96   11:38:07 GCB   SNT EXEC APPT OF SUBST TRUSTEE TO BBW; CY TO FILE
```

CHAPTER 16

000089

312

FORECLOSURE PROCESS NOTES   08/16/96 16:18:30
8974909   FC 8
NES   MAN F   INV 705/400/261758CNC1 TYPE F.H.A.
6   OAK SHORES DR   KINGWOOD   TX 77339   FHAN 703 493-443230
-----------------------# PROCESS NOTES #------------------------
/96 12:29:25 GCN   GV ACTS PYBL FNN INV #74326 $35.00
/96 16:48:47 RE3   RECD PARTIAL ADV OF PYMT-GV TO SPECIALIST
)/96 15:26:38 GCI   PD FNN BILL $20.00
)/96 15:26:21 GCI   PF FNN BILL $45.00
5/96 15:57:01 GCR   SENT HUD PKG TO TX CERTIFIED MAIL; PLACED ALL COPI
                     ES N FLS, PUT FLS N CAROL'S OFFICE BX #33
                     F/C FL & PT A TO ASST TO SND OUT LOCAL HUD PKG
5/96 13:18:56 GDF   FAXED ATTY OC'D COPY OF PART A FOR TITLE PACKAGE.
5/96 13:18:54 GDF   SENT HUD PKG TO WASH
4/96 15:31:17 RE3   GAVE FINAL PRT-A TO CN/////////////////
4/96 10:13:22 GDF   //FL & CLM TO SPEC FOR CORRECTIONS &/OR REPRINT///
4/96 08:17:00 GCK   ###LN REVIEWED BY POST F/C SUPRVSR###############CN
4/96 07:12:30 GCK   PER MEM1 STATES COMM. ASSN FORECLOSED 12-1-95 BUT
                     LFB LIEN SUPERIOR-THEIR F/C SL WS FOR $12K+   THIS
                     MAY CREATE A PROBLEM WHEN IT COMES TIME TO GET
                     TITLE POLICY ISSUED..................IF BBW DID
                     THS F/C & NOT MAKE SURE LFB WS CLEAN ON THIS F/C
                     LFB SHLD PASS ANY LOSSES ON TO BBW/DISCUSSED W-SL
)3/96 14:28:35 GDF GAVE PRT-A TO CN/////////////////

313

Mortgage Insurance Certificate

U.S. Department of Housing and Urban Development
Federal Housing Commissioner

CLAS
DUPLICATE

1. FHA Case Number:	2. ADP Code	3. Amortization Plan	4. Program I.O.	5. LTV Ratio	6. Borrower Type	7. Living Units	8. Control Number
493-4432309	703		00	95.60	1	01	0323444971

1. Name of Mortgagor (last, first, MI):	10. Social Security Number	11. Mortgage Amount	12. Interest rate	13. Monthly Payment (P&I)
JONES, JOHNNIE	████████	$ 75774	10.000 %	$ 664.38

4. Name of Co-Mortgagor (last, first, MI):	15. Social Security Number	16. Maturity Date	17. First Payment	18. Endorsement Date
JONES, HARVELLA	████████	09/18	10/88	09/08/88

3. Address of Property

2026 OAK SHORES DR   KINGWOOD   TX 773390000

1. Mortgagee's Name, Address, & ID Number:

5107701167
LUMBERMENS INVESTMENT CORP TX
C/O LEADER FEDERAL BANK FOR SA
P O BOX 275
MEMPHIS, TN 38101-0275

Beth

Endorsed for insurance when signed below by an authorized agent of the Federal Housing Commissioner (see back).
A copy of this certificate must accompany any claim for insurance benefits submitted to HUD/FHA.

X _Jo Harr_

previous editions are obsolete

8 974909

form HUD-59100 (4/90)
ref. Handbook 4115.3

314

RESIDENTIAL

LISTINGS FOR FORECLOSURE SALE ON MAY 7, 1996

NORTHEAST

NORTHEAST

KINGWOOD

HOUSTON

CHAPTER 16

Plc

316

TO: Diane Floyd

FROM: Angela Richardson

DATE: February 12, 1996

RE: Loan Number   897490-9

Please see the attached documents on the above referenced
loan. This loan is due for December 1, 1995. The
Homeowners's Association apparently foreclosed on the
owners for failure to pay homeowner's dues. However, we
have not been provided any deed conveying title to the
Homeowner's Association. Both parties refuse to be
responsible for this loan. The collection comments appear
to indicate all this. We can do nothing else, at this
time until we receive a transfer deed.

Mr. John C. Clifton is president of the North Woodland
Hills Village Community Association. He has indicated
that the Association was awarded the property in a sale.
He had the locks and the property secured. He informed us
that Leader then had someone come back out to change the
locks. Only the front lock was changed and the back door
was left wide open. Mr Clifton has now had the locks
changed again. He wants reimbursement for this and wants
someone to contact him. He can be reached at:

   phone #'s (713) 635-0871 or 358-8312

   Address: 2170 River Village
             Kingwood, Tx   77339

CHAPTER 16

Plaintij

318

LE FAMILY APPLICATION . DEPARTMENT OF HOUSING
INSURANCE BENEFITS AND URBAN DEVELOPMENT
OFFICE OF FINANCE AND ACCOUNTING

| LAIM TYPE | | | 12. FHA CASE NUMBER |
|)1 - CONVEYANCE | | | 493-4482909 |

| ECT OF ACT CODE | 14. DEFAULT REASON CODE | 15. ENDORSEMENT DATE | 16. DATE FORM PREPARED |
|)09 | 07 | 09-08-88 | 05-30-96 |

| UE DATE OF 1ST PMT | 18. DUE DATE OF LAST PD | 17. TITLE DATE | 110. DEED/ASSGN'T DATE |
| 0-01-88 | 11-01-95 | 05-14-96 | 05-30-96 |

| DATE FC INSTITUTED | 112. HOLDING MTG NO | 119. SERVICING MTG NO | 114. MORTGAGEE REF NO |
| 04-15-96 | 4904409994 | 4904409994 | 8974909 |

| ORIGINAL MTG AMT | 116. HOLDING MTG EIN | 117. UNPAID LOAN BALANCE | 18. DATE OF COMMITMENT |
| 75,774 | | 71,589.34 | |

| EXTENSION EXP DATE | 120. NOTICE/EXT-CONVEY | 121. RELEASE OF BKP | 122. IS PROPERTY VACANT? |
| | | | YES |

| HUD APPROVAL | 124. CONVEYED DAMAGED? | 125A. HUD APPROVAL | 125B. CERTIFICATION |
| | NO | | |

| TYPE OF DAMAGE: | | | 127. ESTIMATE OF DAMAGE: |

| IS MTGE BIDDER? | 129. DEFICIENCY JDG | 130. AUTHORIZED BID AMT | 131. RPTD CURTAILMENT DT |

SCHEDULE OF TAX INFORMATION

YEAR	TYPE OF TAX	COLLECTOR'S PROPERTY ID	AMT PAID	--PERIOD COVERED-- FROM	TO	DATE PAID
	CNTY TAX	EXEMPT 94 07 690 000 0057	.00	12-95	12-96	12-95
	SCHO TAX	1076900000057	544.64	12-95	12-96	12-95
	HUD TAX	1076900000057	482.76	12-95	12-96	12-95

MORTGAGOR'S NAME AND PROPERTY ADDRESS | 194. BRIEF LEGAL DESCRIPTION OF PROPERTY

CHNNIE JONES MARVELLA JONES
024 OAK SHORES DR
INGWOOD TX 77339

LOT - 57
BLOCK - 37
SECTION -
SUBDIVISION - WOODLAND HILLS VILLAGE

IFICATION: THE UNDERSIGNED AGREES THAT IN THE EVENT OF DAMAGE BY FIRE (EXCEPT AS OTHERWISE
IDED IN SECTION 203.379(B) OF THE HUD REGULATIONS); FLOOD, EARTHQUAKE, TORNADO, OR BOILER
OSION, IF APPLICABLE, THE SECRETARY MAY DEDUCT FROM THE SETTLEMENT TO BE MADE TO THE
GAGEE AN AMOUNT COMPUTED IN ACCORDANCE WITH THE APPLICABLE HUD REGULATIONS. THE UNDERSIGNED
HER AGREES: 1) THAT IN THE EVENT THE SECRETARY FINDS IT NECESSARY TO RECONVEY THE ABOVE
RIBED PROPERTY TO THE MORTGAGEE, BECAUSE OF THE MORTGAGEE'S NONCOMPLIANCE WITH HUD
LATIONS, THE MORTGAGEE SHALL REIMBURSE THE SECRETARY FOR ANY SETTLEMENT MADE IN DEBENTURES
OR CASH AND FOR ALL CASH DISBURSEMENTS, INCLUDING THOSE FOR REPAIRS AND REHABILITATION OF
PROPERTY, MADE BY THE SECRETARY; 2) THAT IF A MORTGAGEE DOES NOT COMPLY WITH HUD
LATIONS, THE MORTGAGEE REMAINS RESPONSIBLE FOR THE PROPERTY, AND ANY LOSS OR DAMAGE THERETO,
ITHSTANDING THE FILING OF THE DEED TO THE SECRETARY FOR THE RECORD, AND SUCH RESPONSIBILITY
ETAINED BY THE MORTGAGEE UNTIL HUD REGULATIONS HAVE BEEN FULLY COMPLIED WITH (203.379).

ING: "FEDERAL STATUTES PROVIDE SEVERE PENALTIES FOR ANY FRAUD, INTENTIONAL MISREPRESEN-
ON, OR CRIMINAL CONNIVANCE OR CONSPIRACY PURPOSED TO INFLUENCE THE PAYMENT OR ALLOWANCE OF
CLAIM OR BENEFIT BY THE FEDERAL GOVERNMENT."

IGNING BELOW THE UNDERSIGNED CERTIFIES THAT THE STATEMENTS AND INFORMATION CONTAINED HEREON
H PARTS) ARE TRUE AND CORRECT.

NAME AND ADDRESS OF MORTGAGEE	136. NAME AND ADDRESS OF MORTGAGEE'S SERVICER
EADER FEDERAL BANK	
ORECLOSURE DEPARTMENT	
.O. BOX 1860	
EMPHIS, TENNESSEE 38101-1860	

| MORTGAGEE OFFICIAL SIGNATURE, DATE, TITLE | 138. SERVICER SIGNATURE, DATE, TITLE |

ORECLOSURE SPECIALIST 901-373-2243 05-30-96

. TO: DEPARTMENT OF HOUSING AND URBAN DEVELOPMENT OFA-INSURANCE CLAIMS DIVISION

PART A HUD-27011 (12-84)

CHAPTER 16

100031

E FAMILY APPLICATION   S. DEPARTMENT OF HOUSING
NSURANCE BENEFITS   AND URBAN DEVELOPMENT

OFFICE OF FINANCE AND ACCOUNTING

NUATION OF APPLICATION

MOUNT OF MONTHLY PAYMENT TO:
A INSURANCE |B. TAXES |C. HAZARD INSURANCE |D. INTEREST & PRINCIPAL

DATE BANKRUPTCY	41. IF CONVEYED DAMAGED	42. DATE HIP CANCELLED	43. NUMBER OF LIVING
ILED	DATE OF OCCURANCE	OF REFUSED	UNITS
			1

TATUS OF LIVING UNITS

#1 A. CANT		B. DATE VACATED 01-29-96		C. DATE SECURED 02-06-96
#2 A.		B. DATE VACATED		C. DATE SECURED
#3 A.		B. DATE VACATED		C. DATE SECURED
#4 A.		B. DATE VACATED		C. DATE SECURED

AGEE'S COMMENTS IF ANY
==========================

RED TO ATTY 2-28-96

ZGAL / NOTICE OF SALE 4-15-96

LOSURE SALE 5-7-96

EE DEED 5-14-96

SENT FOR RECORDING 5-30-96

====================

ER MORGAN 901-578-2231

COMMENTS IF ANY

FAX COVER SHEET

Date: 5/6/97   Time: 3:20

Office of Insured Single Family Housing Facsimile Machine
(202) 708-5966

To: Mrs. Harvella Jones

Recipient's phone: (713) 952-0926

From: Leslie Bromer *LmB*
(202) 708-1719

U.S. Department of Housing
and Urban Development
Insured Servicing Branch
Room 9180
451 7th Street, SW
Washington, DC 20410

Subject: FHA 493-4432309
Foreclosure of 2026 Oak Shores Drive
Houston, TX 77339

This fax will confirm our telephone conversation regarding the subject case.

I received the documentation you provided which confirmed that you were <u>not</u> in default of the FHA-insured mortgage at the time that your homeowners association took title through foreclosure in December 1995.

I therefore, have suppressed the Credit Alert reporting which resulted from the subsequent foreclosure of the mortgaged property by Leader Federal (now Union Planters).

As I mentioned, Leader Federal was entitled to receive claim benefits from HUD because of the subsequent default by the new owner of the property, the homeowners association. HUD will review the foreclosure and claim process followed by Leader Federal and if a deficiency is found, appropriate action will be taken.

CHAPTER 16

Comptroller of the Currency
Administrator of National Banks

Washington, DC 20219

April 29, 1998

Mr. Johnnie Jones
Ms. Harvella Jones
Post Office Box 42265
Houston, Texas 77242-2265

Dear Mr. and Ms. Jones:

The Office of the Comptroller of the Currency (OCC) is responding to your correspondence, referred to us by the Office of Thrift Supervision, regarding a mortgage loan held with Union Planters Mortgage, a division of Union Planters National Bank, Memphis, Tennessee. You request assistance in this matter.

The OCC contacted the bank in your behalf and was advised that the matter was resolved in the District Court of Harris County, Texas in favor of the bank. The bank further advised that you have appealed the decision in the United States District Court in Texas, Southern District. Inasmuch as your concerns are being litigated, OCC can provide no further assistance in this matter. As an administrative/regulatory agency of the federal government, the OCC has no authority to intervene in matters which are pending, or which have been the subject of, litigation.

We regret we cannot assist you in this matter. However, if we can be of assistance in the future, please do not hesitate to contact us.

Sincerely,

Judith C. Penn
Senior Consumer Affairs Specialist
Customer Assistance Unit

CHAPTER 16

HARVELLA JONES)   IN THE DISTRICT COURT OF

        Plaintiff)

VS.)   HARRIS COUNTY, TEXAS

LEADER FEDERAL)
BANK FOR SAVINGS)

        Defendant)   295th JUDICIAL DISTRICT

ORDER ON PLAINTIFF'S MOTION TO COMPEL

On the ____ day of _____, 1996, the court considered Plaintiffs' Johnnie Jones and Wife Harvella Jones's Motion to Compel. After considering the motion, response, and after a hearing on the motion and considering the arguments of counsel, the court

GRANTS the motion, orders the Defendant Leader Federal Bank for Savings to respond to the Plaintiffs Johnnie Jones and Wife Harvella Jones's requests on or before ___Aug. 19___, 1996, and orders the Defendant Leader Federal Bank for Savings to pay the Plaintiffs' Johnnie Jones and Wife Harvella Jones's $ __50.00__ for ~~attorney fees~~ expenses incurred in preparing the motion and attending the hearing.

SIGNED this 29th day of July, 1996.

Tracy Christopher
PRESIDING JUDGE

CHAPTER 17

Plaintiffs'

Question No. 1

Did Leader Federal Bank wrongfully foreclose on the Deed of Trust on the property in the name of Johnnie and Harvella Jones?

The Joneses are the original noteholders.
The homeowner's association held a junior lien position on the property in question, and is a junior lienholder.
Leader Federal Bank held the senior lien, and is a senior noteholder. *lien*

If a junior lienholder purchases the property, it must service the senior lien in order for the junior lienholder to retain possession of the property without foreclosure on the senior lien.
If the junior lienholder refuses to service the senior lien, and does not assume the debt, the senior lienholder can foreclose on the original noteholder under the Deed of Trust.

A lienholder does not have to pay cash at a foreclosure sale.

Answer "Yes" or "No"

Answer: No

CHAPTER 17

96-22132

We have enough votes to suppo[rt]
a verdict. Do we need all 12
votes. One person needs more tim[e]
before Voting.

D.F. Kelley

Please follow paragraph 6 on page 2
of the charge.

Tracy Christopher
Judge Presiding
2/25/98

CHAPTER 17

NO. 96-022132

JOHNNIE JONES, ET AL.	§	IN THE DISTRICT COURT OF
VS.	§	HARRIS COUNTY, TEXAS
LEADER FEDERAL BANK FOR SAVINGS	§	295TH JUDICIAL DISTRICT

FINAL JUDGMENT

On February 23, 1998, the court called this case for trial. Plaintiffs JOHNNIE JONES and wife, HARVELLA JONES appeared in person, acted *pro se*, and announced ready for trial. Defendant, LEADER FEDERAL BANK FOR SAVINGS, now known as UNION PLANTERS MORTGAGE CORPORATION, appeared by corporate representative and through its attorney and announced ready for trial. The court determined that it had jurisdiction over the subject matter and the parties to this proceeding. The court then impaneled and swore the jury, which heard the evidence and arguments of the parties. The court submitted questions, definitions, and instructions to the jury. In response, the jury made findings that the court received, filed, and entered of record and incorporates by reference herein. Plaintiffs moved to disregard the jury's findings, or in the alternative that the Plaintiffs be granted judgment non obstante veridecto, and Defendant moved for judgment on the verdict and for its attorneys fees. The court heard and considered the respective parties' motions and arguments thereon. The court finds: that based upon the jury's verdict the subject foreclosure was not wrongful, and that the Defendant is entitled to judgment whereby the Plaintiffs take nothing. The court denies the Plaintiffs' motions and grants the Defendant's motions for judgment; accordingly,

1.   It is ORDERED, ADJUDGED and DECREED that Plaintiffs JOHNNIE JONES and wife, HARVELLA JONES take nothing from Defendant, LEADER FEDERAL BANK FOR

CHAPTER 17

326

SAVINGS, now known as UNION PLANTERS MORTGAGE CORPORATION.

All costs of court are awarded to Defendant, and the Defendant is entitled to such writs of execution in enforcement of this judgment, if same be necessary. The court denies all relief not granted in this judgment.

Signed this 20th day of July, 1998.

Tracy Christopher
PRESIDING JUDGE

327

APPROVED AS TO FORM ONLY:

Kathleen M. Vossler (signature)

KATHLEEN M. VOSSLER
State Bar No. 90001414
3700 North Main Street
Houston, Texas 77009
(713) 861-9447
(713) 236-8801 (fax)

Attorney in Charge for Defendant
Leader Federal Bank for Savings,
now known as Union Planters Mortgage
Corporation

APPROVED AS TO FORM ONLY:

_____
JOHNNIE JONES
P.O. Box 42265
Houston, Texas 77242-2265

_____
HARVELLA JONES
P.O. Box 42265
Houston, Texas 77242-2265

PI# 4479664 UNITED STATES COURT
SOUTHERN DISTRICT OF
FILED

UNITED STATES DISTRICT COURT   **SOUTHERN DISTRICT OF TEX**

JUN 24 1998

Johnnie Jones and Harvella Jones §

MICHAEL N. MILBY, CLERK OF (

Plaintiff(s), §
§
§
VERSUS §
Union Planters Mortgage Corporation §   CAUSE NO. __H 98 - 0818__
(formerly Leader Federal Bank for §
Savings) §
Defendant(s). §

NOTICE OF APPEAL

Notice is hereby given that __Johnnie Jones and Harvella Jon__

appeals to the United States Court of Appeals for the Fifth Circuit from the __June 8, 199__
denying Plaintiffs' Motion for Default Judgment, the June 22, 1998 o
granting Defendants Motion to Dismiss and the June 22, 1
order denying Plaintiffs' Motion for Reconsideration of Plaintiff
Judgment.   __June 24, 1998__   __Harvella Jones, pro se__
Date   (Signature of Counsel for Appellant) I;

Address: __P.O. Box 42265__

__Houston, TX 77242-22__

Telephone: __(713) 952-0926__

Certificate of Service

A true and correct copy of this Notice of Appeal has been mailed via United States
Mails, postage prepaid to counsel for appellee this __24__ day of __June__ ,
__1998__ .

CHAPTER 18   __Harvella Jones__ , pro se
(Counsel for Appellant)

SDTX-DC-34
02/03/98

| UNITED STATES DISTRICT COURT | SOUTHERN DISTRICT OF TEXAS |

JOHNNIE JONES, *et al.*,

              Plaintiffs,

versus

UNION PLANTERS MORTGAGE CORP.,

              Defendant.

CIVIL ACTION H-98-818

UNITED STATES DISTRICT COURT
SOUTHERN DISTRICT OF TEXAS
ENTERED

JUL 2 1998

Michael N. Milby, Clerk

Order

By the Joneses' having delivered a copy of an appellate motion in another case to this court, it has become apparent that they have abused the system with their multiple filings for the same complaints. In the last two years they have filed these cases:

MC 96-666
C.A. 96-1385
C.A. 96-1621
C.A. 96-4368
C.A. 98-818.

Harvella and Johnnie Jones may not file another suit in this district without permission of this judge.

Signed July ___/___, 1998, at Houston, Texas.

Lynn N. Hughes
United States District Judge

CHAPTER 18

#17

JOHNNIE JONES, *et al.*,

               Plaintiffs,

versus

UNION PLANTERS MORTGAGE CORP.,

               Defendant.

CIVIL ACTION H-98-818

UNITED STATES DISTRICT CO
SOUTHERN DISTRICT OF TEX
ENTERED

NOV 9 1998

Michael N. Milby, Clerk

Order

The motions to vacate and to recuse filed by Johnnie Jones and Harvella Jones are denied (18-1, 18-2).

Signed November ___9___, 1998, at Houston, Texas.

Lynn N. Hughes
United States District Judge

CHAPTER 18

BUTLER, EWALT & HAILEY
ATTORNEYS AT LAW

Rick N. Butle
Jeffrey H. Ew
Roy D. Hailey
Mimi A. Lean
Michael J. T
Of Counsel:
David D. Diel

**Board Certified
Civil Trial Law
Texas Board of Le
Specialization
Also Admitted, F
Louisiana

January 26, 1993

Mr. Chuck Venezia   VIA FACSIMILE
Houston Management Service Co.
P. O. Box 38712
Houston, Texas   77238-8712

Re: Woodland Hills Trail Association

Dear Mr. Venezia:

At the end of last year, the attorneys in our firm met to discuss planning for 1993. In the process, we discussed trends in our business and recurring problems experienced by many community associations. This discussion confirmed what we already knew - most community associations constantly face problems with the collection of delinquent maintenance fees and are finding it increasingly difficult to devote portions of their limited budgets for attorney's fees to attempt to collect these delinquent assessments. Even if the attorney's fees are collected, many associations cannot afford to fund the collection effort; further, the uncertainty of the total expense and the recovery of the debt makes planning very difficult. For these reasons, we re-evaluated our fee structure for collection work and decided to offer the following alternative.

We propose to perform collection work on a contingency basis. "Contingency", as used herein, means that our fee will be equal to whatever amount of attorney's fees is collected from the homeowner. It does not mean that we will be paid a percentage of the assessments, late charges, interest and/or court costs recovered. These sums will be paid to the association. Further, we are offering this fee arrangement for all phases of the collection effort, including demand letters. As a result, an association need not budget any amount for attorney's fees for collection work. We will pursue the collection of each account at no cost to the association, regardless of the amount of time devoted to the account. The only out-of-pocket expense that the association will incur for any given collection account is filing fees, court costs, service fees, deposition expenses (if authorized) and similar types of suit fees.

We are of the opinion that this fee arrangement will obviously benefit an association; however, we are not attempting to suggest that it is being proposed solely for that purpose. We anticipate that some associations will pursue collection accounts which might not otherwise be pursued and that other associations may expedite their timetable for commencing legal action. For example, some associations which levy annual assessments wait until a homeowner becomes 2 or 3 years delinquent before commencing legal action simply because the amount owed is not large enough to justify the legal expense. These types of policies may change under the proposed arrangement. Thus, there may be accounts referred to our office for collection which might not otherwise be referred.

5718 Westheimer, Suite 1000, Houston, Texas 77057-5718, Telephone 713/7HU-4150, Telefax 713/7HU-4549

De.Rima   Exhibit 57

Under this fee arrangement, we intend to maintain records of all services provided on a particular account in the same manner as if we were billing the association on an hourly basis. The fees we attempt to collect from a homeowner will be based upon the time devoted to the account at a reasonable hourly rate. We will instruct each homeowner to make his check payable to the association for the total amount due (inclusive of assessments, late charges, interest, court costs and attorney's fees) and forward the check to our office. The total amount collected will then be forwarded to the association with an invoice in an amount equal to the attorney's fees collected. If a payment plan is agreed upon, each payment will be prorated on the basis of the amount owed to the association and the amount of attorney's fees agreed upon. This should simplify the billing process for the association and our office because billing will not occur until the time that the debt, or a portion thereof, is collected. Since the typical review and approval of the content of the invoice and the charges set forth should not be necessary, we merely ask that the association adopt a policy of processing payment of the invoice upon its receipt so that delays in payment are not experienced.

As indicated above, the association will be billed for court costs as those costs are incurred. All costs will be recovered by the association upon the payment of the account. If an account is never collected, the court costs paid by the association will not be recovered. However, aside from the court costs, the association is not at any financial risk.

Please discuss this new fee arrangement and let us know if you have any questions. We look forward to the opportunity of being of service to the Associations.

Very truly yours,

Butler, Ewalt & Hailey

Roy D. Hailey

RDH/era

333

EMPLOYMENT CONTRACT
WITH
BUTLER, EWALT & HAILEY

LAW FIRM RETAINED: Woodland Hills Trail Association ("Client") hereby employs Butler, Ewalt & Hailey, attorneys of Houston, Harris County, Texas, a professional corporation, hereinafter also called ("Attorney") to represent Client in the foregoing matters or cases to-wit:

the collection of delinquent annual and/or monthly general and/or special assessments or charges, together with accrued interest, costs, attorney's fees and other expenses from the owners of property subject to the jurisdiction of the Client, including the enforcement of the Client's lien, if any, securing the payment of said assessments, charges, interest, costs, attorney's fees and expenses, all as may be authorized and more specifically set forth in the applicable restrictive covenants.

ATTORNEY ACCEPTS: Attorneys agree to perform all legal services which are necessary and appropriate on behalf of and in the name of the Client to protect the Client's interest in such legal matters which representation herein contracted for includes advising, counseling, negotiating, investigating, handling, prosecuting, and/or defending the Client in the collection of said delinquent assessments and/or any related matters arising therefrom, attendant thereto, or arising out of the same set of facts or circumstances to final settlement or adjudication.

NO GUARANTEED OUTCOME: The Client understands that the Attorney has made no representations concerning the successful outcome of any contested matter, claim or negotiation or the favorable outcome of any legal action that may be filed or required to be filed on behalf of the Client by Attorney. The Attorney has not guaranteed that it will obtain reimbursement to the client of any of the cost or expenses resulting from the incident out of which the claim may arise.

FEE ARRANGEMENT: In consideration of the services rendered and to be rendered on behalf of Client by Attorney in connection with Client's individual matters or cases, Client agrees that Attorney shall be entitled to a reasonable fee for each such individual matter or case. Since the method of compensation of Attorney is not under the guaranteed hourly rate arrangement, then as consideration of the services heretofore rendered and to be rendered by Attorney to the Client, the Client has agreed and obligated itself to give and allow to Attorney, as their compensation herein, all right and title to any all monies first received over and above the initial retainer for unbilled fees for Attorney's services and unreimbursed expenses incurred by Attorney.

Except as otherwise provided in the paragraphs entitled "Client's Obligations", "Counter-Claims", "Appeals" and "Bankruptcy", the total sum of $250.00, together with any filing fees and out-of-pocket expenses incurred by Attorneys, shall be the only financial obligation of Client for those matters or cases for which Attorney agrees to represent Client.

CHAPTER 19

0 1922

RETAINER AND OTHER FEES: The total sum of $250.00 (together with the initial filing fees) for each individual matter or case for which Attorney agrees to represent Client shall be paid to the firm as a retainer which shall be credited against the fee for time and expenses incurred by Attorneys on Client's behalf. The Attorney's responsibility to provide legal services will be accepted and work will begin when Attorney receives such fees. Except for matters relating to counter or cross-claims against the Client, appeals, or bankruptcy, reasonable hourly fees in excess of the initial retainer shall be deferred and collected all as more fully set forth herein. Client further agrees to reimburse the firm for any and all out-of-pocket expenses associated with the Attorney's representation of Client, including but not limited to, filing fees, copy charges, long distance telephone expenses, document preparation costs, travel costs, West Law or other computerized research expenses, deposition costs, accountant fees, appraisers' fees, consultants' fees, and other professional fees, delivery charges, fax charges and any other out-of-pocket expenses incurred on Client's behalf. In the event the firm elects to advance sums on behalf of Client in order to pay for such expense, Client will reimburse the firm upon request. Client understands that because of the factors enumerated above, no maximum fee for legal services to be provided by the firm can be estimated or guaranteed by the firm. Client acknowledges that the firm has not designated, represented or guaranteed that Client's total fee under this agreement will be more than a certain amount.

BILLING: At monthly or other intervals, the firm will provide the Client with an itemized bill setting forth expenses incurred to date and amounts due from the Client to the extent they exceed the retainer. Client agrees to pay any all such invoices within thirty (30) days of mailing of the bill. In the event Client fails to make full and timely payment of any such billing or provide any requested retainer, Client understands and agrees that the firm may refuse to perform any further legal services until such billing or retainers are paid in full, and further, that the firm may withdraw its representation of Client. Client further agrees that any monies owed to the firm by the Client as described in this Agreement may be deducted from any settlement or award payable to Client. In connection with this Agreement, Client specifically understands and agrees that any settlement or award payable to Client shall be made in care of the firm and that the firm may deduct any fees and expenses owed by the Client from such award before distribution to Client of remaining monies. It is understood by both parties that in the event the Court awarded attorney's fees are less than those actually incurred by the Firm, then the Firm shall only receive the amount so awarded less any retainer paid by client towards such individual matter or case.

ATTORNEY'S FEE RATE: The factors to be considered by the firm as guides in determining the reasonableness of a fee to be charged in connection with Client's case is set out in the Rules of Professional Conduct and approved by the Supreme Court of Texas, include but are not limited to the following:

a.   The time and labor required; the novelty and difficulty of the questions involved, and the skill required to perform the legal services properly;

b.   the likelihood, if apparent to the Client, that the acceptance of particular employment will preclude other employment by the Attorney;

c.   the fees customarily charged in the locality for similar legal services;

d.   the amount involved and the results obtained;

e.   the time limitations imposed by the Client or by the circumstances;

f.   the nature and length of the professional relationship with the Client;

g.   the experience, reputation, and ability of the lawyer or layers performing the services.

To assist in the computation of a reasonable fee, the Client agrees that services rendered by Attorneys will be recorded according to the amount of time spent for work performed on behalf of Client and that such time will be billed at the rates charges by the Attorneys for each individual performing work on behalf of Client at the time services are rendered. Client understands and agrees the firm's minimum amount of time charged for any legal services rendered on behalf of Client will be one tenth (1/10) of one hour. The rates charged by various firm employees are currently set as follows:

Senior Attorney	$150.00 per hour
Associate Attorney	$125.00 per hour
Legal Assistant	$ 60.00 per hour
Other Non-lawyer personnel	$ 40.00 per hour

Client understands and agrees that the rates charged by individuals in the firm may be increased from time to time without prior notice to Client, and that the rates applied for work performed on behalf of Client will be those rates in affect at the time the services are performed. Client further understands that the time spent by individuals and the rates for those individuals shall not be the sole method of computation of a reasonable fee, but shall merely assist in determining a reasonable fee in Client's case. Client understands that all of the factors enumerated above shall be considered in computing a reasonable fee. Client understands and agrees that the firm shall be compensated for all services rendered on behalf of Client including, but not limited to, legal research, drafting of pleadings, conferences, telephone conversations, preparation of documents, investigation of facts, preparation for an appearance in court and any and all other tasks necessary to handle Client's case.

COUNTERCLAIMS: In the event a counter-claim or cross-claim is asserted, Attorney reserves the right to convert the matter or case attendant therewith to an hourly fee basis, whereby Attorney's time will be billed solely at Attorney's hourly rate as set forth herein.

APPEALS: Client understands that in the event an appeal is necessary or desired, the Attorney may require a new contract between the Client and Attorney, or may elect to proceed under the terms of this Agreement, at the Attorney's discretion. Client specifically understands that the Attorney may require an additional appeal retainer and further advancement of anticipated costs associated with an appeal. Client further understands and agrees that nothing in this agreement compels the Attorney to represent Client in any appeal.

BANKRUPTCY: This Agreement shall not extend to fees for any motions, pleadings or hearings in bankruptcy court and any such efforts shall be made solely at Attorney's hourly rate.

SECURITY INTEREST IN RECOVERY: The firm has granted its specific security interest in and to any recovery (whether it be money, property or otherwise) that may come to pass by compromise and settlement agreement, suit or judgment, to secure the payment of its fees.

IOLTA DISCLOSURE: You are hereby notified that all funds deposited in the firm trust account, including your funds draw interest. That interest is paid by the depository to the Texas Equal Access to Justice Foundation under orders of the Texas Supreme Court. This firm received none of the interest so earned and received no benefit from the Foundation except those benefits that all Texas citizens receive as a result of the services rendered by the Foundation.

ATTORNEY OBLIGATION TO COURT SYSTEM: Section 9.001 et. seq. of the Texas Civil Practice and Remedies Code and the Texas Rules of Civil Procedure, Rule 13, provides that the signature of an attorney on any pleading or court document shall constitute a certificate by them that they have read the pleading, motion or other paper; that to the best of their knowledge, information and belief formed after reasonable inquiry that such instrument is not groundless nor brought in bad faith, nor brought for the purposes of harassment. The Rule further provides that should any Attorney or Party bring a fictitious suit as an experiment to get any opinion of the court or who shall file any fictitious pleading in a cause for such a purpose or shall make statements in pleadings which they know to be groundless or false for the purpose of securing a delay in the trial of the cause shall be guilty of contempt of the Court. Groundless, for the purposes of Rule 13, means that there is no basis in law or fact and not warranted by good faith argument for the extension, modification or reversal of existing law. The Federal Rules of Civil Procedure have a similar rule in Rule 13. In light of Section 9.001, Civil Practice and Remedies Code, Rule 13 of the Texas Rules of Civil Procedure and Rule 11 of the Federal Rules of Civil Procedure, the Client agrees that the firm will not advance any spurious claim of fact of law in the advancement of the claim covered by this Employment Agreement. In the event of a conflict between the Attorney and Client as to whether a proposed course of action violated or purports to violate these three (3) rules, or any of them, resolution of that conflict shall be solely vested in the firm. If the Client persists, at any time, in advancing a spurious claim of fact, the firm may treat this contract as breached, may withdraw

337

from the employment, may withdraw from the litigation and shall be entitled to whatever rights that the firm would otherwise have for breach of contract.

CLIENT'S OBLIGATIONS: Client acknowledges Attorney has a security interest in the matters or cases noted hereinbefore and agreed to utilize its best efforts to assist Attorney in a successful and timely resolution of each such matter, including the following:

a. advising Attorney of any and all communications either oral or written, with any person or entity concerning any amount assigned for collection activity;

b. contacting Attorney upon the receipt of any monies or funds to be applied to any account assigned for collection activity prior to the acceptable and deposit of such funds;

c. advising any tax service, title company or similar type organization of pending legal action and the need to confirm additional costs and/or Attorney's fees due and owing on any account assigned for collection activity.

Client agrees that Client shall be responsible to Attorney for any and all Attorney's fees incurred under the following circumstances:

a. Client's receipt, acceptance and deposit of funds constituting an accord and satisfaction of any debt without first notifying Attorney and receiving confirmation of authority from Attorney to deposit such funds.

b. Client's entering into any agreement concerning the payment of any and all charges without first obtained the written consent of Attorney;

c. Accounts which are not capable of being pursued due to the mistake or negligence of the Client, its agents, servants, employees or assigns.

WITHDRAWAL FROM EMPLOYMENT BY ATTORNEY: The firm may withdraw from representation of the Client in any of Client's individual matters or cases at any time if the Client:

a. insists upon presenting a claim that is not warranted under existing law and cannot be supported by good faith argument for an extension, modification or reversal of existing law;

b. seek to pursue an illegal course of conduct;

c. insist that the firm pursue a course of conduct that is illegal or that is prohibited under the disciplinary rules.

338

d.   by other conduct rendered it unreasonably difficult for the firm to carry out its employment;

e.   insist that the firm engage in conduct that is contrary to the judgment and advice of the Attorneys but not prohibited under the disciplinary rules;

f.   fails to honor this Agreement or any obligation under this Agreement including failure to pay any billing within thirty (30) days of mailing or to provide any requested retainer.

If in the judgment of Attorney a particular matter or case cannot be reasonably prosecuted beyond a certain point, Attorney shall turn the entire matter or case file over to client or another attorney of Client's choice, and Client shall not be obligated to pay any additional fee to attorney for services rendered.

In the event the terms determine that it is necessary to withdraw from employment in Client's case or cases, the firm will take reasonable steps to notify Client of its decision, including the basis for the decision.

TERMINATION OF EMPLOYMENT BY CLIENT: In the event of Client's decision to terminate the firm's representation of Client for any reason, Client agrees to pay the firm the total amount of the fee for services rendered on the reasonable fee basis as set forth above, together with all expenses and costs incurred or paid on the Client's behalf. If the Client determines to discharge the firm, such decision shall be communicated in writing to the firm. If permission for withdrawal from employment is required by rules of the Court, the firm shall withdraw upon the granting of permission by the Court. In the event the Client desires to dismiss Attorney and retain other counsel to represent the Client's interest in any matter encompassed by or made the basis of this Agreement after the date of the signing of this Agreement, IT IS AGREED AND UNDERSTOOD THAT THE TERMS OF THIS CONTRACT AS IT PERTAINS TO THE FEE OR FEES AND EXPENSES TO PAID ATTORNEY, SHALL REMAIN IN FULL FORCE AND EFFECT UP TO AND INCLUDING THE DATE OF DISMISSAL, AND THAT IN THE EVENT OF COLLECTION BY CLIENT OF ANY AND ALL SUMS DUE, SAME SHALL BE FIRST APPLIED TO ATTORNEY'S FEES, COSTS OR EXPENSES PURSUANT TO AN ORDER OF THE COURT, VERDICT OF THE JURY, OR BY AGREEMENT OF THE PARTIES SHALL BE CREDITED AGAINST THE AMOUNTS OWED BY THE CLIENT FOR ATTORNEY'S FEES, COSTS AND EXPENSES.

ENTIRE AGREEMENT OF THE PARTIES: This Agreement embodies the entire agreement of the parties hereto with respect to the matter herein contained and it is agreed that the terms, conditions and stipulations herein shall not be modified or revoked unless by written agreement signed by both parties and acknowledged hereto and made a part hereof. Further the Client acknowledges that in addition to having read this Agreement in its entirety, the undersigned Attorney has answered any questions concerning the Agreement raised by the Client and the Client understands the Agreement and considers it to be fair and reasonable. The terms of this Agreement shall be enforceable in Houston, Harris County, Texas.

EXECUTED in multiple originals to be effective on the latter date set forth below.

Butler, Ewalt & Hailey

10/28/92
Date

By: Roy D. Hailey

Woodland Hills Trail Association

Date

Printed Name:

DocNo/9397

COMMITTEES:

Chair, Jurisprudence
State Affairs
Economic Development
Committee of the Whole on Legislative
    and Congressional Redistricting
General Investigating

SENATOR RODNEY ELLIS
District 13

The Senate of
The State of Texas

MEMORANDUM
March 27, 1997

TO: witnesses for Senate Bill 3290
FROM: Amy Chamberlain, Office of Sen. Rodney Ellis
RE: Hearing on Wednesday, April 2

Please meet me in Senator Ellis' office at 1 p.m. on Wednesday, April 2, in room 3E.2 of the Capitol (3rd fl., between the rotunda and Senate Gallery). The hearing will take place in Room E1.016 at 1:30 p.m. or upon adjournment of the Senate. If I am unable to meet you in Sen. Ellis' office at 1 p.m., please proceed to E1.016, by taking the elevator to level E1.

Please fill out the attached witness registration card and bring it with you. If you forget it, that's OK. You can fill out another one here.

Attached is the bill you will be testifying on and the bill as it might look amended.
The bill would **delete** provisions of current law (as it was made in 1995):

1) that explicitly allow associations to charge costs to an owner's account, including attorneys' fees incurred by the association and fees for letters sent to owners to enforce deed restrictions and collect maintenance fees (see page 3 of SB 1864)

2) that explicitly allow associations to increase assessments annually or accumulate and increase the assessment after a number of years without a vote of the membership, if the restrictions allow for an annual increase without a vote (see page 3 of SB 1864)

3) that explicitly allows associations to impose and increase payments, fees, or charges for additional services without a vote of the membership. (see pages 4-5 of SB 1864 as amended).

To drive here from Houston, I usually take I-10 to Highway 71 to I-35, and exit 15th Street. The Capitol is at the intersection of 15th St. and Congress Ave. The best way to get here from I-35 is to exit on 15th St. and turn west. Travel west down 15th Street about 5-6 blocks until you get to Congress and turn right into the Visitor's lot on that corner. Do not worry about the 2-hour maximum; you will not be ticketed.

We are sorry we cannot reimburse you for any travel expenses and appreciate your willingness to travel to Austin for this hearing.

If you need to reach me for any reason, please call me at 512/463-0395. See you there!

Lyric Centre
440 Louisiana, Suite 575
Houston, Texas 77002
(713) 236-0006
FAX: (713) 236-0604

FAX: (51)
E-Mail

2440 Texas Parkway, Suite 280
Missouri City, Texas 77489
(713) 261-2360

CHAPTER 19

FRANK, ELMORE & LIEVENS, P.C.
ATTORNEYS AT LAW
NIELS ESPERSON BUILDING
808 TRAVIS, SUITE 2800
HOUSTON, TEXAS 77002

(713) 224-0

EDWIN H. FRANK, JR., P.C.
JERRY L. ELMORE
RICHARD C. LIEVENS
WILLIAM L. VAN FLEET II
LOYD H. WRIGHT

October 20, 1986

The Supreme Court of the
  State of Texas
P. O. Box 12248
Austin, Texas 78701

Re: Supreme Court Case No. C-5283: Harris; Supreme Court Case No. C-5285:
     Pamilar

To the Honorable Justices of
  The Supreme Court of Texas:

I write individually, and on behalf of the Greater Houston Chapter of The Community Associations Institute (CAI) relative to the pending motion for rehearing filed in connection with the captioned cases. As an attorney, I individually represent numerous community associations (condominium, townhome, single family home subdivisions, etc.). I am also the President-elect of the ~~Greater Houston Chapter of CAI~~ which is a nationwide non-profit organization ~~which promotes education and~~ interaction among community associations, builder-developers, ~~homeowners,~~ public officials, and managers relative to issues involving ~~community associations,~~ including the rights and remedies available to homeowners and/or associations in the collection of maintenance assessments.

With the above introduction, and on behalf of my clients and CAI, I urge this Honorable Court to grant the motion for rehearing as to the captioned cases for the following reasons:

1. The appellate decision has caused tremendous confusion in the community association industry as same concerns the rights and remedies available to homeowner associations in the collection of maintenance assessments against homeowners.

2. Although the appellate decision attempts to distinguish Johnson v. First Southern Property, 687 S.W.2d 399 (Tex.App.--[14th Dist.] 1985, writ ref'd n.r.e.) (wherein the 14th Court of Civil Appeals upheld non-judicial foreclosure of maintenance assessments for a particular condominium regime), the Harris/Pamilar opinions have misinterpreted the facts of Johnson and have distinguished Johnson on an incorrect basis. As a result, the captioned cases also caused considerable confusion relative to the opinion issued in the Johnson case.

CHAPTER 19

342

he United States
Taylor Publisher Services